ESSENTIALS OF COLLEGE ENGLISH

ESSENTIALS OF COLLEGE ENGLISH

MARY ELLEN GUFFEY
Los Angeles Pierce College

SOUTH-WESTERN College Publishing
An International Thomson Publishing Company

Acquisitions Editor: Gary L. Bauer
Senior Acquisitions Editor: Gary Bauer
Production Editors: Shelley Brewer, Kelly Keeler
Production House: WordCrafters Editorial Services, Inc.
Designer: Joseph M. Devine
Marketing Manager: Dreis Van Landuyt
Manufacturing Coordinator: Sue Disselkamp

Annotated Instructor's Edition ISBN: 0-538-86003-0
Student Edition ISBN: 0-538-86002-2
2 3 4 5 6 7 8 9 BN 3 2 1 0 9 8
Printed in the United States of America

I(T)P™
International Thomson Publishing
South-Western College Publishing is an ITP Company.
The ITP trademark is used under license.

CONTENTS

PREFACE TO STUDENT

Mary Ellen Guffey

Dear Student:

Essentials of College English was written to assist you in reviewing English grammar, punctuation, style, and usage. By improving your control of these language principles, you'll feel more confident about yourself. You'll also have a strong foundation for becoming an effective communicator in a world that is increasingly dependent on the exchange of information.

You can get the most out of this book by following this three-step plan:

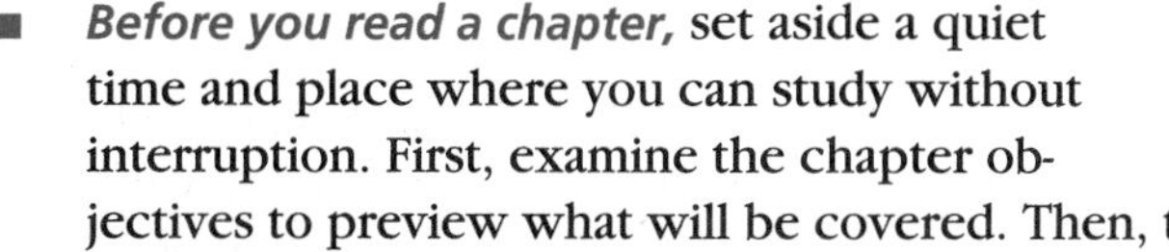

- ***Before you read a chapter,*** set aside a quiet time and place where you can study without interruption. First, examine the chapter objectives to preview what will be covered. Then, take the pretest to assess your knowledge. Next, check your answers (given at the bottom of the page).
- ***As you read a chapter,*** use a marking pencil to highlight important concepts and examples. If you don't understand a principle or if you have a question, write your question in the margin so that you can ask about it in class. Because the chapters are fairly short, you'll probably read them quickly.
- ***After reading a chapter,*** review the passages you highlighted. Ask yourself if you understand the concepts presented. Then, take the posttest and compare it with your pretest performance. Next, complete Exercise A and immediately check your answers at the bottom of the page. If you have more than three incorrect responses out of ten, reread the chapter before continuing with the other reinforcement exercises. Complete all the assigned exercises before going to class.

Some students try to fill in answers for the reinforcement exercises without first reading a chapter. This is like trying to program a VCR without reading the instruction manual. You'll be much more successful if you read the chapter first!

The following features in *Essentials of College English* will help you understand and remember the language concepts presented.

- ***Three-Level Approach.*** Beginning with Chapter 4, language concepts appear in levels. These levels progress from fundamental, frequently used concepts in Level I to more complex concepts in Level III. Each level has its own trial exercises as well as numerous reinforcement exercises. Dividing a chapter into three levels provides you with small, easily mastered learning segments.

- ***Hot Line Queries.*** A significant feature of *Essentials of College English* is its questions and answers from grammar hot line services across the country. These authentic questions — and the author's suggested answers to them — illustrate communication problems just like the ones you meet every day. As you read the questions, imagine how you would answer them.
- ***Pretests and Posttests.*** Each chapter includes a brief pretest to preview concepts, stimulate interest, and enable you to recognize your strengths and weaknesses. The posttests help you to judge your achievement and improvement.
- ***Marginal Annotations.*** These helpful, interesting marginal notes identified by the following icons:

Memory devices and learning suggestions appear as study tips. They help you understand and retain the many language principles you will be reviewing.

SPOT THE BLOOPER

To provide humorous relief from the sometimes heavy load of grammar and mechanics, these bloopers demonstrate common language errors.

Thought-provoking quotations provide moments of reflection at the same time they enhance your total learning experience.

These inquisitive tidbits relate interesting trivia to English language concepts.

When you finish reading and studying this book, I personally guarantee that your language skills will be much better than when you started. However, your mind is not a computer and can't record everything for instant recall. Like most professionals, you will occasionally need reference books to find answers. That's why you'll probably want to keep this book, along with a good dictionary and a reference manual, for review and use after you leave this class.

If you have any comments about this book or suggestions for improvement, please write to me. I wish you well in your studies!

Dr. Mary Ellen Guffey
Professor of Business
23852 Pacific Coast Highway, Suite 307
Malibu, CA 90265

UNIT 1 Laying a Foundation

1 Reference Skills

OBJECTIVES When you have completed the materials in this chapter, you will be able to do the following:

- Describe three types of dictionaries.
- Use a dictionary confidently to determine spelling, meaning, pronunciation, syllabication, accent, word usage, and word history.
- Select a dictionary to suit your needs.
- Anticipate what information is included in dictionaries and what information is not.
- Understand the value of reference manuals.

PRETEST

Each chapter begins with a brief pretest. Answer the questions in the pretest to assess your prior knowledge of the chapter content and also to give yourself a preview of what you will learn. Compare your answers with those at the bottom of the page. When you complete the chapter, take the posttest to measure your improvement.

Write *T* (true) or *F* (false) after the following statements.

1. Dictionaries, reference manuals, and English textbooks are significantly different in content and organization. _____
2. Most college students would find a current unabridged dictionary best for daily use. _____
3. Nearly all dictionaries present word definitions in the same order. _____
4. The usage label *colloquial* means that a word is informal. _____
5. Most dictionaries contain the plural spellings of all nouns. _____

Your success in college, in your career, and in today's information society demands good communication skills. Communicating well means listening carefully, understanding what you read, and expressing yourself effectively in writing and in speech.

Communication skills are especially important in today's careers. Just take a look at the want ads. You'll see that one of the most frequent requests is for good communication skills. Why are employers screaming for employees who can listen, read, write, and speak effectively? Because nearly all of today's careers involve generating, processing, and exchanging information. We live in the age of information. Estimates

1.T 2.F 3.F 4.T 5.F

suggest that as many as 95 percent of all new jobs will be in service or information industries. To thrive in these environments, you need polished communication skills.

Essentials of College English helps you review and polish fundamental communication skills. You'll develop a firm foundation by studying the basics of grammar, usage, punctuation, capitalization, and number style. But your mind is not a computer. It won't remember everything you study. That's why it is especially important to know where to find answers.

One of the goals of your education is to know where to find answers and how to interpret the information you find. Even experts do not know *all* the answers. Attorneys refer to casebooks. Doctors consult their medical libraries. And you, as a student of the language, must develop skill and confidence in using reference materials. These reference materials may be printed or electronic. We'll focus on printed reference materials in this book. But you should be aware that excellent software programs can help you verify spelling, define words, and even check some grammar and style usage.

SPOT THE BLOOPER

On résumés that crossed the desk of personnel expert Robert Half: "I am a rabid typist." "Here are my qualifications for you to overlook." "Hope to hear from you shorty."

Whether you use electronic or printed references, you'll want to develop the habit of verifying information. Such verification is easy if you have your own personal library of reference materials. At a minimum, you'll need a current desk or college dictionary and a good reference manual. Another helpful reference book is a thesaurus, which is a collection of *synonyms* (words with similar meanings) and *antonyms* (words with opposite meanings). Specific career fields may require additional materials.

The dictionary is probably the most used and the most useful of all reference materials. Here are some suggestions for selecting and using your dictionary.

DICTIONARIES

Types

Dictionaries can be grouped into three categories: pocket, desk (college), and unabridged. In choosing one for yourself, consider your needs. A *pocket* dictionary is handy and efficient. However, since it usually has no more than 75,000 entries, it may prove inadequate for college reference homework.

A *desk* or *college-level* dictionary generally contains over 170,000 entries plus extra features. Both pocket and desk dictionaries are abridged; that is, they are condensed or shortened dictionaries. For college work you should own a current desk dictionary. The following list shows some of the best-known desk dictionaries. Notice that the titles of three dictionaries contain the name *Webster.* Because names cannot be copyrighted, any publisher may use the word *Webster* on its dictionary. Definitions and usage in this textbook are based on *Merriam-Webster's Collegiate Dictionary,* Tenth Edition. Many publishers rely on this dictionary as their standard. Some readers, however, prefer *The American Heritage College Dictionary* because it provides more plural spellings, more usage labels, and more opinions about appropriate usage than other dictionaries.

Name	Approximate Number of Definitions
The American Heritage College Dictionary	200,000
Random House Webster's College Dictionary	180,000
Merriam-Webster's Collegiate Dictionary, Tenth Edition*	200,000 plus
Webster's New World Dictionary	170,000

*The standard dictionary for definitions and usage in this book.

To *abridge* means to "shorten"; a bridge shortens the distance between points. An "unabridged" book has not been shortened.

Unabridged, or complete, dictionaries are large, heavy volumes that contain nearly all English words. Schools, libraries, newspapers, and business offices that are concerned with editing or publishing use unabridged dictionaries. One of the best-known unabridged dictionaries is *Merriam-Webster's New International Dictionary.* It includes over 450,000 entries. Another famous unabridged dictionary is the *Oxford English Dictionary* (*OED*). This 13-volume set shows the historical development of all English words; it is often used by professional writers, scholars of the language, and academics. A computer version on CD-ROM is now available for easy access.

Copyright Date

If the copyright date of your current dictionary shows that the dictionary was published ten or more years ago, consider investing in a more recent edition. English is a responsive, dynamic language that admits new words and recognizes changes in meanings and usage of familiar words. These changes are reflected in an up-to-date dictionary.

Features

In selecting a dictionary, check the features it offers in addition to vocabulary definitions. Many editions contain biographical and geographical data, abbreviations, standard measurements, signs, symbols, foreign words and phrases, lists of colleges and universities, and information about the language.

"Language is the dress of thought. Every time you talk, your mind is on parade."
— Samuel Johnson, creator of the first dictionary

Entry

This example from *The American Heritage College Dictionary** illustrates some of the ten points we will discuss here to help you use your dictionary more effectively.

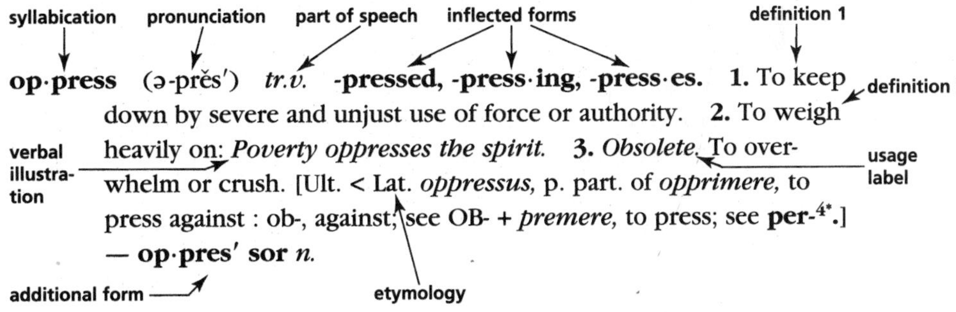

Dictionary Use

■ ***Introduction.*** Before using your dictionary, take a few moments to read the instructions located in the pages just before the beginning of the vocabulary entries. Pay particular attention to the order of definitions. Some dictionaries show the most common definitions first. Other dictionaries develop meanings historically; that is, the first known meaning of the word is shown first.

■ ***Guide words.*** In boldface type at the top of each dictionary page are two words that indicate the first and last entries on the page. When searching for a word, look *only* at these guide words until you locate the desired page.

■ ***Syllabication.*** Most dictionaries show syllable breaks with a centered dot, as shown for the word *oppress.* Compound words are sometimes troublesome to dictionary users. If a compound word is shown with a centered dot, it is one word, as in *drop·out* (dropout). If a compound word is shown with a hyphen, it is hyphenated, as in *drop-off.* If two words appear without a centered dot or a hyphen, they should be written as two words, as in *drop kick.* If you find no entry for a word or phrase in a college-level dictionary, you may usually assume that the words are written separately, for example, *drop cloth.*

■ ***Pronunciation.*** Special symbols (diacritical marks) are used to help you pronounce words correctly. A detailed explanation of pronunciation symbols is found in the front pages of a dictionary; a summary of these symbols may appear at the bottom of each set of pages. If two pronunciations are possible, the preferred one is usually shown first.

■ ***Accent.*** Most dictionaries show accents with a raised stress mark immediately following the accented syllable, as in the word ***i den′ ti fy***. Other dictionaries use a raised stress mark immediately *preceding* the accented syllable (i ′den ti fy). Secondary stress may be shown in lighter print, as illustrated on the syllable *fy* (i den′ ti fy′), or it may be shown with a *lowered* accent mark (*i ′den ti ˌfy*).

■ ***Etymology.*** College-level dictionaries provide in square brackets [ ] the brief history or etymology of the word. For example, the word *oppress* ultimately derived its meaning from the Latin *oppressus,* which is the past participle form of *opprimere* (meaning "to press against"). Keys to etymological abbreviations may be found in the introductory notes in your dictionary. Do not confuse the etymological definition shown in brackets with the actual word definition(s).

■ ***Part of speech.*** Following the phonetic pronunciation of an entry word is an italicized or boldfaced label indicating what part of speech the entry word represents. The most common labels are the following:

adj	(adjective)	*prep*	(preposition)
adv	(adverb)	*pron*	(pronoun)
conj	(conjunction)	*v* or *vb*	(verb)
interj	(interjection)	*vt* or *v tr*	(verb transitive)
n	(noun)	*vi* or *v int*	(verb intransitive)

Spelling, pronunciation, and meaning may differ for a given word when that word functions as different parts of speech. Therefore, check its grammatical label carefully. If the parts of speech seem foreign to you at this time, don't despair. Chapter 2 and successive chapters will help you learn more about the parts of speech.

■ ***Labels.*** Not all words listed in dictionaries are acceptable in business or other writing. Usage labels are used to warn readers about the use of certain words. In the dictionary entry for the word *oppress,* one meaning is labeled *obsolete.* The following list defines *obsolete* and other usage labels:

SPOT THE BLOOPER

In a Chinese fortune cookie: "You will gain admiration from your pears."

LABEL	EXAMPLE
archaic: words once common but now rare; only sporadic evidence of use since 1755	*goodwife* (meaning *female head of household*)
obsolete: no longer in active use	*entertain* (meaning *to hire*)
colloquial or *informal*:* used in casual writing or conversation	*glitz* (*showiness, flashiness*)
slang: very informal but may be sparingly used for effect	*glop* (*soft, soggy mixture*)
nonstandard and *substandard:* not conforming to usage among educated speakers	*irregardless* (*regardless*)
dialect, Brit., South, Scot., etc.: used in certain regions	*bonnet* (used in Britain to mean *car hood*)

*Some dictionaries no longer use the labels *colloquial* or *informal.*

If no usage label appears, a word is considered standard; that is, it is acceptable for all uses. However, it should be noted that many lexicographers have substantially reduced the number of usage labels in current editions. Lexicographers, by the way, are those who make dictionaries.

■ ***Inflected forms.*** When nouns, verbs, adverbs, or adjectives change form grammatically, they are said to be *inflected,* as when *child* becomes *children.* Because of limited space, dictionaries usually show only irregular inflected forms. Thus, nouns with irregular or unusual plurals (*wife, wives*) will be shown. Verbs with irregular tenses or difficult spelling (*gratified, gratifying*) will be shown. Adverbs or adjectives with irregular comparatives or superlatives (*good, better, best*) will also be shown. But regular noun plurals, verb tenses, and comparatives generally will *not* be shown in dictionaries. Succeeding chapters will elucidate regular and irregular parts of speech.

■ ***Synonyms and antonyms.*** *Synonyms,* words having similar meanings, are often provided after word definitions. For example, a synonym for *elucidate* is *explain.* Synonyms are helpful as word substitutes. *Antonyms,* words having opposite meanings, appear less frequently in dictionaries; when included, they usually follow synonyms. One antonym for *elucidate* is *confuse.* The best place to find synonyms and antonyms is in a thesaurus.

"Luck is a matter of preparation meeting opportunity."
— Oprah Winfrey

REFERENCE MANUALS

Reference Manual Versus Dictionary

In addition to one or more dictionaries, writers and information workers should have a good reference manual or handbook readily available. In it one can find helpful information not available in dictionaries. Most reference manuals provide the following information:

■ ***Punctuation.*** Detailed explanations of punctuation rules are presented logically. A well-written manual will also provide ample illustrations of punctuation usage so that the reader can readily find solutions to punctuation dilemmas.

■ ***Hyphenation.*** Dictionaries provide syllable breaks. Words, however, cannot be divided at all syllable breaks. A reference manual will supply rules for, and examples of, word division. Moreover, a good reference manual will explain when compound adjectives like *up-to-the-minute* should be hyphenated.

SPOT THE BLOOPER

Advertisement from Bullock's Department Store describing ten appliances: Top 10 Best Cellars! [Would a computer spell checker have caught this blooper?]

■ *Capitalization.* Complete rules with precise examples illustrating capitalization style will be shown.

■ *Numbers.* Deciding whether to write a number as a figure or as a word can be very confusing. A reference manual will provide both instruction and numerous examples illustrating number and word styles.

Other topics covered in reference manuals are confusing words (such as *effect* and *affect*), abbreviations, contractions, literary and artistic titles, forms of address, and letter and report formats. In addition, some manuals contain sections devoted to English grammar and office procedures.

Reference Manual Versus Textbook

You may be wondering how a reference manual differs from an English textbook such as the one you are now reading. Although content is similar, the primary difference is one of purpose. A textbook is developed *pedagogically*—that is, for teaching—so that the student understands and learns concepts. A reference manual is organized *functionally,* so that the reader finds accurate information efficiently. A well-written reference manual is complete, coherent, and concise.

Most of the language and style questions that perplex writers and students could be answered quickly by a trained person using a reliable dictionary and a well-written reference manual.

Now complete the reinforcement exercises on the following pages.

2 Parts of Speech

OBJECTIVES When you have completed the materials in this chapter, you will be able to do the following:

- Define the eight parts of speech.
- Recognize how parts of speech function in sentences.
- Compose sentences showing words playing more than one grammatical role.

PRETEST

Study the following sentence and identify selected parts of speech. For each word below underline the correct part of speech. Compare your answers with those at the bottom of the page.

Rob and Ellen eagerly completed job applications for assistant manager.

1. and	(a) prep	(b) conj	(c) verb	(d) adverb
2. eagerly	(a) prep	(b) conj	(c) verb	(d) adverb
3. completed	(a) prep	(b) conj	(c) verb	(d) adverb
4. job	(a) adj	(b) pronoun	(c) noun	(d) adverb
5. for	(a) prep	(b) conj	(c) noun	(d) adverb

As you learned in Chapter 1, this review of basic English will cover the fundamentals of grammar, current usage, and appropriate style. Such a study logically begins with the eight parts of speech, the building blocks of our language. This chapter will provide a brief overview of the parts of speech; the following chapters will deal with these topics more thoroughly. The goal of this chapter is to help you develop a foundation vocabulary so that you will have the tools necessary to study the language and to improve your effectiveness in communication.

THE EIGHT PARTS OF SPEECH

Nouns

In elementary school you probably learned that *nouns* are the names given to persons, places, and things. In addition, though, nouns name qualities, concepts, and activities.

1. (b) conjunction 2. (d) adverb 3. (c) verb 4. (c) noun 5. (a) preposition

The words *a, an,* and *the* are sometimes called "noun markers" because they identify or "mark" nouns.

PERSONS:	Sherry, Mr. Thomas, vice president, Mark
PLACES:	Albany, park, England, college
THINGS:	bicycle, computers, desk, blanket
QUALITIES:	reliability, honor, virtue, credibility
CONCEPTS:	truth, faith, freedom, enthusiasm
ACTIVITIES:	traveling, working, sleeping, communication

Nouns are important words in our language. Sentences revolve around nouns since they function both as subjects and as objects of verbs. To determine if a word is really a noun, try using it with the verb *is* or *are.* Notice that all the nouns listed here would make sense if used in this way: *Sherry is, Albany is, computers are,* and so on. In Chapter 4 you will learn four classes of nouns and rules for making nouns plural.

Pronouns

As substitutes for nouns, *pronouns* are used in our language for variety and efficiency. Compare these two versions of the same sentence:

WITHOUT PRONOUNS:	Jeff used Jeff's credit card to pay Jeff's library fines when Jeff received Jeff's bill.
WITH PRONOUNS:	Jeff used his credit card to pay his library fines when he received his bill.

In sentences pronouns may function as subjects (for example, *I, we, they*) or as objects of verbs (*me, us, them*). They may show possession (*mine, ours, his*), and they may act as connectors (*that, which, who*). Only a few examples are given here. More examples, along with functions and classifications of pronouns, will be presented in Chapters 6 and 7.

To test whether a word is truly a verb, try using it with a noun or pronoun, such as *Kim eats, she seems,* or *it is. He food* doesn't make sense because *food* is not a verb.

Verbs

Verbs do two things: (a) they show the action of a sentence, or (b) they join or "link" to the subject of the sentence words that describe it. Some action verbs are *runs, studies, works,* and *fixes.* Some linking verbs are *am, is, are, was, were, be, being,* and *been.* Other linking verbs express the senses: *feels, appears, tastes, sounds, seems, looks.*

Verbs will be discussed more fully in Chapters 8–11. At this point it is important that you be able to recognize verbs so that you can determine whether sentences are complete. All sentences have at least one verb; many sentences will have more than one verb. Verbs may appear singly or in phrases.

Becky wrote a check for her purchase. (Action verb.)

Becky's check is good. (Linking verb.)

She has been making regular deposits. (Verb phrase.)

Adjectives

Words that describe nouns or pronouns are called *adjectives.* They often answer the questions *what kind? how many?* and *which one?* The adjectives in the following sentences are italicized. Observe that the adjectives all answer questions about the nouns that they describe.

SPOT THE BLOOPER

From *The Wall Street Journal* comes a report that Marshall Field's, the big Chicago retailer, announced it would serve hot chocolate to "tiresome" shoppers. [The store later blamed this misused adjective on a computer spell checker. Did the computer get a bum rap?]

Large and *small* employers are recruiting graduates. (What kind of employers?)

Fifteen students responded to the *three* job openings. (How many students? How many job openings?)

That employer wants *trustworthy, dependable,* and *well-organized* candidates. (Which employer? What kind of candidates?)

The president of *the profitable* company is *energetic.* (Which president? Which company?)

Adjectives usually precede nouns and pronouns. They may, however, follow the words they describe, especially when used with linking verbs, as shown in the last example above.

Here is a brief list of words often used as adjectives:

effective	important	best
specific	short	long
good	real	harmful

Three words (*a, an,* and *the*) form a special group of adjectives called *articles.*

To remember more easily what an *adverb* does, think of its two syllables: *ad* suggests that you will be adding to or amplifying the meaning of a *verb.* Hence, adverbs often modify verbs.

Adverbs

Words that modify (describe or limit) verbs, adjectives, or other adverbs are *adverbs.* Adverbs often answer the questions *when? how? where?* and *to what extent?*

Yesterday I was interviewed. (Interviewed when?)

The recruiter began the interview *slowly.* (Began how?)

He asked questions *very carefully.* (Asked questions how?)

I planned to be *there* at 1 p.m. (Where?)

I wanted to pursue the matter of benefits *further.* (Pursue the matter to what extent?)

Here are additional examples of common adverbs:

here	only	really
then	never	not
quickly	rather	greatly

Many, but not all, words ending in *ly* are adverbs. Some exceptions are *friendly, costly,* and *ugly,* all of which are adjectives.

SPOT THE BLOOPER

The menu of a restaurant in Columbia, South Carolina, offers "A humongous baked potato, slightly hallowed and stuffed."

Prepositions

Prepositions join nouns and pronouns to other words in a sentence. As the word itself suggests (*pre* meaning "before"), a preposition is a word in a position *before* its object (a noun or pronoun). Prepositions are used in phrases to show a relationship between the object of the preposition and another word in the sentence. In the following sentence notice how the preposition changes the relation of the object (*the owner*) to the verb (*spoke*):

Maria spoke *with* the owner.

Maria spoke *about* the owner.

Maria spoke *for* the owner.

The most frequently used prepositions are *to, by, for, at, from, with,* and *of.* A more complete list of prepositions can be found in Chapter 13. Learn to recognize objects of prepositions so that you won't confuse them with sentence subjects.

Conjunctions

Words that connect other words or groups of words are *conjunctions.* The most common conjunctions are *and, or, but,* and *nor.* These are called *coordinating conjunctions* because they join equal (coordinate) parts of sentences. Other kinds of conjunctions will be presented in Chapter 15. Study the examples of coordinating conjunctions shown here:

> Ellen, Kent, *and* Ali submitted their résumés. (Joins equal words.)
>
> You may call the manager, *or* you may send her an E-mail message. (Joins equal groups of words.)

The vocabulary of American English is constantly growing, and some Britishers criticize our eagerness to accept new words and meanings. Prince Charles recently pronounced American English "very corrupting" and to be avoided at all costs. He told the British Council that Americans tend to "invent all sorts of new nouns and verbs and make words that shouldn't be."

Interjections

Words expressing strong feelings are *interjections.* Interjections standing alone are followed by exclamation marks. When woven into a sentence, they are usually followed by commas.

> *Look!* Here is the missing disk!
>
> *Gosh,* the car won't move!

SUMMARY

The sentence below illustrates all eight parts of speech.

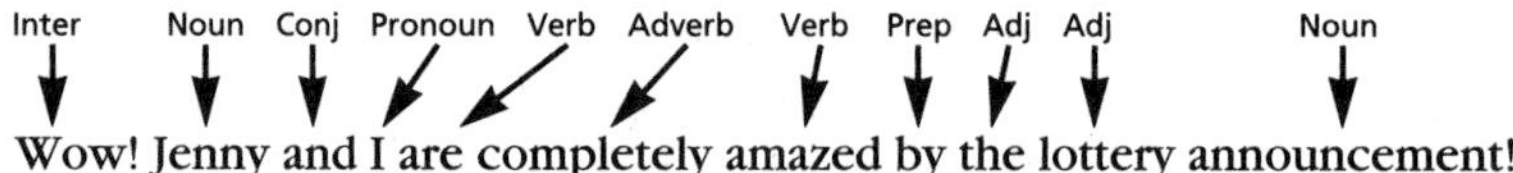

You need to know the functions of these eight parts of speech so that you will be able to understand the rest of this textbook and profit from your study of basic English. The explanation of the parts of speech has so far been kept simple. This chapter is meant to serve as an introduction to later, more fully developed chapters. At this stage you should not expect to be able to identify the functions of *all* words in *all* sentences.

A word of caution: English is a wonderfully flexible language. As we noted in discussing dictionaries, many words in our language can serve as more than one part of speech. Notice how flexible the word *box* is in these sentences:

> That *box* is very heavy. (Noun — serves as subject of sentence.)
>
> Music from the boom *box* startled the librarian. (Noun — serves as object of preposition.)
>
> Pick up your tickets at the *box* office. (Adjective — identifies what kind of office.)
>
> The featherweight fighters will *box* first. (Verb — serves as action word in the sentence.)

SPOT THE BLOOPER

Headline in *The Daily Aztec,* the student newspaper at San Diego State University: "Juveniles Arrested for Attempted Parking Structure Theft."

Now complete the reinforcement exercises for this chapter.

HOT LINE QUERIES

Students, writers, and businesspeople are very concerned about appropriate English usage, grammar, and style. This concern is evident in the number and kinds of questions called in to grammar hot line services across the country.

DID YOU KNOW

You can receive a directory of grammar hot line services across the country. Send a self-addressed, stamped envelope to Grammar Hotline Director, Writing Center, Humanities Division, Tidewater Community College, Virginia Beach, VA 23456.

Among the callers are business supervisors, managers, executives, secretaries, clerks, and word processing specialists. Writers, teachers, librarians, students, and other community members also seek answers to language questions.

Some of the questions asked and appropriate answers to them will be presented in the following chapters. In this way you, as a student of the language, will understand the kinds of everyday communication problems encountered in the real world.

The original questions in our Hot Line Queries came from the Los Angeles Pierce College hot line. More recently, questions were selected from the following grammar hot line services: University of Delaware, Purdue University, Eastern Illinois University, Broward Community College, Moorpark College, Illinois State University at Normal, University of Arkansas at Little Rock, and Wright State University.

QUESTION Help! How do I write *fax?* Small letters? Capital letters? Periods? And is it proper to use it as a verb, such as *May we fax the material to you?*

ANSWER The shortened form of *facsimile* is *fax,* written in small letters without periods. Yes, it may be used as a verb, as you did in your sentence.

QUESTION I saw this sentence recently in the newspaper: *At the movie premiere the crowd scanned the limousines for glitterati.* Is *glitterati* a real word?

ANSWER A new noun to our vocabulary, *glitterati* means "celebrities or beautiful people." New words are generally considered legitimate when their use is clear and when they are necessary (that is, when no other word says exactly what they do). If educated individuals begin to use such words, the words then appear in dictionaries, and *glitterati* has made it.

QUESTION Which word should I use in this sentence? *Our department will* disburse *or* disperse *the funds shortly.*

ANSWER Use *disburse. Disperse* means "to scatter" or "to distribute" (*information will be dispersed to all divisions*). *Disburse* means "to pay out." Perhaps this memory device will help you keep them straight: associate the *b* in *disburse* with *bank* (*banks disburse money*).

QUESTION How should I address a person who signed a letter *J. R. Henderson?*

ANSWER Use *Dear J. R. Henderson.*

QUESTION What's the difference between *toward* and *towards?*

ANSWER None. They are interchangeable in use. However, it's more efficient to use the shorter word *toward.*

QUESTION Is *every day* one word or two in this case? *We encounter these problems every day.*

ANSWER In your sentence it is two words. When it means "ordinary," it is one word (*she wore everyday clothes*). If you can insert the word *single* between *every* and *day* without altering your meaning, you should be using two words.

QUESTION I work in an office where we frequently send letters addressed to people on a first-name basis. Should I use a comma or a colon after a salutation like *Dear Mike?*

ANSWER The content of the letter, not the salutation (greeting), determines the punctuation after the salutation. If the letter is a business letter, always use a colon. If the letter is totally personal, a comma may be used, although a colon would also be appropriate.

QUESTION What is the name of a group of initials that form a word? Is it an abbreviation?

ANSWER A word formed from the initial letters of an expression is called an *acronym* (pronounced ACK-ro-nim). Examples: *snafu* from *situation normal, all fouled up,* and *DOS* from *disk operating system.* Acronyms are usually pronounced as a single word and are different from abbreviations. Expressions like *FBI* and *dept.* are abbreviations, not acronyms.

3 Sentences: Elements, Patterns, Types

OBJECTIVES When you have completed the materials in this chapter, you will be able to do the following:

- Recognize subjects and predicates.
- Convert fragments into complete sentences.
- Recognize basic sentence faults such as comma splices and run-on sentences.
- Complete sentences in three basic sentence patterns.
- Punctuate statements, commands, questions, and exclamations.

PRETEST

Write the correct letter after each of the numbered groups of words below to identify it.

a = correctly punctuated sentence   c = comma splice
b = fragment   d = run-on sentence

1. Carole Peck, who represents the ideal of the committed American chef. ____

2. Carole chooses ingredients carefully, her goal is healthful meals. ____

3. On her menus are clear, distinct, and aggressive flavors. ____

4. Carole concentrates on healthful dishes James prefers classic, minimally processed foods. ____

5. Since she uses natural ingredients rather than technologically engineered foods. ____

Sentences are groups of words that express complete thoughts. In this chapter you'll review the two basic elements of every sentence. In addition, you'll learn to recognize sentence patterns and types. This knowledge will help you use and punctuate sentences correctly. This chapter also introduces proofreading marks and provides a message for you to edit.

SENTENCE ELEMENTS

Subjects and Predicates

Good writers know that sentences are composed of two essential elements: subjects and predicates. The *subject* of a sentence is the person or thing being talked about,

1. b 2. c 3. a 4. d 5. b

and the *predicate* tells what the subject is, what the subject is doing, or what is being done to the subject. Study the following sentence:

The new driver of the limousine	observed the speed limit carefully.
complete subject	complete predicate

The *complete subject* of the sentence includes the subject (in this case a noun) plus all the words that describe or limit the subject (its modifiers). The *complete predicate* includes the verb plus its modifiers.

The heart of the complete subject is the simple subject (*driver*), and the heart of the predicate is the simple predicate, or verb (*observed*). The following sentences are divided into complete subjects and complete predicates. Simple subjects are underlined once; simple predicates (verbs) are underlined twice.

COMPLETE SUBJECTS	COMPLETE PREDICATES
Sales of sunglasses	jumped over 20 percent last year.
All branches of the company	are connected by E-mail.
A Florida pilot program	will be launched next month.
Most sunglass manufacturers	stress fashion and styling.

STUDY TIP

Many linking verbs also serve as helping verbs. Note that a verb phrase is *linking* only when the final verb is a linking verb, such as in the phrase *might have been.*

Notice in the previous sentences that the verbs may consist of one word or several. In a verb phrase the principal verb is the final one; the other verbs are ***helping*** or ***auxiliary verbs.*** The most frequently used helping verbs are *am, is, are, was, were, been, have, has, had, must, ought, can, might, could, would, should, will, do, does,* and *did.*

Sentence Sense

In addition to a subject and a predicate, a group of words must possess one additional element to qualify as a sentence: the group of words must make sense. Observe that the first two groups of words that follow express complete thoughts and make sense; the third does not.

> Athletic shoe makers convinced us that we need $100 tennis shoes. (Subject plus predicate making sense = sentence.)
>
> Kevin now owns different sneakers for every sport. (Subject plus predicate making sense = sentence.)
>
> Although sunglass makers promote different sunglasses for different activities (Subject plus predicate but NOT making sense = no sentence.)

In the third case a reader or listener senses that the idea expressed is incomplete. We do not have a sentence; instead, we have a fragment.

The English language has about three times as many words as any other language on earth. English is estimated to include at least 450,000 words. German has 185,000, Russian 130,000, and French 100,000.

SENTENCE FAULTS

Three typical sentence faults are fragments, comma splices, and run-on sentences.

Fragment

Fragments are groups of words that have been broken off from preceding or succeeding sentences. They cannot function as complete sentences. Avoid fragments by making certain that each sentence contains a subject and a verb and makes sense by itself. In the examples below, the fragments are italicized. Notice how they can be revised to make complete sentences.

SPOT THE BLOOPER

From a local church bulletin: "Mrs. Betty Larkin is poorly this spring, her smiling face is much missed in church. It being always there when she is able to be present."

FRAGMENT: Suzie spends a lot of time in the sun. *Which is why she is shopping for a good sunscreen product.*

REVISION: Suzie spends a lot of time in the sun, which is why she is shopping for a good sunscreen product.

REVISION: Because Suzie spends a lot of time in the sun, she is shopping for a good sunscreen product.

FRAGMENT: High thin clouds that let most of the ultraviolet rays pass through.

REVISION: High thin clouds let most of the ultraviolet rays pass through.

FRAGMENT: If you can see through a fabric when it is held up to the light. The cloth probably offers scant protection from UV rays.

REVISION: If you can see through a fabric when it is held up to the light, it probably offers scant protection from UV rays.

Comma Splice

A *comma splice* results when two sentences are incorrectly joined or spliced together with a comma. The sentences below show how comma splices could be revised into acceptable sentences.

SPOT THE BLOOPER

In a newspaper article: "He is recovering from a near-fatal accident that sent him into a comma."

COMMA SPLICE: Always prepare for a job interview, never go in cold.

REVISION: Always prepare for a job interview; never go in cold. (You'll learn more about semicolons in Chapters 14 and 17.)

REVISION: Always prepare for a job interview. Never go in cold.

COMMA SPLICE: First you must fill out an application, then you may submit your résumé.

REVISION: First you must fill out an application; then you may submit your résumé.

REVISION: First you must fill out an application. Then you may submit your résumé.

COMMA SPLICE: Many candidates applied, however, none had the proper background.

REVISION: Many candidates applied; however, none had the proper background.

Run-On Sentence

A *run-on sentence* joins two complete thoughts without proper punctuation. Notice how the following run-on sentences can be corrected by dividing the two thoughts into separate sentences.

RUN-ON SENTENCE: Please write me a letter of reference I need it by June 20.

REVISION: Please write me a letter of reference. I need it by June 20.

RUN-ON SENTENCE: Thoughtful interviewees send thank-you letters they make sure to spell the interviewer's name correctly.

REVISION: Thoughtful interviewees send thank-you letters. They make sure to spell the interviewer's name correctly.

SENTENCE PATTERNS

Three basic word patterns are used to express thoughts in English sentences.

Pattern No. 1: Subject–Verb

In the most basic sentence pattern, the subject is followed by its verb. No additional words are needed for the sentence to make sense and be complete.

SPOT THE BLOOPER

TV promo for upcoming program: "Yoko Ono will talk about her husband, John Lennon, who was killed in an interview with Barbara Walters."

SUBJECT	VERB
We	listened.
Someone	is knocking.
He	might have called.
All of the witnesses	are being investigated.

Pattern No. 2: Subject–Action Verb–Object

In this kind of sentence, the subject is followed by an action verb and its direct object. The object usually answers the question *what?* or *whom?*

SUBJECT	ACTION VERB	OBJECT
Marta	ate	chocolates.
Her brother	played	tennis.
Employees	send	E-mail messages.

This basic sentence pattern may also employ an indirect object that usually answers the question *to whom?*

SUBJECT	ACTION VERB	INDIRECT OBJECT	DIRECT OBJECT
This organization	pays	workers	high salaries.
LaDonna	had given	him	the data.

"The most important thing I learned in college was how to communicate."
— Lee Iacocca, former CEO, Chrysler Corporation

Pattern No. 3: Subject–Linking Verb–Complement

In the third kind of sentence, the subject is followed by a linking verb and its complement. A *complement* is a noun, pronoun, or adjective that renames or describes the subject. A complement *completes* the meaning of the subject.

SUBJECT	LINKING VERB	COMPLEMENT	
The manager	is	Jeffrey.	(Noun complements.)
These packages	are	books.	
Your instructor	is	she.	(Pronoun complements.)
The callers	might have been	they.	
This monitor	looks	satisfactory.	(Adjective complements.)
Tiffany	feels	bad.	

The sentences shown here have been kept simple so that their patterns can be recognized easily. Although most speakers and writers expand these basic patterns with additional phrases and clauses, the basic sentence structure remains the same. Despite its length, the following sentence follows the basic subject–verb–object order:

Citizens in the world's economic superpowers—the U.S., Germany, and Japan—answered survey questions ranging from job security to health care. (The simple subject is *Citizens,* the verb is *answered,* and the object is *questions.*)

Inverted Order

In some sentences the elements appear in inverted order, with the verb preceding the subject.

Parked in front are sports cars.

Selling the most vans is Ryan.

In questions the verb may precede the subject or may be interrupted by the subject.

How are light utility trucks selling?

Do you offer price quotes by fax?

In sentences beginning with *here* or *there,* the normal word order is also inverted.

Here are the latest prices.

There is no single answer.

To locate the true subject in any inverted sentence, mentally rearrange the words. Place them in the normal subject-verb order.

Sports cars are parked in front.

Ryan is selling the most vans.

The latest prices are here.

No single answer is there.

FOUR SENTENCE TYPES

NOTABLE QUOTABLE

"Trim sentences, like trim bodies, usually require far more effort than flabby ones."
— Claire K. Cook

Statements

Statements make assertions and end with periods.

We are expanding our markets beyond our shores.

Laws passed by Congress require truth in advertising.

Questions

Direct questions are followed by question marks.

Where will you move?

What does the manufacturer's label say?

Commands

Commands end with periods or, occasionally, with exclamation points. Note that the subject in all commands is understood to be *you.* The subject *you* is not normally stated in the command.

Close the window. ([You] close the window.)

Send for your new credit card. ([You] send for your . . .)

"Cut out all those exclamation marks. An exclamation mark is like laughing at your own joke."
— F. Scott Fitzgerald

Exclamations

Showing surprise, disbelief, or strong feelings, exclamations may or may not be expressed as complete thoughts. Both subject and predicate may be implied.

Look! Isn't that Elizabeth?

What a wonderful day [it is]!

How extraordinary [that is]!

Now complete the reinforcement exercises for this chapter.

HOT LINE QUERIES

QUESTION A fellow worker insists on saying, *I could care less.* Seems to me that it should be *I couldn't care less.* Who is right?

ANSWER The phrase *I couldn't care less* has been in the language a long time. It means, of course, "I have little concern about the matter." Recently, though, people have begun to use *I could care less* with the same meaning. Most careful listeners realize that the latter phrase says just the opposite of its intent. Although both phrases are clichés, stick with *I couldn't care less* if you want to be clear.

QUESTION This sentence just doesn't sound right to me, but I can't decide how to improve it: *The reason for the delay is because we have a new computer program.*

ANSWER The problem lies in this construction: *the reason . . . is because . . .* Only nouns or adjectives may act as complements following linking verbs. In your sentence an adverbial clause follows the linking verb and sounds awkward. One way to improve the sentence is to substitute a noun clause beginning with *that: The reason for the delay is that we have a new computer program.* An even better way to improve the sentence would be to make it a direct statement: *Our new computer program caused the delay.*

QUESTION My friend says that this sentence is correct: *Jill will first print all the letters, then she will prepare the envelopes.* I think something is wrong, but I'm not sure what.

ANSWER You're right. This sentence has two short independent clauses, and some writers attempt to join them with a comma. But this construction produces a comma splice. The adverb *then* cannot function as a conjunction, such as *and,* to join these two clauses. Start a new sentence or use a semicolon between the clauses.

QUESTION My boss dictated a report with this sentence: *Saleswise, our staff is excellent.* Should I change it?

ANSWER Never change wording without checking with the author. You might point out, however, that the practice of attaching *-wise* to nouns is frowned on by many language experts. Such combinations as *budgetwise, taxwise,* and *productionwise* are considered commercial jargon. Suggest this revision: *On the basis of sales, our staff is excellent.*

QUESTION At the end of a letter I wrote: *Thank you for attending to this matter immediately.* Should I hyphenate *thank you?*

ANSWER Do not hyphenate *thank you* when using it as a verb (*thank you for writing*). Do hyphenate it when using it as an adjective (*I sent a thank-you note*). It is also hyphenated when used as a noun (*I sent four thank-yous*). Since *thank you* is used as a verb in your sentence, do not hyphenate it. Notice that *thank you* is never written as a single word.

NAME ______________________

UNIT 1 REVIEW ■ Chapters 1–3 (Self-Check)

Begin your review by rereading Chapters 1–3. Then check your comprehension of those chapters by writing *T* (true) or *F* (false) in the blanks below. Compare your responses with those at the end of the review.

1. Nearly all dictionaries present word definitions in the same sequence. F

2. Usage labels such as *obsolete, archaic,* and *informal* warn dictionary users about appropriate usage. T

3. An unabridged dictionary is a shortened or condensed form of a longer dictionary. F

4. The etymology code helps you to pronounce a word correctly. F

5. Most dictionaries show noun plurals only if the plurals are irregular, such as the word *men.* F

6. A thesaurus is a collection of words and their definitions. F

7. Most college students would find a current pocket dictionary best for their assignments. F

8. The usage label *nonstandard* means that a word is no longer in use. F

9. The terms *desk* and *college-level* refer to the same kind of dictionary. T

10. A summary of diacritical marks is often found at the bottom of dictionary pages. F

Read the following sentence carefully. Identify the parts of speech for the words as they are used in this sentence.

She glanced quickly at the message and then wrote two notes.

11. She	(a) noun	(b) pronoun	(c) adverb	(d) adj	B
12. glanced	(a) conj	(b) prep	(c) verb	(d) adverb	C
13. quickly	(a) conj	(b) prep	(c) adj	(d) adverb	D
14. at	(a) conj	(b) prep	(c) adj	(d) adverb	B
15. message	(a) noun	(b) pronoun	(c) conj	(d) adverb	A
16. and	(a) noun	(b) pronoun	(c) conj	(d) prep	C
17. then	(a) noun	(b) adverb	(c) conj	(d) prep	B
18. wrote	(a) verb	(b) adverb	(c) conj	(d) prep	A
19. two	(a) verb	(b) adverb	(c) adj	(d) prep	C
20. notes	(a) noun	(b) pronoun	(c) adj	(d) prep	A

For each of the following statements, determine the word or phrase that correctly completes that statement and write its letter in the space provided.

21. In the sentence ***A new global network was established,*** the simple subject is (a) new, (b) global, (c) network, (d) established. C

22. In the sentence ***Here are both messages,*** the simple subject is (a) Here, (b) both, (c) messages, (d) you. C

23. In the sentence ***I feel good,*** the verb ***feel*** is a (a) linking verb, (b) helping verb, (c) subject, (d) predicate. A

24. The sentence *He sent an E-mail message* represents what sentence pattern: (a) subject-verb, (b) subject-action verb-object, (c) subject-linking verb-complement, (d) subject-linking verb-object. ____

25. In the sentence *All branches of the bank will close on the holiday,* the simple subject is (a) all, (b) branches, (c) bank, (d) holiday. ____

26. The sentence *The president is she* represents what sentence pattern? (a) subject-verb, (b) subject-action verb-object, (c) subject-linking verb-complement, (d) subject-linking verb-object. ____

From the list below select the letter(s) to accurately describe each of the following groups of words.

a = command	c = fragment	e = run-on sentence
b = complete sentence	d = comma splice	

27. We must install one more computer, then our equipment will be complete. ____
28. Whether the election is scheduled this year or next year. ____
29. Take the dog for a walk and bring back some ice cream. ____
30. That company's printers are excellent its service is slow, however. ____
31. Many applicants are interested in submitting electronic résumés. ____
32. Since many résumés must be scanned by our computer program first. ____
33. Complete the application and return it with your résumé. ____
34. The hurricane hit Bermuda, we're not sure how much damage occurred. ____
35. Your limousine just arrived the driver is waiting for you outside. ____
36. The first toothbrush was the "chew stick," and such frayed twigs are still used by people in remote parts of the world today. ____
37. Make a dental appointment, and write it on your calendar. ____
38. Although fingernail polish originated in ancient China where the color of a person's nails indicated social rank. ____
39. Early Egyptian and Roman military commanders spent hours before a battle having their hair lacquered and curled, they also had their nails painted the same shade as their lips. ____

Hot Line Review

Select the word or phrase that correctly completes each statement, and write its letter in the corresponding blank.

40. (a) Thankyou, (b) Thank-you, (c) Thank you for returning my wallet. ____
41. Informative literature and coupons will be (a) dispersed, (b) disbursed at the beginning of the sales campaign. ____
42. Newspapers are delivered (a) everyday, (b) every day, (c) every-day except Sunday. ____
43. The reason he was delayed is (a) because, (b) that an accident created a traffic jam. ____
44. The horse and its owner moved (a) toward, (b) towards the winner's circle. ____
45. The expression *snafu* is known as a(n) (a) abbreviation, (b) acronym, (c) cliché. ____

1. F 2. T 3. F 4. T 5. T 6. F 7. F 8. F 9. T 10. T 11. b 12. c 13. d 14. b 15. a 16. c 17. b 18. a 19. c
20. a 21. c 22. c 23. a 24. b 25. b 26. c 27. d 28. c 29. a or b 30. e 31. b 32. c 33. a or b 34. d 35. e 36. b
37. a or b 38. c 39. d 40. c 41. a 42. b 43. b 44. a 45. b

UNIT

2

Knowing the Namers

4 Nouns

OBJECTIVES When you have completed the materials in this chapter, you will be able to do the following:

Level I
- Recognize four kinds of nouns.

Level II
- Spell troublesome plural nouns ending in *y, o,* and *f.*
- Form the plurals of compound nouns, numerals, letters, degrees, and abbreviations.

Level III
- Recognize and use correctly foreign plural nouns and selected special nouns.
- Create sentences using plural personal titles.

PRETEST

Underline any incorrectly spelled noun in the following sentences. Write the correct spelling in the space provided.

1. It seemed that all the mice in the building had found the cheese on our two bottom shelfs. ______

2. Beetle's kitchen duties included sharpening knifes and chopping potatos. ______

3. Won't our taxes pay for school lunchs for the children who need them? ______

4. The attornies demanded run-offs in both elections. ______

5 Because no candidate can meet all the criterions, we use certain formulas to narrow the field. ______

As you will recall from Chapter 1, nouns *name* persons, places, things, qualities, and concepts. In this chapter you'll learn to distinguish concrete from abstract nouns and common from proper nouns. The principal emphasis, however, will be on forming and spelling plural nouns, an area of confusion for many writers.

Beginning with this chapter, concepts are presented in levels, progressing from basic, frequently used concepts at Level I to more complex and less frequently used concepts at Level III. This unique separation of concepts has proved very effective in helping students understand, retain, and apply basic language principles.

1. shelves 2. knives, potatoes 3. lunches 4. attorneys 5. criteria

KINDS OF NOUNS

Concrete and Abstract Nouns

Concrete nouns name specific objects that can actually be seen, heard, felt, tasted, or smelled. Abstract nouns name qualities and concepts. Because concrete nouns are precise, they are more forceful in writing and talking than abstract nouns.

Concrete Nouns		
car	teacher	pencil
rose	cookie	clock
garage	catalog	spoon
Abstract Nouns		
comfort	honesty	creativity
violence	talent	anger
time	fear	courage

"An abstract noun neither smiles nor sings nor tells bedtime stories."
— Lewis Lapham

Common and Proper Nouns

Common nouns name *generalized* persons, places, and things. Proper nouns, on the other hand, name *specific* persons, places, and things. They are always capitalized. Rules for capitalization are presented in Chapter 19.

Common Nouns		
college	candy	planet
car	pen	computer
newspaper	city	book
Proper Nouns		
Michigan State University	Snickers candy bar	Jupiter
Corvette	Paper Mate pen	IBM Personal Computer
USA Today	New York	*The American Heritage College Dictionary*

Note: Common nouns following proper nouns are not capitalized.

Basic Plurals

Singular nouns name *one* person, place, or thing. Plural nouns name *two* or more. At Level I you will learn basic rules for forming plurals. At Level II you will learn how to form the plurals of nouns that create spelling problems.

- ***Most regular nouns*** form the plural with the addition of *s*.

project, projects	document, documents	chair, chairs
pencil, pencils	keyboard, keyboards	letter, letters
office, offices	Jane, Janes	Miller, Millers

Note: Most proper nouns (*Jane, Miller*) become plural the same way that common nouns do.

SPOT THE BLOOPER

Advertisement for Kimberly Woods Apartment Houses, San Jose, CA: "MAKE THE JONES JEALOUS."

- ***Nouns ending in* s, x, z, ch, *or* sh** form the plural with the addition of *es.*

lunch, lunches	blintz, blintzes	tax, taxes
wish, wishes	process, processes	switch, switches
index, indexes	Mendez, Mendezes	boss, bosses

- ***Irregular nouns*** form the plural by changing the spelling of the word.

child, children	foot, feet	goose, geese
mouse, mice	ox, oxen, oxes	woman, women

SPOT THE BLOOPER

Nabisco introduced a new product as *Teddy Graham Bearwich's.* Not long after, it quietly gave the box a new design and new name, *T. G. Bearwiches.*

Because of space restrictions most dictionaries do *not* show plurals of *regular* nouns. Thus, if you look up the plural of *ranch,* you probably will not find it. Dictionaries *do* show the plurals of nouns that might be confusing or difficult to spell.

Be careful not to use apostrophes (') to form plural nouns. Reserve the apostrophe to show possession. (Chapter 5 discusses possessive nouns in detail.)

INCORRECT: The season ended when owner's and player's could not agree on salary's.

CORRECT: The season ended when owners and players could not agree on salaries.

In using plural words, do not confuse nouns with verbs (*He saves* [verb] *his money in two safes* [noun]). Be especially mindful of the following words:

SPOT THE BLOOPER

Headline from [The Bellefontaine, OH] *Examiner:* "Leaders shelf plan to reduce bomber force."

NOUNS	VERBS
belief, beliefs	believe, believes
leaf, leaves (foliage)	leave, leaves (to depart)
loaf, loaves (of bread)	loaf, loafs (to be idle)
proof, proofs	prove, proves

Now complete the reinforcement exercises for Level I.

LEVEL II

TROUBLESOME NOUN PLURALS

Your ability to spell certain troublesome nouns can be greatly improved by studying the following rules and examples.

- ***Common nouns ending in* y** form the plural in two ways.

a. When the *y* is preceded by a vowel (*a, e, i, o, u*), the plural is formed with the addition of *s* only.

attorney, attorneys	essay, essays	play, plays
survey, surveys	valley, valleys	Murray, Murrays

b. When the *y* is preceded by a consonant (all letters other than vowels), the plural is formed by changing the *y* to *ies.*

baby, babies	company, companies	copy, copies
laboratory, laboratories	policy, policies	specialty, specialties

In making surnames plural, never change the original spellings. Adding *s* or *es* is acceptable, but changing *Kennedy* to *Kennedies* changes the original spelling.

Note: This rule does *not* apply to the plural forms of proper nouns: Sally, Sallys; January, Januarys; Billy, Billys; Henry, Henrys.

■ *Nouns ending in* f *or* fe follow no standard rules in the formation of plurals. Study the examples shown here, and use a dictionary when in doubt. When two forms are shown, the preferred appears first.

ADD *s*	CHANGE TO *ves*	BOTH FORMS RECOGNIZED
brief, briefs	half, halves	calves, calfs
proof, proofs	knife, knives	dwarfs, dwarves
safe, safes	leaf, leaves	wharves, wharfs
handkerchief, handkerchiefs	shelf, shelves	scarves, scarfs
sheriff, sheriffs	wife, wives	
Wolf, Wolfs	wolf, wolves	

■ *Nouns ending in* o may be made plural by adding *s* or *es.*

a. When the *o* is preceded by a vowel, the plural is formed by adding *s* only.

studio, studios   curio, curios   radio, radios

b. When the *o* is preceded by a consonant, the plural is formed by adding *s* or *es.* Study the following examples and again use your dictionary whenever in doubt. When two forms are shown, the preferred one appears first.

ADD *s*	ADD *es*	BOTH FORMS RECOGNIZED
photo, photos	echo, echoes	cargoes, cargos
typo, typos	embargo, embargoes	commandos, commandoes
logo, logos	hero, heroes	mosquitoes, mosquitos
patio, patios	potato, potatoes	tornadoes, tornados
ratio, ratios	tomato, tomatoes	volcanos, volcanoes
Angelo, Angelos	veto, vetoes	zeros, zeroes

c. Musical terms ending in *o* always form the plural with the addition of *s* only.

alto, altos   banjo, banjos   cello, cellos

concerto, concertos   piano, pianos   solo, solos

SPOT THE BLOOPER

In an advertisement for Accelerated Schools in Colorado's *Rocky Mountain News:* "STUDENT'S DON'T HAVE TO FAIL."

■ *Compound nouns* may be written as single words, may be hyphenated, or may appear as two words.

a. When written as single words, compound nouns form the plural by appropriate changes in the final element.

bookshelf, bookshelves   classmate, classmates   letterhead, letterheads

payroll, payrolls   photocopy, photocopies   stockholder, stockholders

b. When written in hyphenated or open form, compound nouns form the plural by appropriate changes in the principal noun.

accounts payable   bills of lading   boards of directors

editors in chief   leaves of absence   hangers-on

mayors-elect   brothers-in-law   runners-up

c. If the compound noun has no principal noun at all, the final element is made plural.

cure-alls get-togethers go-betweens
hang-ups has-beens know-it-alls
so-and-sos trade-offs walk-throughs

d. Some compound noun plurals have two recognized forms. In the following list, the preferred form is shown first.

attorneys general, attorney generals
cupfuls, cupsful; teaspoonfuls, teaspoonsful
courts-martial, court-martials; notaries public, notary publics

■ ***Numerals, alphabet letters, isolated words, and degrees*** are made plural by adding *s, es,* or *'s.* The trend is to use the *'s* only when necessary for clarity.

a. Numerals and uppercase letters (with the exception of *A, I, M,* and *U*) require only *s* in plural formation.

1990s all Cs and Ds the three Rs
401Ks W-2s and 1040s 7s and 8s

b. Isolated words used as nouns are made plural with the addition of *s* or *es,* as needed for pronunciation.

ands, ifs, or buts dos and don'ts pros and cons
yeses and noes (or yeses and nos) ups and downs whys and wherefores

c. Degrees are made plural with the addition of *s.*

A.A.s B.S.s Ph.D.s
R.N.s M.B.A.s M.D.s

d. Isolated lowercase letters and the capital letters *A, I, M,* and *U* require *'s* for clarity.

M&M's p's and q's A's

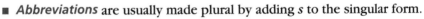

"The English language has far more lives than a cat. People have been murdering it for years."
— *Farmers' Almanac*

■ ***Abbreviations*** are usually made plural by adding *s* to the singular form.

bldg., bldgs. CEO, CEOs RSVP, RSVPs
IOU, IOUs mgr., mgrs. No., Nos.
wk., wks. yr., yrs. VCR, VCRs

The singular and plural forms of abbreviations for units of measurement are, however, often identical.

deg. (degree or degrees) in. (inch or inches)
ft. (foot or feet) oz. (ounce or ounces)

Some units of measurement have two plural forms.

lb. or lbs. yd. or yds. qt. or qts.

Now complete the reinforcement exercises for Level II.

SPECIAL PLURAL FORMS

Language purists contend that the word *data* can only be plural (*the data are*). However, see the Hot Line Queries for another view.

■ ***Nouns borrowed from foreign languages*** may retain a foreign plural. A few, however, have an Americanized plural form, shown in parentheses below. Check your dictionary for the preferred form.

SINGULAR	PLURAL
analysis	analyses
alumna (feminine)	alumnae (pronounced a-LUM-nee)
alumnus (masculine)	alumni (pronounced a-LUM-ni)
bacterium	bacteria
basis	bases
cactus	cacti (or cactuses)
criterion	criteria
curriculum	curricula (or curriculums)
datum	data*
diagnosis	diagnoses
erratum	errata
formula	formulae (or formulas)
genus	genera
larva	larvae
memorandum	memoranda (or memorandums)
opus	opera
parenthesis	parentheses
phenomenon	phenomena
radius	radii (or radiuses)
syllabus	syllabi (or syllabuses)
thesis	theses
vertebra	vertebrae (or vertebras)

*See discussion on p. 45.

■ ***Personal titles*** may have both formal and informal plural forms.

SINGULAR	FORMAL PLURALS	INFORMAL PLURALS
Miss	the Misses Kelly	the Miss Kellys
Mr.	Messrs.* Sanchez and Larson	Mr. Sanchez and Mr. Larson
Mrs.	Mmes.† Stokes and Aboud	Mrs. Stokes and Mrs. Aboud
Ms.	Mses.‡ Freeman and Moya	Ms. Freeman and Ms. Moya

* Pronounced MES-erz (abbreviation of Messieurs).
† Pronounced May-DAHM (abbreviation of Mesdames).
‡ Pronounced MIZ-ez (Ms. is probably a blend of Miss and Mrs.).

You can practice these special nouns by using them with the singular verb *is* or the plural verb *are*. For example, *Aeronautics is fascinating* (sing.); *scissors are useful* (plural).

■ ***Special nouns,*** many of which end in *s,* may normally be *only* singular *or* plural in meaning. Other special nouns may be considered *either* singular *or* plural in meaning.

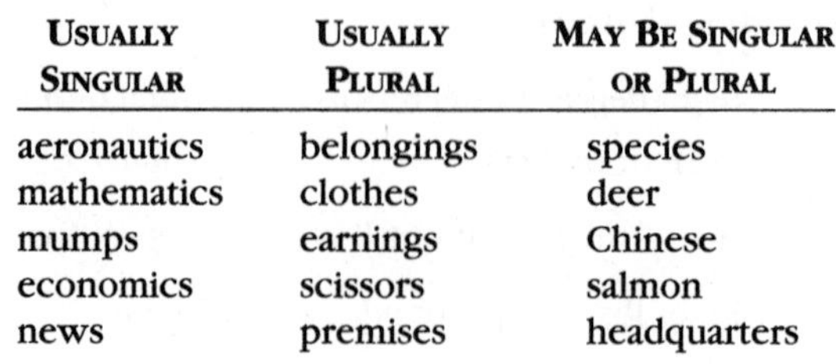

USUALLY SINGULAR	USUALLY PLURAL	MAY BE SINGULAR OR PLURAL
aeronautics	belongings	species
mathematics	clothes	deer
mumps	earnings	Chinese
economics	scissors	salmon
news	premises	headquarters

- *Single-letter abbreviations* may be made plural by doubling the letter.

pp. (pages)	See pp. 18–21. (pages 18 through 21)
ff. (and following)	See pp. 18 ff. (page 18 and following pages)

Now complete the reinforcement exercises for Level III.

HOT LINE QUERIES

QUESTION It seems to me that the meaning of the word *impact* has changed. I thought it meant "an effect." But now I hear this use: *How does this policy impact on the Middle East?* What's happening to this word?

ANSWER In our language, nouns often become verbs (to *bridge* the gap, to *corner* a market, to *telephone* a friend). Whether a noun-turned-verb is assimilated into the language seems to depend on its utility, its efficiency, and the status of the individuals who use it. Skilled writers, for example, avoid the word *prioritize* because it is inefficient and sounds bureaucratic. Transformation of the noun *impact* into a verb would appear to be unnecessary, since the word *affect* clearly suffices in most constructions (*How does this program affect the Middle East?*). Although we hear *impact* used frequently as a verb today, many language specialists find it offensive.

QUESTION Could you help me spell the plurals of *do* and *don't?*

ANSWER In forming the plurals of isolated words, the trend today is to add *s* and no apostrophe. Thus, we have *dos* and *don'ts.* Formerly, apostrophes were used to make isolated words plural. However, if no confusion results, make plurals by adding *s* only.

QUESTION One member of our staff consistently corrects our use of the word *data.* He says the word is plural. Is it never singular?

ANSWER The word *data* is indeed plural; the singular form is *datum.* Through frequent usage, however, *data* has recently become a collective noun. Collective nouns may be singular or plural depending on whether they are considered as one unit or as separate units. For example, *These data are much different from those findings.* Or, *This data is conclusive.*

QUESTION I don't have a dictionary handy. Can you tell me which word I should use in this sentence: *A [stationary/stationery] circuit board will be installed.*

ANSWER In your sentence use *stationary,* which means "not moving" or "permanent" (*the concrete columns are stationary*). *Stationery* means "writing paper" (*his stationery has his address printed on it*). You might be able to remember the word *stationery* by associating *envelopes* with the *e* in *stationery.*

QUESTION My mother is always correcting me when I say, *I hate when that happens.* What's wrong with this? I hear it on TV all the time.

ANSWER Your mother wants you to speak standard English, the written and spoken language of educated people. Hearing an expression on TV is no assurance that it's acceptable. The problem with an expression like *I hate when that happens* is that an adverbial phrase (*when that happens*) is used as the object of a verb (*hate*). Only nouns, noun clauses, or pronouns may act as objects of verbs. Correction: *I hate it when that happens,* or *I hate this to happen.*

QUESTION As a sportswriter, I need to know the plural of *hole-in-one.*

ANSWER Make the principal word plural, *holes-in-one.*

5 Possessive Nouns

OBJECTIVES When you have completed the materials in this chapter, you will be able to do the following:

Level I

- Distinguish between possessive nouns and noun plurals.
- Follow five steps in using the apostrophe to show ownership.

Level II

- Use apostrophe construction for animate nouns.
- Distinguish between descriptive nouns and possessive nouns.
- Pluralize compound nouns, combined ownership nouns, organization names, and abbreviations.
- Understand incomplete possessives.
- Avoid awkward possessives.

Level III

- Determine if an extra syllable can be pronounced in forming a possessive.
- Make proper nouns possessive.

PRETEST

Underline any incorrect possessive forms. Write correct versions in the spaces provided.

1. Only one doctors prescription can be filled at a time. ____________
2. Were all the questions answered by the Sale's Department? ____________
3. The newspapers slogan reads, "Tomorrows news today." ____________
4. How did the Sanchez dog get into Mr. Taylor's yard? ____________
5. Neil's and Shelley's party was the hit of this year's season. ____________

"Everything comes to those who hustle while they wait."
— Will Rogers

Thus far you have studied four kinds of nouns (concrete, abstract, common, and proper), and you have learned how to make nouns plural. In this chapter you will learn how to use the apostrophe in making nouns possessive.

1. doctor's 2. Sales 3. newspaper's; Tomorrow's 4. Sanchezes' 5. Neil

LEVEL I

SHOWING POSSESSION WITH APOSTROPHES

Notice in the following phrases how possessive nouns show ownership, origin, authorship, or measurement:

the carpenter's hammer (ownership)
Mexico's currency (origin)
Clancy's novels (authorship)
two months' time (measurement)

In expressing possession, speakers and writers have a choice. They may show possession with an apostrophe construction, or they may use a prepositional phrase with no apostrophe:

the hammer of the carpenter
the currency of Mexico
the novels of Clancy
the time of two months

The use of a prepositional phrase to show ownership is more formal and tends to emphasize the ownership word. The use of the apostrophe construction to show ownership is more efficient and more natural, especially in conversation. In writing, however, placing the apostrophe can be perplexing. Here are five simple but effective steps that will help you write possessives correctly.

Five Steps in Using the Apostrophe Correctly

SPOT THE BLOOPER

From Lois and Selma DeBakey's collection of bad medical writing: "The receptionist called the patients names." (*How does the omitted apostrophe alter the meaning?*)

■ ***Look for possessive construction.*** Usually two nouns appear together. The first noun shows ownership of (or special relationship to) the second noun.

the woman['s] briefcase
the children['s] toys
a month['s] wages
several printers['] quotes
the singers['] voices

Whenever you have any doubt about using an apostrophe, always put the expression into an "of" phrase. You'll immediately recognize the ownership word and see whether it ends in an *s.*

■ ***Reverse the nouns.*** Use the second noun to begin a prepositional phrase. The object of the preposition is the ownership word.

briefcase of the woman
toys of the children
wages of a month
quotes of several printers
voices of the singers

■ ***Examine the ownership word.*** To determine the correct placement of the apostrophe, you must know whether the ownership word ends in an *s* sound (such as *s, x,* or *z*).

■ ***If the ownership word does not end in an* s *sound, add an apostrophe and* s.**

the woman's briefcase
the children's toys
a month's wages

SPOT THE BLOOPER

Headline in the [Bellefontaine, OH] *Examiner:* "One Man's Harem Is Anothers' Tax Burden."

■ ***If the ownership word does end in an s sound, usually add only an apostrophe.***

several printers' quotes

the singers' voices

A word of caution: Once students begin to study apostrophes, they tend to use a shotgun approach on passages with words ending in *s,* indiscriminately peppering them with apostrophes. Do *not* use apostrophes for nouns that simply show more than one of something. In the sentence *These companies are opening new branches in the West,* no apostrophes are required. The words *companies* and *branches* are plural; they are not possessive. In addition, be careful to avoid changing the spelling of singular nouns when making them possessive. For example, the *secretary's* desk (meaning one secretary) is *not* spelled *secretaries'.*

Pay particular attention to the following possessive constructions. Perhaps the explanations and hints in parentheses will help you understand and remember these expressions.

a year's experience (the experience of one year)

ten years' experience (the experience of ten years)

a dollar's worth (the worth of one single dollar)

your money's worth (the worth of your money)

today's newspaper (there can be only one today)

tomorrow's appointments (there can be only one tomorrow)

the stockholders' meeting (we assume that a meeting involves more than one person)

The guides for possessive construction presented thus far cover the majority of possessives found in writing.

Now complete the reinforcement exercises for Level I.

"Even if you're on the right track, you'll get run over if you just sit there."
— Thomas Edison

LEVEL II

PROBLEM POSSESSIVE CONSTRUCTIONS

■ ***Animate versus inanimate nouns.*** As a matter of style, some careful writers prefer to reserve the apostrophe construction for people and animals. For other nouns use prepositional phrases or simple adjectives.

wing of the airplane or airplane wing (better than airplane's wing)

style of the suit or suit style (better than suit's style)

terms of the contract or contract terms (better than contract's terms)

To identify descriptive nouns, ask if ownership is involved. Does *Department* belong to *Sales?* Is *industry* possessed by *electronics?* When the answer is no, omit the apostrophe.

■ ***Descriptive versus possessive nouns.*** When nouns provide description or identification only, the possessive form is *not* used. Writers have most problems with descriptive nouns ending in *s,* such as *Claims* Department. No apostrophe is needed, just as none is necessary in *Personnel* Department.

Sales Department (not Sales' Department)

graphics design (not graphic's design)

Arkansas Razorbacks (not Arkansas' Razorbacks)

■ *Compound nouns.* Make compound nouns possessive by adding an apostrophe or an *'s* to the final element of the compound.

editor-in-chief's desk

board of directors' decision

attorney general's office

■ *Incomplete possessives.* When the second noun in a possessive noun construction is unstated, the first noun is nevertheless treated as possessive.

I left my umbrella at Colleen's [house].

They are meeting at the lawyer's [office] to discuss the testimony.

His score beat the champion's [score] by 20 points.

STUDY TIP

Look at the object owned (*agreement, home*). If that object is singular, ownership is usually combined.

■ *Separate or combined ownership.* When two names express separate ownership, make both names possessive. When two names express combined ownership, make only the *second* name possessive.

SEPARATE OWNERSHIP	COMBINED OWNERSHIP
nurses' and doctors' orders	actor and agent's agreement
Nadine's and Katie's birthdays	my father and mother's home

■ *Names of organizations.* Organizations with possessives in their names may or may not use apostrophes. Follow the style used by the individual organization. (Consult the organization's stationery or a directory listing.)

Farmers Insurance Group	McDonald's
U.S. Department of Veterans Affairs	Macy's

■ *Abbreviations.* Make abbreviations possessive by following the same guidelines as for animate nouns.

AMA's annual convention	both CEOs' signatures
MTV's fall schedule	Marketing Dept.'s memo

To avoid an awkward possessive, use an *of* phrase starting with the object owned, such as *prizes.*

■ *Awkward possessives.* When the addition of an apostrophe results in an awkward construction, show ownership by using a prepositional phrase.

AWKWARD: runners-up's prizes
IMPROVED: prizes of the runners-up

AWKWARD: my roommate's dog's collar
IMPROVED: the collar of my roommate's dog

AWKWARD: her boss, Mr. Wilde's, office
IMPROVED: office of her boss, Mr. Wilde

Now complete the reinforcement exercises for Level II.

LEVEL III

You have learned to follow five steps in identifying possessive constructions and in placing the apostrophe correctly. The guides presented thus far cover most possessive constructions. The possessive form of a few nouns, however, requires a refinement of the final step.

ADDITIONAL GUIDELINE

Let us briefly review the five-step plan for placing the apostrophe in noun possessives. Having done so, we will then add a refinement to the fifth step.

SPOT THE BLOOPER

Announcement pasted on top of each Domino's pizza box: "We accept all competitors coupons."

- Look for possessive construction. (Usually, but not always, two nouns appear together.)
- Reverse the nouns.
- Examine the ownership word.
- If the ownership word does *not* end in an *s* sound, add an apostrophe and *s.*
- If the ownership word *does* end in an *s* sound, usually add just an apostrophe. *However, if an extra syllable can be easily pronounced in the possessive form, most writers will add an apostrophe and an* s *to singular nouns.*

Singular Noun Ending in an *s* Sound; Extra Syllable Can Be Easily Pronounced	Add Apostrophe and *s*
role of the actress	actress's role
request of the boss	boss's request
yoke of the ox	ox's yoke

MAKING DIFFICULT PROPER NOUNS POSSESSIVE

Of all possessive forms, individuals' names—especially those ending in *s* sounds—are the most puzzling to students, and understandably so. Even experts don't always agree on the possessive form for singular proper nouns.

Traditionalists, as represented in *The Chicago Manual of Style* and *The Modern Language Association Style Manual,* prefer adding *'s* to troublesome *singular proper* nouns that end in *s* sounds. On the other hand, writers of more popular literature, as represented in *The Associated Press Stylebook and Libel Manual,* prefer the simpler style of adding just an apostrophe to singular proper nouns. You may apply either style, but be consistent. Please note in the examples below that the style choice applies *only* to singular names ending in *s* sounds. Plural names are always made possessive with the addition of an apostrophe only. Study the examples shown here.

The word *the* preceding a name is a clue that the name is being used in a plural sense. For example, *the Harrises* means the entire *Harris* family.

Singular Name	Singular Possessive — Traditional	Singular Possessive — Popular	Plural Possessive
Mr. Harris	Mr. Harris's	Mr. Harris'	the Harrises'
Mrs. Sanchez	Mrs. Sanchez's	Mrs. Sanchez'	the Sanchezes'
Mr. Lewis	Mr. Lewis's	Mr. Lewis'	The Lewises'
Ms. Horowitz	Ms. Horowitz's	Ms. Horowitz'	the Horowitzes'

SUMMARY

Here's a summary of the possessive rule that should be easy to remember. If an ownership word does not end in an *s,* add an apostrophe and *s.* If the ownership word does end in an *s,* add just an apostrophe—unless you can easily pronounce an extra syllable. If you can pronounce that extra syllable, add an apostrophe and *s.*

HOT LINE QUERIES

QUESTION Where should the apostrophe go in *employee's handbook?*

ANSWER This is tricky because the writer of that phrase must decide whether he or she considers the handbook from one employee's point of view or from all employees' points of view. Depending on the point of view, the apostrophe could be justified for either position. The trend today seems to favor the singular construction (*employee's handbook*).

QUESTION I'm addressing a letter to the American Nurses Association. What salutation shall I use? One person in our office suggested *Gentlewomen.* Is this being used?

ANSWER I recommend that you use *Ladies and Gentlemen* since both male and female nurses are members of the association. In fact, this salutation is appropriate for any organization in which men and women may be represented in management. I would not use *Gentlewomen* because it sounds stilted and artificial. In response to the women's movement, many businesses and individuals are trying to avoid sexism in language. Salutations such as *Dear Sir* and *Gentlemen* are rarely used. Today we are more sensitive to women as employees, managers, and executives. The use of awkward terms like *Gentlewomen* or *Gentlepersons,* however, is an overreaction and should be avoided. To solve the problem of sexism in letter salutations, consider using the AMS (American Management Society) simplified letter style. It substitutes a subject line for the salutation.

QUESTION Should *undercapitalized* be hyphenated? I can't find it in my dictionary.

ANSWER The prefixes *under* and *over* are not followed by hyphens.

QUESTION Is there an apostrophe in *Veterans Day,* and if so, where does it go?

ANSWER *Veterans Day* has no apostrophe, but *New Year's Day* does have one.

QUESTION My boss has dictated, *I respectfully call <u>you</u> and your client's attention to . . . .* What's wrong with this? How can I make *you* possessive?

ANSWER The best way to handle this awkward wording is to avoid using the possessive form. Instead, use a prepositional phrase (*I respectfully call to the attention of you and your client . . .*).

QUESTION Here at the Cancer Society we have a bureau of speakers. Where should the apostrophe go when we use the possessive form of the word *speakers?*

ANSWER *Speakers' bureau.*

6 Personal Pronouns

OBJECTIVES When you have completed the materials in this chapter, you will be able to do the following:

Level I
- Use personal pronouns correctly as subjects and objects.
- Distinguish between personal possessive pronouns (such as *its*) and contractions (such as *it's*).

Level II
- Choose the correct pronoun in compound constructions, comparatives, and appositives.
- Use reflexive pronouns correctly.

Level III
- Use nominative case pronouns with subject complements.
- Select the correct pronouns for use with the infinitive *to be.*

PRETEST

Underline the correct pronouns.

1. The budgets were submitted by Noel and (I, me, myself) on Monday.
2. Nominations were made by (we, us) students.
3. Nobody does it better than (she, her).
4. Do you know if it was Sarah and (he, him) who spoke at the rally?
5. Just between you and (I, me), which horse will win the race?

"The only place success comes before work is in the dictionary."
— Donald Kendall, former chair, PepsiCo

As you will remember from Chapter 2, pronouns are words that substitute for nouns and other pronouns. They enable us to speak and write without awkward repetition. Grammatically, pronouns may be divided into seven types (personal, relative, interrogative, demonstrative, indefinite, reflexive, and reciprocal). Rather than consider all seven pronoun types, this textbook will be concerned only with those pronouns that cause difficulty in use.

1. me 2. us 3. she 4. he 5. me

LEVEL I

PERSONAL PRONOUNS

Personal pronouns indicate the person speaking, the person spoken to, or the person or object spoken of. Notice in the following table that personal pronouns change their form (or *case*) depending on who is speaking (called the *person*), how many are speaking (the *number*), and the sex (or *gender*) of the speaker. For example, the third person feminine objective singular case is *her.* Most personal pronoun errors by speakers and writers involve faulty usage of case forms. Study this table to avoid errors in personal pronoun use.

This list is so important that you must memorize it. You must also know how these pronouns function in sentences.

	Nominative Case*		Objective Case		Possessive Case	
	Sing.	Plural	Sing.	Plural	Sing.	Plural
First person (person speaking)	I	we	me	us	my, mine	our, ours
Second person (person spoken to)	you	you	you	you	your, yours	your, yours
Third person (person or thing spoken of)	he, she, it	they	him, her, it	them	his, her, hers, its	their, theirs

*Some authorities prefer the term *subjective case.*

SPOT THE BLOOPER

Vanity Fair interview with famous Hollywood action hero: "If I got married, it would be a unique situation where me and the woman would have a certain kind of format . . ."

Basic Use of the Nominative Case

Nominative case pronouns are used primarily as the subjects of verbs. Every verb or verb phrase, regardless of its position in a sentence, has a subject. If that subject is a pronoun, it must be in the nominative case.

I thought *she* would pay me back.

We wondered if *they* would ever arrive.

Basic Use of the Objective Case

Objective case pronouns most commonly are used in two ways.

- ***Object of a verb.*** When pronouns act as direct or indirect objects of verbs, they must be in the objective case.

Offer *her* the job.

Ellen took *him* to the doctor.

SPOT THE BLOOPER

A host on NBC's "Today" show: "Willard Scott is praying for Katie and I."

- ***Object of a preposition.*** The objective case is used for pronouns that are objects of prepositions.

Brandon bought the ring for *her.*

The instructions were given to *us.*

Just between *you* and *me,* the negotiations have stalled.

SPOT THE BLOOPER

From Marilyn Monroe in *Seven-Year Itch:* "A girl like I hardly ever gets to meet interesting men."

When the words *between, but, like,* and *except* are used as prepositions, errors in pronoun case are likely to occur. To avoid such errors, isolate the prepositional phrase, and then use an objective case pronoun as the object of the preposition. (*Every employee* [*but Tom and him*] *completed the form.*)

Never use *it's* unless you can substitute *it is*. Because they'd rather be safe than sorry, many writers mentally say *it is* every time they use *it's*.

Basic Use of the Possessive Case

Possessive pronouns show ownership. Unlike possessive nouns, possessive pronouns require no apostrophes. Study these five possessive pronouns: ***hers, yours, ours, theirs, its.*** Notice the absence of apostrophes. Do not confuse possessive pronouns with contractions. Contractions are shortened (contracted) forms of subjects and verbs, such as ***it's*** (for ***it is***), ***there's*** (for ***there is***), and ***they're*** (for ***they are***). In these contractions the apostrophes indicate omitted letters.

SPOT THE BLOOPER

From the side of a box of General Mills' Cinnamon Toast Crunch cereal: "What gives Cinnamon Crunch it's totally intense taste?"

Possessive Pronouns	Contractions
Those seats are *theirs.*	*There's* not a seat left in the theater.
My iguana has escaped from *its* cage.	*It's* an unusual pet.

Now complete the reinforcement exercises for Level I.

LEVEL II

PROBLEMS IN USING PERSONAL PRONOUNS

SPOT THE BLOOPER

Well-known football coach in *The Arizona Republic:* "We — my wife and I — used to have dinner with he [Governor Bill Clinton] and Hillary."

Compound Subjects and Objects

When a pronoun appears in combination with a noun or another pronoun, special attention must be given to case selection. Use this technique to help you choose the correct pronoun case: Ignore the extra noun or pronoun and its related conjunction, and consider separately the pronoun in question to determine what the case should be.

> Mindy asked [you and] ***me*** for help. (Ignore *you and.*)
>
> [Allison and] ***he*** went to the concert. (Ignore *Allison and.*)
>
> Will you allow [Janna and] ***them*** to come along? (Ignore *Janna and.*)

Notice in the first sentence, for example, that when *You and* is removed, the pronoun ***me*** must be selected because it functions as the object of the verb.

SPOT THE BLOOPER

Television commercial for Continental Insurance Co.: "Nobody does it better than us."

Comparatives

In statements of comparison, words are often implied but not actually stated. To determine pronoun case in only partially complete comparative statements introduced by ***than*** or ***as,*** always mentally finish the comparative by adding the implied missing words.

> Shelley earns as much as ***he.*** (Shelley earns as much as ***he*** [not ***him***] earns.)
>
> Michael is a better cook than ***she.*** (. . . better cook than ***she*** [not ***her***] is.)
>
> Does her attitude annoy you as much as ***me?*** (. . . annoy you as much as it annoys ***me*** [not ***I***].)

SPOT THE BLOOPER

From the KOB-TV [Albuquerque, NM] weather reporter: "Good news for we skiers!"

Appositives

Appositives explain or rename previously mentioned nouns or pronouns. A pronoun in apposition takes the same case as that of the noun or pronoun with which it is in apposition. In order to determine more easily what pronoun case to use for a pronoun in combination with an appositive, temporarily ignore the appositive.

We [students] must protest these fee hikes. (Ignore *students.*)

The responsibility belongs to *us* [citizens]. (Ignore *citizens*).

SPOT THE BLOOPER

Classified advertisement from local newspaper: "For Sale. Three canaries of undermined sex"

Reflexive (or Compound Personal) Pronouns

Reflexive pronouns that end in *-self* emphasize or reflect on their antecedents (the nouns or pronouns previously mentioned).

I will take care of this problem *myself.* (Reflects on *I.*)

Oprah *herself* presented the award. (Emphasizes *Oprah.*)

Errors result when reflexive pronouns are used instead of personal pronouns. If no previously mentioned noun or pronoun is stated in the sentence, use a personal pronoun instead of a reflexive pronoun.

Address your questions to your manager or *me.* (Not *myself.*)

Brenda and *I* wrote the proposal. (Not *myself.*)

Please note that *hisself* is substandard and should always be avoided.

Now complete the reinforcement exercises for Level II.

LEVEL III

ADVANCED USES OF NOMINATIVE CASE PRONOUNS

Whenever a pronoun follows a linking verb, that pronoun will always be in the nominative case.

Subject Complement

As we have already seen earlier in this chapter, nominative case pronouns usually function as subjects of verbs. Less frequently, nominative case pronouns also perform as subject complements. A pronoun that follows a linking verb and renames the subject must be in the nominative case. Be especially alert to the linking verbs *am, is, are, was, were, be, being,* and *been.*

It was *I* who called the meeting.

Is it *he* who has the key?

If you were *I,* would you go?

When a verb of several words appears in a phrase, look at the final word of the verb. If it is a linking verb, use a nominative pronoun.

It may have been *they* who asked the question.

The culprit could have been *he.*

If the owner had been *I,* your money would have been refunded.

STUDY TIP

This memory device may help you remember the correct pronoun to use with the infinitive *to be:* No subject, then nominative. That is, if the infinitive *to be* has no subject, supply a nominative pronoun. For example, *I was thought to be she.*

In conversation it is common to say, *It is me,* or more likely, *It's me.* Careful speakers and writers, though, normally use nominative case pronouns after linking verbs. If the resulting constructions sound too "formal," revise your sentences appropriately. For example, instead of *It is I who placed the order,* use *I placed the order.*

Infinitive *To Be* Without a Subject

Infinitives are the present forms of verbs preceded by *to* — for example, *to sit, to run,* and *to walk.* Nominative pronouns are used following the infinitive *to be* when the infinitive has no subject. In this instance the infinitive joins a complement (not an object) to the subject.

Her twin sister was often taken to be *she.* (The infinitive *to be* has no subject; *she* is the complement of the subject *sister.*)

Darrell was mistakenly thought to be *I.* (The infinitive *to be* has no subject; *I* is the complement of the subject *Darrell.*)

Why would Jennifer want to be *she?* (The infinitive *to be* has no subject; *she* is the complement of the subject *Jennifer.*)

ADVANCED APPLICATIONS OF PERSONAL CASE PRONOUNS

When the infinitive *to be* has a subject, any pronoun following it will function as an object. Therefore, the pronoun following the infinitive will function as its object and take the objective case.

The teacher believed Jennifer to be *her.* (The subject of the infinitive *to be* is Jennifer; therefore, the pronoun functions as an object. Try it another way: *The teacher believed her to be Jennifer.* You would not say, *The teacher believed she to be Jennifer.*)

John expected the callers to be *us.* (The subject of the infinitive *to be* is *callers;* therefore, the pronoun functions as an object.)

Colonel Dunn judged the winner to be *him.* (The subject of the infinitive *to be* is *winner;* therefore, use the objective case pronoun *him.*)

Whenever you have selected a pronoun for the infinitive *to be* and you want to test its correctness, try reversing the pronoun and its antecedent. For example, *We thought the winner to be her* (*We thought her [not she] to be the winner*) or *Cheryl was often taken to be she* (*She [not her] was often taken to be Cheryl*).

SUMMARY

The following table summarizes the uses of nominative and objective case pronouns.

SPOT THE BLOOPER

Sign at Bob's Big Boy restaurant in Monrovia (CA): One side says "There back!" The other side says "Their back!" [Which side is correct?]

NOMINATIVE CASE	
Subject of the verb	*They* are sky divers.
Subject complement	That is *he.*
Infinitive *to be* without a subject	Josh pretended to be *he.*

OBJECTIVE CASE	
Direct or indirect object of the verb	Give *him* another chance.
Object of a preposition	Send the order to *him.*
Object of an infinitive	Ann hoped to call *us.*
Infinitive *to be* with subject	We thought the guests to be *them.*

Now complete the reinforcement exercises for Level III.

TYPES OF PRONOUNS

For students of the language interested in a total view, here is a summary of the seven types of pronouns, with sentences illustrating each type. This list is presented for your interest alone, not for potential testing.

■ *Personal pronouns* replace nouns or other pronouns. Examples:

NOMINATIVE CASE:	I, we, you, he, she, it, they
OBJECTIVE CASE:	me, us, you, him, her, it, them
POSSESSIVE CASE:	my, mine, our, ours, your, yours, his, hers, its, their, theirs
	Mr. Benton said *he* put *his* signature on *it* yesterday.

SPOT THE BLOOPER

Picture caption from travel brochure: "Mt. Kilimanjaro, the breathtaking backdrop for the Serena Lodge. Swim in the lovely pool while you drink it all in."

■ *Relative pronouns* join subordinate clauses to antecedents. Examples: *who, whose, whom, which, that, whoever, whomever, whichever, whatever.*

He is the candidate *whom* we all admire.

■ *Interrogative pronouns* replace nouns in a question. Examples: *who, whose, whom, which, what.*

Whose seat is this?

■ *Demonstrative pronouns* designate specific persons or things. Examples: *this, these, that, those.*

This must be the work request we need.

■ *Indefinite pronouns* replace nouns. Examples: *everyone, anyone, someone, each, everybody, anybody, one, none, some, all,* and so on.

Everybody needs adequate nourishment.

■ *Reflexive pronouns (compound personal)* emphasize or reflect on antecedents. Examples: *myself, yourself, himself, herself, itself, oneself,* and so on.

The president *himself* answered that letter.

■ *Reciprocal pronouns* indicate mutual relationship. Examples: *each other, one another.*

All three chief executive officers consulted *one another* before making the announcement.

HOT LINE QUERIES

QUESTION On the radio I recently heard a talk-show host say, *My producer and myself. . .* A little later that same host said, *Send any inquiries to the station or myself at this address.* This sounded half right and half wrong, but I would have trouble explaining the problem. Can you help?

ANSWER The problem is a common one: use of a reflexive pronoun (*myself*) when it has no preceding noun on which to reflect. Correction: *My producer and I* and *Send inquiries to the station or me.* Reflexive pronouns like *myself* should be used only with obvious antecedents, such as *I, myself, will take the calls.* Individuals in the media often misuse reflexive pronouns, perhaps to avoid sounding egocentric with overuse of *I* and *me.*

QUESTION I have a question about the use of *etc.* in this sentence: *We are installing better lighting, acoustical tile, sound barriers, and etc.* Should I use two periods at the end of the sentence, and does a comma precede *etc.?*

ANSWER Although the use of *etc.* (meaning "and so forth") is generally avoided, do not, if it is to be used, include the redundant word *and.* When *etc.* is found at the end of a sentence, one comma should precede it. When *etc.* appears in the middle of a sentence, two commas should set it off. For example, *Better lighting, acoustical tile, and sound barriers, etc., are being installed. Never* use two periods at the end of a sentence, even if the sentence ends with an abbreviation such as *etc.*

QUESTION We're having a disagreement in our office about the word *healthy.* Is it correct to write *Exercise is healthy?*

ANSWER Strictly speaking, *healthy* means "to have or possess good health." For example, *The rosy-cheeked schoolchildren look healthy.* The word *healthful* means "to promote or be conducive to good health." Your sentence should read: *Exercise is healthful.*

QUESTION Should a hyphen be used in the word *dissimilar?*

ANSWER No. Prefixes such as *dis, pre, non,* and *un* do not require hyphens. Even when the final letter of the prefix is repeated in the initial letter of the root word, no hyphens are used: *disspirited, preenroll, nonnutritive.*

QUESTION I thought I knew the difference between *to* and *too,* but could you provide me with a quick review?

ANSWER *To* may serve as a preposition (*I'm going to the store*), and it may also serve as part of an infinitive construction (*to sign his name*). The adverb *too* may be used to mean "also" (*Andrea will attend too*). In addition, the word *too* may be used to indicate "to an excessive extent" (*the letter is too long*).

QUESTION I have a lot of trouble with the word *extension,* as in the expressions *extension* cord and telephone *extension.* Is the word ever spelled *extention?*

ANSWER You are not alone in having trouble with *extension.* No, it is never spelled with the familiar suffix *tion.* Perhaps you could remember it better if you associate the word *tension* with *extension.*

7 Pronouns and Antecedents

OBJECTIVES When you have completed the materials in this chapter, you will be able to do the following:

Level I
- Make personal pronouns agree with their antecedents in number and gender.
- Understand the traditional use of common gender and be able to use its alternatives with sensitivity.

Level II
- Make personal pronouns agree with subjects joined by *or* or *nor.*
- Make personal pronouns agree with indefinite pronouns, collective nouns, and organization names.

Level III
- Understand the functions of *who* and *whom.*
- Follow a three-step plan in selecting *who* or *whom.*

PRETEST

Underline the correct word.

1. Every one of the men was given (his, their) own locker.
2. Our staff asked (its, their) members to vote before leaving.
3. Neither of the committees would have (its, their) members' names included.
4. (Who, Whom) would you recommend for the manager's position?
5. Give the supplies to (whoever, whomever) needs them.

Pronouns enable us to communicate efficiently. They provide short forms that save us from the boredom of repetitious nouns. But they can also get us in trouble if the nouns to which they refer — their *antecedents* — are unclear. This chapter shows you how to avoid pronoun-antecedent problems. It also presents solutions to a major problem for sensitive communicators today — how to handle the *his/her* dilemma.

"Be like a postage stamp. Stick to something until you get there."
— Josh Billings

LEVEL I

FUNDAMENTALS OF PRONOUN–ANTECEDENT AGREEMENT

When pronouns substitute for nouns, the pronouns must agree with their antecedents in number (either singular or plural) and gender (either masculine, feminine, or neuter). Here are suggestions for using pronouns effectively.

1. his 2. its 3. its 4. Whom 5. whoever

Making Pronoun References Clear

Do not use a pronoun if your listener or reader might not be able to identify the noun it represents.

UNCLEAR: Roger's manager said that his report was incomplete.
CLEAR: Roger's manager said that Roger's report was incomplete.

UNCLEAR: In the computer lab they do not allow you to eat.
CLEAR: The administration does not allow anyone to eat in the computer lab. *Or:* Eating is not allowed in the computer lab.

UNCLEAR: When Clinton suceeded Bush, many of his policies were reversed.
CLEAR: When Clinton suceeded Bush, many of Bush's policies were reversed.

SPOT THE BLOOPER

From a letter to members of the National Council of Teachers of English: "It takes a special person to choose teaching as their life goal."

Making Pronouns Agree with Their Antecedents in Number

Pronouns must agree in number with the nouns they represent. For example, if a pronoun replaces a singular noun, that pronoun must be singular.

Columbus thought that *he* had reached India. (Singular antecedent and pronoun.)

Many explorers believed *they* could find a faster route. (Plural antecedent and pronoun.)

If a pronoun refers to two nouns joined by *and,* the pronoun must be plural.

Rocky and *Bullwinkle* enjoyed *their* adventures. (Plural antecedent and pronoun.)

Mitchell and *Nancy* asked that questions be directed to *them.* (Plural antecedent and pronoun.)

Pronoun-antecedent agreement can be complicated when words or phrases come between the pronoun and the word to which it refers. Disregard phrases such as those introduced by *as well as, in addition to,* and *together with.* Find the true antecedent and make the pronoun agree with it.

The *teacher,* along with her students, is composing *her* reply to the dean. (Singular antecedent and pronoun.)

The *students,* together with their teacher, delivered *their* reply to the dean. (Plural antecedent and pronoun.)

The *members* of the group voiced *their* grievances. (Plural antecedent and pronoun.)

Making Pronouns Agree with Their Antecedents in Gender

Pronouns exhibit one of three *genders:* masculine (male), feminine (female), or neuter (neither masculine nor feminine). Pronouns must agree with their antecedents in gender.

Natalie ate *her* lunch. (Feminine gender.)

Jeremy brought *his* books. (Masculine gender.)

The plan had *its* advantages. (Neuter gender.)

Choosing Alternatives to Common-Gender Antecedents

Occasionally, writers and speakers face a problem in choosing pronouns of appropriate gender. English has no all-purpose singular pronoun to represent indefinite nouns (such as *a student* or *an employee*). For this reason writers and speakers have, over the years, used masculine, or common-gender, pronouns to refer to nouns that might be either masculine or feminine. For example, in the sentence

DID YOU KNOW

Despite efforts for the past 140 years, no one has yet come up with an acceptable multipurpose, unisex pronoun. Suggested replacements: *ne* (1850), *le* (1884), *se* (1938), *ve* (1970), *e* (1977), and *ala* (1988). What would you suggest to fill the void in our language?

SPOT THE BLOOPER

Television commercial for *Encyclopedia Britannica:* "Every parent has a wish list for their child."

A student has his rights, the pronoun ***his*** referred to its antecedent *student,* which might name either a feminine or masculine person.

Communicators today, however, avoid masculine pronouns (*he, his*) when referring to indefinite nouns that could be masculine or feminine. Critics call these pronouns "sexist" because they exclude women. To solve the problem, sensitive communicators rewrite those sentences requiring such pronouns. Although many alternatives exist, here are three common options:

COMMON GENDER:	A passenger must show ***his*** ticket before boarding.
ALTERNATIVE NO. 1:	Passengers must show ***their*** tickets before boarding.
ALTERNATIVE NO. 2:	A passenger must show ***a*** ticket before boarding.
ALTERNATIVE NO. 3:	A passenger must show ***his or her*** ticket before boarding.
WRONG:	A passenger must show ***their*** ticket before boarding.

In Alternative No. 1 the subject has been made plural to avoid the need for a singular common-gender pronoun. In Alternative No. 2 the pronoun is omitted, and an article is substituted, although at the cost of making the original meaning less emphatic. In Alternative No. 3 both masculine and feminine references (*his* or *her*) are used. Because the latter construction is wordy and clumsy, frequent use of it should be avoided. Substituting the plural pronoun ***their*** is incorrect since it does not agree with its singular antecendent, *passenger.*

Now complete the reinforcement exercises for Level I.

LEVEL II

PROBLEMS WITH PRONOUN–ANTECEDENT AGREEMENT

Antecedents Joined by *or* or *nor*

When antecedents are joined by *or* or *nor,* the pronoun should agree with the antecedent closer to it.

> Either Sondra or *Janine* left ***her*** backpack in the classroom.
>
> Neither the teacher nor the ***students*** wanted to give up ***their*** vacations.

You may be wondering why antecedents joined by *and* are treated differently from antecedents joined by *or/nor.* The conjunction *and* joins one plus one to make two antecedents; hence, a plural pronoun is used. The conjunctions *or/nor* require a choice between two antecedents. Always match the pronoun to the closer antecedent.

Indefinite Pronouns as Antecedents

Pronouns such as *anyone, something,* and *anybody* are called *indefinite* because they refer to no specific person or object. Some indefinite pronouns are always singular; others are always plural.

Always Singular		Always Plural
anybody	everything	both
anyone	neither	few
anything	nobody	many
each	no one	several
either	nothing	
everybody	somebody	
everyone	someone	

When indefinite pronouns function as antecedents of pronouns, make certain that the pronoun agrees with its antecedent. Do not let prepositional phrases obscure the true antecedent.

Someone on the men's volleyball team left *his* sneakers on the court.

Each of the schools had *its* own specialty.

Few of the employees agreed to give up *their* raises.

Several of the lawyers filed *their* papers after the deadline.

STUDY TIP

When *either* or *neither* is followed by an "of" phrase, it's functioning as a singular pronoun. For example, *either of the books is available.*

The words *either* and *neither* can be confusing. When these words stand alone and function as pronoun subjects, they are always considered singular. When they are joined with *or* or *nor* to form conjunctions, however, they may connect plural subjects. These plural subjects, then, may act as antecedents to plural pronouns.

Has *either* of the boys joined *his* little league team? (*Either* is a pronoun and functions as the subject of the sentence.)

Either the professor *or* her colleagues expressed *their* support for the project. (*Either/or* is used as a conjunction; *colleagues* is the pronoun antecedent.)

Collective Nouns as Antecedents

Words such as *jury, faculty, committee, union, team,* and *group* are called *collective* nouns because they refer to a collection of people, animals, or objects. Such words may be either singular or plural depending on the mode of operation of the collection to which they refer. When a collective noun operates as a unit, it is singular. When the elements of a collective noun operate separately, the collective noun is plural.

No action can be taken until the *committee* announces *its* decision. (*Committee* operating as one unit.)

The *jury* delivered *its* verdict. (*Jury* operating as one unit.)

Our *staff* wanted *their* own reserved parking spaces. (*Staff* operating as individuals.)

However, if a collective noun is to be used in a plural sense, the sentence can often be made to sound less awkward by the addition of a plural noun (*The staff* members *wanted their own reserved parking spaces*).

DID YOU KNOW

English is the first language in history in which the majority of speakers are nonnative. Of the 750 million people who use English regularly, only 300 million are native speakers. It is the universal language of scholarship, science, and trade.

Company and Organization Names as Antecedents

Company and organization names are generally considered singular. Unless the actions of the organization are attributed to individual representatives of that organization, pronouns referring to organizations should be singular.

Abercrombie & Fitch is having *its* annual half-price sale.

The United Nations is expanding *its* campaign to fight world hunger.

Brackman Information Services plans to open *its* new branch in Chicago this year.

The Antecedents *each, every,* and *many a*

If the limiting adjectives *each, every,* and *many a* describe either noun or both nouns in a compound antecedent, that antecedent is considered singular.

Each player and coach on the men's team has *his* assigned duties.

Many a man has found *his* career to be less important than his family.

Now complete the reinforcement exercises for Level II.

LEVEL III

ADVANCED PRONOUN USE

The Problem of *who* and *whom*

SPOT THE BLOOPER

Famous singer on NBC's "Today" show: "I began to recognize whom I am, and I wasn't afraid of whom I was."

The use of *who* and *whom* presents a continuing dilemma for speakers and writers. In conversation the correct choice of *who* or *whom* is especially difficult because of the mental gymnastics necessary to locate subjects and objects. In writing, however, an author has ample time to analyze a sentence carefully and make a correct choice — if the author understands the traditional functions of *who* and *whom*. *Who* is the nominative case form. Like other nominative case pronouns, *who* may function as the subject of a verb or as the subject complement of a noun following the linking verb. *Whom* is the objective case form. It may function as the object of a verb or as the object of a preposition.*

SPOT THE BLOOPER

From *Newsweek:* "Why did Clinton nominate someone whom advisers knew would be a lightning rod?"

Who does he think will be elected? (*Who* is the subject of *will be elected.*)

Susan wondered *who* my boss is. (*Who* is the complement of *boss.*)

Whom should we choose? (*Whom* is the object of *should choose.*)

Edmund is the one to *whom* I wrote. (*Whom* is the object of *to.*)

How to Choose Between *who* and *whom*

The choice between *who* and *whom* becomes easier if the sentence in question is approached according to the following procedure:

- Isolate the *who/whom* clause.
- Invert the clause, if necessary, to restore normal subject-verb-object order.
- Substitute the nominative pronoun *he* (*she* or *they*) for *who.* Substitute the objective pronoun *him* (*her* or *them*) for *whom.* If the sentence sounds correct with *him,* replace *him* with *whom.* If the sentence sounds correct with *he,* replace *he* with *who.*

Study the following sentences and notice how the choice of *who* or *whom* is made:

	Here are the addresses of those (who/whom) we are inviting.
ISOLATE:	________ we are inviting
INVERT:	we are inviting ________
SUBSTITUTE:	we are inviting __him__
EQUATE:	we are inviting __whom__
COMPLETE:	Here are the addresses of those whom we are inviting.

SPOT THE BLOOPER

Heading in the [Cleveland] *Browns News/Illustrated:* "Whom Will It Be?"

	Do you know (who/whom) your true friends are?
ISOLATE:	________ your true friends are
INVERT:	your true friends are ________
SUBSTITUTE:	your true friends are __they__
EQUATE:	your true friends are __who__
COMPLETE:	Do you know who your true friends are?

**Whom* may also function as the subject or object of an infinitive. Since little confusion results from these constructions, they will not be discussed.

In choosing *who* or *whom,* ignore parenthetical expressions such as *I hope, we think, I believe,* and *you know.*

Larry is the applicant (who/whom) we believe is best qualified.

ISOLATE:	______ we believe is best qualified
IGNORE:	we believe ______ is best qualified
SUBSTITUTE:	we believe __he__ is best qualified
EQUATE:	we believe __who__ is best qualified
COMPLETE:	Larry is the applicant who we believe is best qualified.

EXAMPLES:

Whom do you think we should call? (Invert: you do think we should call him/*whom.*)

The person to whom we gave our evaluation was Sherry. (Invert: we gave our evaluation to her/*whom.*)

Do you know who the plaintiff is? (Invert: the plaintiff is he/*who.*)

Whom would you like to include in the acknowledgments? (Invert: you would like to include him/*whom.*)

"What is written without effort is, in general, read without pleasure."
— Samuel Johnson

The Use of *whoever* and *whomever*

Whoever, of course, is nominative and *whomever* is objective. The selection of the correct form is sometimes complicated when *whoever* or *whomever* appears in clauses. These clauses may act as objects of prepositions, objects of verbs, or subjects of verbs. Within the clauses, however, you must determine how *whoever* or *whomever* is functioning in order to choose the correct form. Study the following examples and explanations.

Offer the clothes to *whoever* needs them. (The clause *whoever needs them* is the object of the preposition to. Within the clause itself, *whoever* acts as the subject of *needs* and is therefore in the nominative case.)

A scholarship will be given to *whoever* has the qualifications. (The clause *whoever has the qualifications* is the object of the preposition *to.* Within the clause *whoever* acts as the subject of *has* and is therefore in the nominative case.)

The baker will add to the cake the names of *whomever you wish.* (The clause *whomever you wish* is the object of the preposition *of.* Within the clause *whomever* acts as the object of *you wish* and is therefore in the objective case.)

Now complete the reinforcement exercises for Level III.

HOT LINE QUERIES

QUESTION My friend insists that the combination *all right* is shown in her dictionary as one word. I say that it's two words. Who's right?

ANSWER *All right* is the only acceptable spelling. The listing *alright* is shown in many dictionaries to guide readers to the acceptable spelling, *all right.* Do not use *alright.* By the way, some individuals can better remember that *all right* is two words by associating it with *all wrong.*

QUESTION I don't seem to be able to hear the difference between *than* and *then.* Can you explain it to me?

ANSWER The conjunction *than* is used to make comparisons (*your watch is more accurate than mine*). The adverb *then* means "at that time" (*we must complete this task; then we will take our break*) or "as a consequence" (*if all the angles of the triangle are equal, then it must be equilateral as well*).

QUESTION What is the order of college degrees and which ones are capitalized?

ANSWER Two kinds of undergraduate degrees are commonly awarded: the associate's degree, a two-year degree; and the bachelor's degree, a four-year degree. A variety of graduate degrees exist. The most frequently awarded are the master's degree and the doctorate. Merriam-Webster dictionaries do not capitalize the names of degrees: associate of arts degree, bachelor of science, master of arts, doctor of philosophy. However, when used with an individual's name, the abbreviations for degrees are capitalized: Bruce Gourlay, M.A.; Cynthia L. Phillips, Ph.D.

QUESTION Why does the sign above my grocery market's quick-check stand say *Ten or less items?* Shouldn't it read *Ten or fewer items?*

ANSWER Right you are! *Fewer* refers to numbers, as in *fewer items. Less* refers to amounts or quantities, as in *less food.* Perhaps markets prefer *less* because it has fewer letters.

QUESTION If I have no interest in something, am I *disinterested?*

ANSWER No. If you lack interest, you are *uninterested.* The word *disinterested* means "unbiased" or "impartial" (*the judge was disinterested in the cases before him*).

QUESTION Everyone says "consensus of opinion." Yet, I understand that there is some objection to this expression.

ANSWER Yes, the expression is widely used. However, since *consensus* means "collective opinion," the addition of the word *opinion* results in a redundancy.

QUESTION I'm disgusted and infuriated at a New York University advertisement I just saw in our newspaper. It says, *It's not just <u>who</u> you know. . . .* Why would a leading institution of learning use such poor grammar?

ANSWER Because it sounds familiar. But familiarity doesn't make it correct. You're right in recognizing that the proper form is *whom* (isolate the clause *you know him* or *whom*). The complete adage — or more appropriately, cliché — correctly stated is: *It's not what you know but <u>whom</u> you know.*

NAME ______________________________

UNIT 2 REVIEW ■ Chapters 4–7 (Self-Check)

Begin your review by rereading Chapters 4–7. Then test your comprehension of those chapters by filling in the blanks in the exercises that follow. Compare your responses with those at the end of the review.

LEVEL I

1. Do you think the (a) Schwartzes, (b) Schwartz, (c) Schwartz's have been asked to attend? ______
2. Each summer I search the farmers' market for the best (a) peachs, (b) peaches. ______
3. We dropped the (a) childs, (b) children, (c) childrens off at the playground on our way over. ______
4. With only two (a) years', (b) years, (c) year's experience, she received a 10 percent salary increase. ______
5. My (a) companies', (b) company's benefits get better every year. ______
6. How did the (a) sales, (b) sale's (c) sales' department manage to avoid layoffs? ______
7. Many of our (a) students', (b) students, (c) student's have difficulty with possessive constructions. ______
8. Can you turn the table on (a) its, (b) it's side? ______
9. That blue Mustang convertible is (a) theirs, (b) there's, (c) their's. ______
10. I think we should offer (a) her, (b) she the position of product manager. ______
11. Evelyn gave the checks to (a) we, (b) us to deposit after work. ______
12. Just between you and (a) me, (b) I, what should I do? ______
13. Everyone except Mitch and (a) he, (b) him received one-year pins. ______
14. Tell both of the champions that (a) he, (b) he or she, (c) they should prepare for the next round. ______
15. For an employee to be fired, (a) he or she, (b) they must have received warnings. ______

LEVEL II

16. Several of the (a) attorneys, (b) attornies were on the mediation panel. ______
17. Regina and Kim asked their (a) mother-in-laws, (b) mothers-in-law to join them. ______
18. In her five years with the company, she had learned the (a) do's and don't's, (b) dos and don'ts of dealing with the board. ______
19. (a) Diana's and Charles', (b) Diana and Charles' children hoped for reconciliation. ______
20. I certainly hope that today's weather is better than (a) yesterday's, (b) yesterdays. ______
21. Sarah was studying for a degree in (a) economic's, (b) economics. ______

22. Brad and (a) I, (b) me will be there by 4:30. _____

23. Can you give the schedule to Anna and (a) he, (b) him? _____

24. Ernesto earns almost as much as (a) he, (b) him. _____

25. Beverly ordered the books for you and (a) I, (b) me. _____

26. Either Captain Picard or (a) I, (b) me, (c) myself will lead the mission. _____

27. (a) We, (b) Us honor students must set a good example. _____

28. It was (a) he, (b) him who asked us to be here early for the meeting. _____

29. Neither the father nor his sons wanted (a) his, (b) their business to be sold. _____

30. Every doctor and every nurse planned to cast (a) his or her, (b) their vote for the new information system. _____

LEVEL III

31. Several (a) analysises, (b) analyses, (c) analysis were offered to explain the problem. _____

32. The (a) curriculum, (b) curricula offered by the two schools are quite similar. _____

33. Because of its excellent work, thanks (a) is, (b) are in order for our organizing committee. _____

34. Is it the (a) Morrises, (b) Morrises' (c) Morris's home that won the landscaping award? _____

35. I am certain that my (a) bosses, (b) boss's, (c) bosses' signature will be forthcoming. _____

36. The IRS is checking Mr. (a) Gross's, (b) Grosses' return. _____

37. The composer who wrote the score was believed to be (a) him, (b) he. _____

38. Laura was often taken to be (a) her, (b) she. _____

39. If you were (a) I, (b) me, would you take the class? _____

40. To (a) who, (b) whom have you decided to offer the position? _____

41. (a) Who, (b) Whom has been chosen for the scholarship? _____

42. Take the canned goods to (a) whoever, (b) whomever needs them. _____

43. (a) Who, (b) Whom would you prefer to cut your hair? _____

44. Can you believe (a) who, (b) whom I saw at the supermarket? _____

45. It may have been she (a) who, (b) whom wrote the memo. _____

Hot Line Review

46. (a) To, (b) Too many cooks spoil the stew. _____

47. Check your (a) owner's, (b) owners' warranty carefully. _____

48. A diet rich in beta-carotene is (a) healthful, (b) healthy. _____

49. This frozen yogurt has (a) fewer, (b) less calories than your ice cream. _____

50. It's (a) alright, (b) all right, (c) allright with me if you borrow my camera. _____

1.a 2.b 3.b 4.a 5.b 6.a 7.b 8.a 9.a 10.a 11.b 12.a 13.b 14.c 15.a 16.a 17.b 18.b 19.b 20.a
21.b 22.a 23.b 24.a 25.b 26.a 27.a 28.a 29.b 30.a 31.b 32.b 33.b 34.b 35.b 36.a 37.b
38.b 39.a 40.b 41.a 42.a 43.b 44.b 45.a 46.b 47.a 48.a 49.a 50.b

UNIT

3

Showing the Action

8 Verbs: Kinds, Voices, Moods

OBJECTIVES When you have completed the materials in this chapter, you will be able to do the following:

Level I
- Distinguish between transitive and intransitive verbs.
- Identify at least ten linking verbs.

Level II
- Recognize active and passive voice verbs.
- Convert sentences written in the passive voice to sentences in the active voice.

Level III
- Recognize sentence constructions requiring the subjunctive verb mood.
- Create sentences using the subjunctive mood correctly.

PRETEST

Underline the appropriate answers.

1. In the sentence *Reuben played by the rules,* the verb *played* is (a) transitive, (b) intransitive, (c) linking.
2. In the sentence *Many cupcakes were eaten,* the verb phrase *were eaten* is in the (a) active voice, (b) passive voice, (c) subjunctive mood, (d) intransitive mood.
3. In the sentence *Alex brought the supplies,* the verb *brought* is in the (a) active voice, (b) passive voice, (c) subjunctive mood, (d) intransitive mood.
4. Allen acts as if he (a) was, (b) were the teacher.
5. I move that the proposal (a) is, (b) be approved.

SPOT THE BLOOPER
From *The Denver Post,* a city councilperson is quoted as saying, "I will not be guilted into this idea." (Is this a correct verb?)

A verb is a word that expresses action or a state of being. In relation to subjects, verbs tell what the subject is doing or what is being done to the subject. Verbs may also link to the subject words that describe the subject or identify it.

The verb is the most complex part of speech. A complete treatment of its forms and uses would require at least a volume. Our discussion of verbs will be limited to four chapters.

In our discussion of sentences in Chapter 3, you became familiar with three basic sentence patterns: (1) subject-verb, (2) subject-active verb-object, and

1. (b) intransitive 2. (b) passive voice 3. (a) active voice 4. (b) were 5. (b) be

(3) subject-linking verb-complement. Sentence patterns are determined by their verbs. You have already learned to identify active and linking verbs. Let's now consider how these verbs actually function.

First we'll deal with active verbs. They express their action either transitively or intransitively. When active verbs are transitive, they may create subject-active verb-object sentence patterns. When active verbs are intransitive, they may create subject-verb sentence patterns.

KINDS OF VERBS

Transitive Verbs

A verb expressing an action directed toward a person or thing is said to be *transitive.* An action verb used transitively needs, in addition to its subject, a noun or pronoun to complete its meaning. This noun or pronoun functions as the direct object of the transitive verb. Notice in the following sentences that the verbs direct action toward objects.

The students demanded lower fees.

Meredith asked him to the dance.

Our team won the game.

Objects usually answer the questions *what?* or *whom?* In the first example, the students demanded *what?* The object is *fees.* In the second example, Meredith asked *whom?* The object is *him.*

"Kind words can be short and easy to speak, but their echoes are truly endless."
— Mother Teresa

Intransitive Verbs

An action verb that does not require an object to complete its action is said to be *intransitive.*

Karl typed in the personnel office last summer.

Juanita competed in the winter Olympics.

Profits increased steadily last year.

Notice that the verbs in these sentences do not express actions directed toward persons or things. Prepositional phrases (*in the personnel office* and *in the winter Olympics*) and adverbs (*steadily*) do not receive the action expressed by the verbs. Therefore, prepositional phrases and adverbs do not function as objects of verbs.

Linking Verbs

You will recall that linking verbs *link* to the subject words that rename or describe the subject. A noun, pronoun, or adjective that renames or describes the subject is called a *complement* because it *completes* the meaning of the subject.

Nancy is the captain of the team. (*Captain* is a noun complement that completes the meaning of the sentence by renaming *Nancy*.)

This salsa is spicy. (*Spicy* is an adjective complement that completes the meaning of *salsa.*)

Her professor is he. (*He* is a pronoun complement that completes the meaning of *professor.*)

Here's a mnemonic (memory) device to help you remember the verbs of the senses. Call them the FATS verbs, an acronym (word formed of initials) made from the first letters of *feel, appear, taste,* and *seem.*

Notice in the preceding sentences that the noun, pronoun, or adjective complements following these linking verbs do not receive action from the verb; instead, the complements *complete* the meaning of the subject.

You are already familiar with those linking verbs that are derived from the *to be* verb form: *am, is, are, was, were, be, being, been.* Other words that often serve as linking verbs are *feels, appears, tastes, seems, sounds, looks,* and *smells.* Notice that many of these words describe sense experiences. Verbs expressing sense experiences may be followed by complements just as the *to be* linking verbs often are.

> Mario feels bad about leaving the company. (*Bad* is an adjective complement following the linking verb *feel.*)
>
> Your perfume smells good. (*Good* is an adjective complement following the linking verb *smells.*)

The use of adjectives following such verbs will be discussed more completely in Chapter 12.

SPOT THE BLOOPER

From the *Alameda* [CA] *Times-Star:* "There are those who think the fates are perspiring against the Oakland A's as they seek their moment in the sun."

The function of a verb in a sentence determines its classification. The verb *typed,* for example, is intransitive when it has no object (*Karl typed*). The same verb is transitive when an object *follows* (*Karl typed a letter*). The verb *felt* is linking when it is used to connect a complement describing the subject (*Lorna felt good*). The same verb is transitive when it directs action to an *object* (*Lorna felt the puppy's soft fur*). To distinguish between classifications, study carefully the constructions in which the verbs appear.

To review briefly:

- Action verbs — two kinds:
  - a. Transitive: need objects to complete their meaning
  - b. Intransitive: do not need objects to complete their meaning
- Linking verbs: form a link to words that rename or describe the subject

Now complete the reinforcement exercises for Level I.

LEVEL II

VERB VOICES

You will recall that a verb expressing an action directed toward a person or thing is said to be transitive. Transitive verbs fall into two categories depending on the receiver of the action of the verbs.

"Your attitude, not your aptitude, will determine your altitude."
—Zig Ziglar

Active Voice

When the verb expresses an action directed by the subject toward the object of the verb, the verb is said to be in the *active voice.*

> Maggie opened the door. (Action directed to the object, *door*).

Verbs in the active voice are direct and forceful; they clearly identify the doer of the action. For these reasons, writing that frequently uses the active voice is vigorous and effective. Writers of business and professional communications strive to use the active voice; in fact, it is called the *voice of business.*

In the passive voice, verbs always require a *helper,* such as *is, are, was, were, being,* or *been.*

Passive Voice

When the action verb is directed toward the subject, the verb is said to be in the *passive voice.* Study the following pairs:

PASSIVE: Verbs are used to express action.
ACTIVE: We use verbs to express action.

PASSIVE: The students are being taught by Ms. Crowley.
ACTIVE: Ms. Crowley is teaching the students.

PASSIVE: Mistakes were made in the campaign.
ACTIVE: The aides made mistakes in the campaign.

SPOT THE BLOOPER

Headline from newspaper article on nutrition: "COLLEGIANS TURN TO VEGETABLES"

Because the passive voice can be used to avoid mentioning the performer of the action, the passive voice is sometimes called the *voice of tact.* Notice how much more tactful the passive version of the last example shown above is. Although directness in business writing is generally preferable, in certain instances the passive voice is used when indirectness is desired.

Now complete reinforcement exercises for Level II.

LEVEL III

VERB MOODS

Three verb moods are available to enable a speaker or writer to express an attitude toward a subject: (a) the *indicative mood* is used to express a fact; (b) the *imperative mood* is used to express a command; (c) the *subjunctive mood* is used to express a doubt, a conjecture, or a suggestion. The subjunctive mood may cause speakers and writers difficulty and therefore demands special attention.

Subjunctive Mood

Although the subjunctive mood is seldom used today, it is still employed by careful individuals in the following constructions.

- **If *and* wish *clauses.*** When a statement that is doubtful or contrary to fact is introduced by *if, as if,* or *wish,* the subjunctive form *were* is substituted for the indicative form *was.*

  If I *were* you, I would not go. (I am *not* you.)

  Rafael wishes he *were* able to sing like Tony Bennett. (Rafael does *not* sing like Tony Bennett.)

  Martin acts as if he *were* my father. (Martin is *not* my father).

  But if the statement could possibly be true, use the indicative form.

  If Angela *was* here, I did not see her. (Angela might have been here.)

- **That *clauses.*** When a *that* clause follows a verb expressing a command, recommendation, request, suggestion, or requirement, the subjunctive verb form *be* is used.

  The company requires that all employees *be* tested.

  Her babysitter requested that she *be* home by midnight.

"One should aim not at being possible to understand but at being impossible to misunderstand."
— Quintillian

■ *Motions.* When a motion is stated, a subjunctive verb form should be used in the *that* clause in the sentence.

I move that she *be* elected.

Do I hear a motion that the minutes *be* approved?

Caution: In a sentence without *that* clauses, do not mix subjunctive and indicative verbs.

RIGHT: If he *were dissatisfied,* he *would apply* for other jobs. (Both verbs are subjunctive.)

RIGHT: If he *is dissatisfied,* he *will apply* for other jobs. (Both verbs are indicative.)

WRONG: If he *were dissatisfied,* he *will apply* for other jobs. (One subjunctive verb and one indicative verb.)

Now complete the reinforcement exercises for Level III.

HOT LINE QUERIES

QUESTION Which is better: *The truck carried canisters of highly flammable or inflammable liquid?*

ANSWER Actually, both *flammable* and *inflammable* mean "easily set on fire." Either would be correct in your sentence. However, *flammable* is preferred because its meaning is less likely to be confused. Since the prefix *in* often means "not," the word *inflammable* could be misunderstood. Therefore, use *flammable* in technical matters, particularly if you wish to suggest a warning. You may use *inflammable* or its derivatives for nontechnical descriptions, such as *Her words were inflammatory.*

QUESTION I have a sentence that begins *Beside(s) providing financial aid. . . .* Is there any real difference between *beside* and *besides?*

ANSWER Yes, indeed! *Beside* is a preposition meaning "by the side of" (*come sit beside me*). *Besides* is an adverb meaning "in addition to" (*besides paper we must order ribbons*). In your sentence use *besides.*

QUESTION I received a magazine advertisement recently that promised me a *free gift* and a *15 percent off discount* if I subscribed. What's wrong with this wording?

ANSWER You've got a double winner here in the category of redundancies. The word *gift* suggests *free;* therefore, to say *free gift* is like saying *I'm studying English English.* It would be better to say *special gift.* In the same way, *15 percent off discount* repeats itself. Omit *off.*

QUESTION When do you use *may* and when do you use *can?*

ANSWER Traditionally, the verb *may* is used in asking or granting permission (*yes, you may use that desk*). *Can* is used to suggest ability (*you can succeed in business*). In informal writing, however, authorities today generally agree that *can* may be substituted for *may.*

QUESTION I just checked the dictionary and found that *cooperate* is now written as one word. It seems to me that years ago it was *co-operate* or *coöperate.* Has the spelling changed?

ANSWER Yes, it has. And so has the spelling of many other words. As new words become more familiar, their spelling tends to become more simplified. For example, *per cent* and *good will* are now shown by most dictionaries as *percent* and *goodwill.* By the same token, many words formerly hyphenated are now written without hyphens: *strike-over* is now *strikeover, to-day* is *today, editor-in-chief* is *editor in chief, vice-president* is *vice president,* and *passer-by* is now *passerby.* Current dictionaries reflect these changes.

QUESTION On my computer I'm using a program that checks the writer's style. My problem is that it flags every passive voice verb and tells me to consider using active voice verbs. Are passive voice verbs totally forbidden in business and professional writing?

ANSWER Of course not! Computer style checkers capitalize on language areas that can be detected mechanically, and a passive voice verb is easily identified by a computer. Although active voice verbs are considered more forceful, passive voice verbs have a genuine function. Because they hide the subject and diffuse attention, passive verbs are useful in sensitive messages where indirect language can develop an impersonal, inconspicuous tone. For example, when a lower-level employee must write a persuasive and somewhat negative message to a manager, passive voice verbs are quite useful.

QUESTION What's the correct verb in this sentence? *Tim recognized that, if his company (was or were) to prosper, it would require considerable capital.*

ANSWER The verb should be *were* because the clause in which it functions is not true. Statements contrary to fact that are introduced by words like *if* and *wish* require subjunctive mood verbs.

9 Verb Tenses and Parts

OBJECTIVES When you have completed the materials in this chapter, you will be able to do the following:

Level I
- Write verbs in the present, past, and future tenses correctly.
- Use the emphatic tense correctly.

Level II
- Recognize and use present and past participles.
- Write the correct forms of 60 irregular verbs.

Level III
- Supply correct verb forms in the progressive and perfect tenses.

PRETEST

Underline the correct verb.

1. Antonia and he (came, come) to watch our soccer match.

2. He has (swam, swum) every day for over three years.

3. Those checks have (laid, lain) in the drawer for months.

4. You can (rise, raise) the window if you are warm.

5. Thomas has (wore, worn) the Warrior uniform with pride.

English verbs change form (inflection) to indicate number (singular or plural), person (first, second, or third), voice (active or passive), and tense (time). In contrast to French and German, English verbs today are no longer heavily inflected; that is, our verbs do not change form extensively to indicate number or person.

To indicate precise time, however, English employs four rather complex sets of tenses: primary tenses, emphatic tenses, perfect tenses, and progressive tenses. Level I will focus on the primary and emphatic tenses. Level II will consider participles and irregular verbs. Level III will treat the perfect and progressive tenses.

1. came 2. swum 3. lain 4. raise 5. worn

LEVEL I

PRIMARY TENSES

Present Tense

Verbs in the present tense express current or habitual action. Present tense verbs may also be used in constructions showing future action.

I *pay* my rent on the first of each month. (Current or habitual action.)

We *leave* for vacation tomorrow. (Future action.)

Past Tense

Verbs in the past tense show action that has been completed. Regular verbs form the past tense with the addition of *d* or *ed.*

Sheila *passed* the test with flying colors.

He *lifted* the barbell over his head.

The report *focused* on changes in our department.

Future Tense

Verbs in the future tense show actions that are expected to occur at a later time. Traditionally, the helper verbs *shall* and *will* have been joined with principal verbs to express future tense. In most writing today, however, the verb *will* is generally used as the helper to express future tense. Careful writers continue to use *shall* in appropriate first-person constructions. (*I/we shall attend the meeting*.)

Patrick *will* need help with his next assignment.

Vanessa *will* run in next week's 10-K race.

Problems with Primary Tenses

Most adult speakers of our language have few problems using present, past, and future tense verbs. A few considerations, however, merit mention:

- Present tense verbs are used to express "timeless" facts, even if these verbs occur in sentences with other past tense verbs.

When did you learn that he *snores?* (Not *snored,* if he continues to snore.)

My mother told me that a stitch in time *saves* nine. (Not *saved.*)

What did you say the name of that book *is?* (Not *was.*)

- A dictionary should be used to verify spelling of verbs that change form. One must be particularly careful in spelling verbs ending in *y* (*hurry, hurries, hurried*) and verbs for which the final consonant is doubled (*occurred, expelled*).

Summary

The following table summarizes the various forms employed to express the primary tenses:

Note carefully that singular third-person verbs require an *s* ending (*he needs*) and plural third-person verbs do *not* (*they need*).

	PRESENT TENSE		PAST TENSE		FUTURE TENSE	
	SING.	PLURAL	SING.	PLURAL	SING.	PLURAL
FIRST PERSON:	I need	we need	I needed	we needed	I will need	we will need
SECOND PERSON:	you need	you need	you needed	you needed	you will need	you will need
THIRD PERSON:	he, she, it, needs	they need	he, she, it needed	they needed	he, she, it will need	they will need

SPOT THE BLOOPER

From the Princeton Review Book for the Scholastic Aptitude Test II: "You don't have to be a genus."

EMPHATIC TENSES

To express emphasis, place *do, does,* or *did* before the present tense form of a verb.

She *does have* the qualifications for the job. (Present emphatic tense.)

I *do hope* you brought your raincoat. (Present emphatic tense.)

He stated that he *did help* you with the project. (Past emphatic tense.)

You *did say* you had enough supplies. (Past emphatic tense.)

Now complete the reinforcement exercises for Level I.

LEVEL II

"For good or ill, your conversation is your advertisement. Every time you open your mouth, you let me look into your mind."
— Bruce Barton

PRESENT AND PAST PARTICIPLES

To be able to use all the tenses of verbs correctly, you must understand the four principal parts of verbs: present, past, present participle, and past participle. You have already studied the present and past forms. Now, let's consider the participles.

Present Participle

The present participle of a regular verb is formed by adding *ing* to the present part of the verb. When used in a sentence as part of a verb phrase, the present participle is always preceded by some form of the helping verb *to be (am, is, are, was, were, be, been)*.

I *am printing* the proposal.

You *are wasting* good paper.

SPOT THE BLOOPER

From a CNN interview: "The warden has came out and gave us his view of the execution."

Past Participle

The past participle of a regular verb is usually formed by adding a *d* or *t* sound to the present part of the verb. Like present participles, past participles may function as parts of verb phrases.

Beth *has locked* her keys in the car.

The keys *have been locked* in the car by Beth.

We *should have finished* the project earlier.

The project *should have been finished* earlier.

IRREGULAR VERBS

Up to this point, we have considered only regular verbs. Regular verbs form the past tense by the addition of *d* or *ed* to the present tense form. Many verbs, however, form the past tense and the past participle irregularly. (More specifically, irregular verbs form the past tense by a variation in the root vowel and, commonly, the past participle by the addition of *en*.) A list of the more frequently used irregular verbs follows. Learn the forms of these verbs by practicing in patterns such as:

PRESENT TENSE: Today I write.
PAST TENSE: Yesterday I wrote.
PAST PARTICIPLE: In the past I have written.

Frequently Used Irregular Verbs

PRESENT	PAST	PAST PARTICIPLE
arise	arose	arisen
be (am, is, are)	was, were	been
bear (to carry)	bore	borne
become	became	become
begin	began	begun
bite	bit	bitten
blow	blew	blown
break	broke	broken
bring	brought	brought
build	built	built
choose	chose	chosen
come	came	come
do	did	done
draw	drew	drawn
drink	drank	drunk
drive	drove	driven
eat	ate	eaten
fall	fell	fallen
fly	flew	flown
forbid	forbade	forbidden
forget	forgot	forgotten *or* forgot
forgive	forgave	forgiven
freeze	froze	frozen
get	got	gotten *or* got
give	gave	given
go	went	gone
grow	grew	grown
hang (to suspend)	hung	hung
hang (to execute)	hanged	hanged
hide	hid	hidden *or* hid
know	knew	known
lay (to place)	laid	laid
leave	left	left
lie (to rest)	lay	lain
lie (to tell a falsehood)	lied	lied
pay	paid	paid
prove	proved	proved *or* proven
raise (to lift)	raised	raised
ride	rode	ridden
ring	rang	rung

SPOT THE BLOOPER

From the *Journal* [Albany, CA]: "Board member Ed McManus . . . expressed concern that classified staff would have to bare the brunt of budget cuts."

SPOT THE BLOOPER

From a Dunkin' Donuts advertisement: "The trouble with supermarket doughnuts is there's no telling how long they've been laying around."

SPOT THE BLOOPER

From *The Times-Union* [Albany, NY]: "Jane Fonda's Beverly Hills hairdresser sweared the thick blond braid she's been sporting . . . is her real hair."

SPOT THE BLOOPER

From Walt Disney Company: "Honey, I Shrunk the Kids."

PRESENT	PAST	PAST PARTICIPLE
rise (to move up)	rose	risen
run	ran	run
see	saw	seen
set (to place)	set	set
shake	shook	shaken
shrink	shrank	shrunk
sing	sang	sung
sink	sank	sunk
sit (to rest)	sat	sat
speak	spoke	spoken
spring	sprang	sprung
steal	stole	stolen
strike	struck	struck *or* stricken
swear	swore	sworn
swim	swam	swum
take	took	taken
tear	tore	torn
throw	threw	thrown
wear	wore	worn
write	wrote	written

THREE PAIRS OF FREQUENTLY MISUSED IRREGULAR VERBS

The key to the correct use of the following pairs of verbs lies in developing the ability to recognize the tense forms of each and to distinguish transitive verbs and constructions from intransitive ones.

Lie–Lay

These two verbs are confusing because the past tense of *lie* is spelled in exactly the same way that the present tense of *lay* is spelled. Memorize these verb forms:

STUDY TIP

Whenever you use *lay* in the sense of "placing" something, you must provide a receiver of the action: *Please lay the book down.*

	PRESENT	PRESENT PARTICIPLE	PAST	PAST PARTICIPLE
INTRANSITIVE:	lie (to rest)	lying	lay	lain
TRANSITIVE:	lay (to place)	laying	laid (*not layed*)	laid

The verb *lie* is intransitive; therefore, it requires no direct object to complete its meaning.

I *lie* down for a nap every afternoon. (Note that *down* is not a direct object.)

"*Lie* down," he told his dog. (Commands are given in the present tense.)

Last week I *lay* down on the grass in the sunshine. (Past tense.)

My shoes are *lying* on the floor. (Present participle.)

They have *lain* there since I took them off yesterday. (Past participle.)

SPOT THE BLOOPER

From *The Detroit News:* "Emerick allegedly fired one shot in his wife's back as she lied on the floor."

The verb *lay* is transitive and must have a direct object to complete its meaning.

Lay the bricks over there. (Command in the present tense.)

The mason is *laying* bricks. (Present participle.)

He *laid* the bricks in a row. (Past tense.)

He has *laid* bricks all his life. (Past participle.)

To help you remember that these verbs are intransitive, look at the second letter of each:
lie
sit
rise
Associate *i* with *i*ntransitive.

Sit–Set

Less troublesome than *lie-lay,* the combination of *sit-set* is nevertheless perplexing because the sound of the verbs is similar. The intransitive verb *sit* (past tense, *sat;* past participle, *sat*) means "to rest" and requires no direct object.

> Do you *sit* on this park bench every day? (Used intransitively.)
>
> Are you *sitting* on my jacket? (Present participle.)

The transitive verb *set* (past tense, *set;* past participle, *set*) means "to place" and must have a direct object.

> Please *set* the flowers on the table. (*Flowers* is the direct object.)
>
> We are *setting* the vase where Sal can see it. (Present participle.)

Rise–Raise

The intransitive verb *rise* (past tense, *rose;* past participle, *risen*) means "to go up" or "to ascend" and requires no direct object.

> He *rises* early every morning. (*Every morning* is an adverbial phrase, not an object.)
>
> The tide is *rising* rapidly. (Present participle.)
>
> The president *rose* from his chair to greet us. (Past tense.)
>
> Interest rates have *risen* steadily. (Past participle.)

The transitive verb *raise* (past tense, *raised;* past participle, *raised*) means "to lift up" or "to elevate" and must have a direct object.

> Please *raise* the curtain for the second act. (*Curtain* is a direct object.)
>
> The manufacturer is *raising* prices next month. (*Prices* is a direct object.)

Now complete the reinforcement exercises for Level II.

LEVEL III

PROGRESSIVE AND PERFECT TENSES

Thus far in this chapter, you have studied the primary tenses, the emphatic verb tenses, and irregular verbs. The remainder of this chapter focuses on two additional sets of verb tenses: the perfect and the progressive. Most native speakers and writers of English have little difficulty controlling these verb forms because they have frequently heard them used correctly. For individuals who are not native speakers and for those who are eager to study the entire range of verb tenses, this largely descriptive section is thus presented.

Progressive Tenses

Present Progressive Tense

	First Person	Second Person	Third Person
Active:	I am asking we are asking	you are asking	he, she, it is asking they are asking
Passive:	I am being asked we are being asked	you are being asked	he, she, it is being asked they are being asked

	Past Progressive Tense		
	First Person	**Second Person**	**Third Person**
ACTIVE:	I was asking we were asking	you were asking	he, she, it was asking they were asking
PASSIVE:	I was being asked we were being asked	you were being asked	he, she, it was being asked they were being asked

	Future Progressive Tense		
	First Person	**Second Person**	**Third Person**
ACTIVE:	I will be asking we will be asking	you will be asking	he, she, it will be asking they will be asking
PASSIVE:	I will be being asked we will be being asked	you will be being asked	he, she, it will be being asked they will be being asked

We *are sending* the fax right now. (Present progressive tense expresses action in progress.)

Federal Express *was testing* its systems last week. (Past progressive tense indicates action begun in the past.)

They *will be announcing* the winner tomorrow. (Future progressive tense indicates action in the future.)

SPOT THE BLOOPER

In *Skyway News/Freeway News,* describing a restaurant in Mantonville, Minnesota: "Proprietor Paul J. Pappas extends his hostility to tour groups. Call for reservations."

Perfect Tenses

	Present Perfect Tense		
	First Person	**Second Person**	**Third Person**
ACTIVE:	I have asked we have asked	you have asked	he, she, it has asked they have asked
PASSIVE:	I have been asked we have been asked	you have been asked	he, she, it has been asked they have been asked

	Past Perfect Tense		
	First Person	**Second Person**	**Third Person**
ACTIVE:	I had asked we had asked	you had asked	he, she, it had asked they had asked
PASSIVE:	I had been asked we had been heard	you had been asked	he, she, it had been asked they had been asked

	Future Perfect Tense		
	First Person	**Second Person**	**Third Person**
ACTIVE:	I will have asked we will have asked	you will have asked	he, she, it will have asked they will have asked
PASSIVE:	I will have been asked we will have been asked	you will have been asked	he, she, it will have been asked they will have been asked

Miriam has just *left* the building. (Present perfect tense expresses action just completed or *perfected.*)

The letter had *reached* your office by the time I called. (Past perfect tense shows an action finished before another action in the past.)

The polls *will have been closed* two hours when the results are telecast. (Future perfect tense indicates action that will be completed before another future action.)

SPOT THE BLOOPER

Headline from classified advertisements: "Illiterate? Write today for free help."

SUMMARY

The following table summarizes the four sets of tenses.

PRIMARY TENSES	EMPHATIC TENSES
Present	Present emphatic
Past	Past emphatic
Future	

PROGRESSIVE TENSES	PERFECT TENSES
Present progressive	Present perfect
Past progressive	Past perfect
Future progressive	Future perfect

Now complete the reinforcement exercises for Level III.

HOT LINE QUERIES

QUESTION We're having a big argument in our office. What's correct? *E-mail, e-mail, email,* or *Email*? And is it *on-line* or *online*?

ANSWER When technology thrusts new concepts and language on us, we sometimes experience a state of flux until standardized usage patterns develop. Although I've seen *e-mail* and *online* in reputable publications, I recommend *E-mail* and *on-line* because they are the forms shown in *Merriam-Webster's Collegiate Dictionary*, Tenth Edition (our standard reference). By the way, *Webster's* Tenth also shows *database* as one word. Some organizations have style manuals showing preferred usage for these words.

QUESTION We have a new electronic mail system, and one of the functions is "messaging" people. When folks say, *I'll message you*, it really grates on my nerves. Is this correct?

ANSWER "Messaging" is certainly a hot term with the explosion of E-mail. As to its correctness, I think we've caught language in the act of evolving. What's happened here is the reinstitution of a noun (*message*) as a verb. Converting nouns into verbs is common in English (he *cornered* the market, we *tabled* the motion, I *penciled* it in on my calendar, the farmer *trucked* the vegetables to market). Actually, *message* was sometimes used as a verb nearly a century ago (in 1896 *the bill was messaged over from the house*). However, its recent use has been almost exclusively as a noun. Today, it is increasingly being used again as a verb. New uses of words usually become legitimate when the words fill a need and are immediately accepted. Some word uses, though, appear to be mere fads, like *The homeless child could not language her fears*. Forcing the noun *language* to function as a verb is unnecessary since a good word already exsists for the purpose: *express*. But other "nouns-made-verbs" have been in use long enough to sound reasonable: I *faxed* the document, he *videotaped* the program, she *keyboarded* the report.

QUESTION I'm embarrassed to ask this because I should know the answer — but I don't. Is there an apostrophe in this: *its relevance to our program?*

ANSWER No. Use an apostrophe only for the contraction *it's,* meaning *it is* (*it's a good plan*). The possessive pronoun *its,* as used in your example, has no apostrophe (*the car had its oil changed*).

QUESTION I thought I knew the difference between *principal* and *principle,* but now I'm not so sure. In a report I'm typing I find this: *The principal findings of the research are negative.* I thought principal always meant your "pal," the school principal.

ANSWER You're partly right and partly wrong. *Principal* may be used as a noun meaning *chief* or *head person.* In addition, it may be used as an adjective to mean *chief* or *main.* This is the meaning most people forget, and this is the meaning of the word in your sentence. The word *principle* means a *law* or *rule.* Perhaps it is easiest to remember *principle* rule. All other uses require *principal:* the *principal* of the school, the *principal* of the loan, the *principal* reason.

QUESTION Even when I use a dictionary, I can't tell the difference between *affect* and *effect.* What should the word be in this sentence? *Changes in personnel (affected/effected) our production this month.*

ANSWER No words generate more calls to the Hot Line than do *affect/effect.* In your sentence use *affected.* Let's see if we can resolve the *affect/effect* dilemma. *Affect* is a verb meaning "to influence" (*smoking affects health; government policies affect citizens*). *Affect* may also mean "to pretend or imitate" (*he affected a British accent*). *Effect* can be a noun or a verb. As a noun, it means "result" (*the effect of the law is slight*). As a verb (and here's the troublesome part) *effect* means "to produce a result" (*small cars effect gasoline savings; GM effected a new pricing policy*).

QUESTION I'm editing a screenplay for a studio, and I know something is grammatically wrong with this sentence: *The old man left the room hurriedly after discovering a body laying near the window.*

ANSWER As you probably suspected, the verb *laying* should be *lying. Lay* means "to place" and requires an object (*he is laying the report on your desk now*). *Lie* means "to rest" and requires no object (*the document is lying on your desk).*

QUESTION As the holiday season approaches, I'm wondering whether it's *Season's Greetings* or *Seasons' Greetings.*

ANSWER If you are referring to one season, it's *Season's Greetings.*

QUESTION I learned that the verb *set* is transitive and requires an object. If that's true, how can we say that the sun *sets* in the west?

ANSWER Good question! The verb *set* is generally transitive, but it does have some standardized intransitive uses, such as the one you mention. Here's another: *Glue sets up quickly.* I doubt that anyone would be likely to substitute *sit* in either of these unusual uses. While we're on the subject, the verb *sit* also has some exceptions. Although generally intransitive, *sit* has a few transitive uses: *Sit yourself down* and *The waiter sat us at Table 1.*

10 Verb and Subject Agreement

OBJECTIVES When you have completed the materials in this chapter, you will be able to do the following:

Level I
- Locate the subjects of verbs despite intervening elements and inverted sentence structure.
- Make verbs agree with true subjects.
- Make verbs agree with subjects joined by *and.*

Level II
- Make verbs agree with subjects joined by *or* or *nor.*
- Select the correct verbs to agree with collective nouns and indefinite pronouns.

Level III
- Make verbs agree with quantities, fractions, portions, clauses, and *a number/the number.*
- Achieve subject-verb agreement within *who* clauses.

PRETEST

Underline the correct verb.

1. One of our managers (is, are) preparing the budget.
2. The president, along with members of the staff, (is, are) attending the briefing.
3. Neither the students nor the teachers (are, is) protesting the fee hike.
4. At the entrance of the estate (stand, stands) two large columns.
5. The number of students enrolled (are, is) decreasing each year.

SPOT THE BLOOPER

On the label of Heinz 57 Sauce: "Its' unique tangy blend of herbs and spices bring out the natural taste of steak." (Did you find two bloopers?)

Subjects must agree with verbs in number and person. Beginning a sentence with *He don't* damages a speaker's credibility and limits a communicator's effectiveness.

If an error is made in subject-verb agreement, it can generally be attributed to one of three lapses: (a) failure to locate the subject, (b) failure to recognize the number (singular or plural) of the subject after locating it, or (c) failure to recognize the number of the verb. Suggestions for locating the true subject and determining the number of the subject and its verb follow.

1. is 2. is 3. are 4. stand 5. is

LEVEL I

LOCATING SUBJECTS

Prepositional Phrases

All verbs have subjects. Locating these subjects can be difficult, particularly if a prepositional phrase comes between the verb and its subject. Subjects of verbs are not found in prepositional phrases. Therefore, you must learn to ignore such phrases in identifying subjects of verbs. Some of the most common prepositions are *of, to, in, from, for, with, at,* and *by.* Notice in these sentences that the italicized prepositional phrases do not contain the subjects of the verbs.

> Each *of our products* is unconditionally guaranteed. (The verb *is* agrees with its subject *each.*)
>
> I asked if her report *on the benefits* was copied. (The verb *was* agrees with its subject *report.*)
>
> The variety *of papers and inks available* makes choosing letterhead difficult. (The verb *makes* agrees with the subject *variety.*)

SPOT THE BLOOPER

Headline in *The Democrat and Chronicle* [Rochester, NY]: "In Keshequa, Drop in Scores Are No Surprise."

Some of the less easily recognized prepositions are *except, but, like,* and *between.* In the following sentences, distinguish the subjects from the italicized prepositional phrases.

> All the students *but one* are scheduled to take the tests. (The verb *are* agrees with its subject *students.*)
>
> Everyone *except the managers* is expected to attend. (The verb *is* agrees with its subject *everyone.*)

SPOT THE BLOOPER

From Inmac computer catalog: "WORD is full of new automatic features that really does simplify your workday."

SPOT THE BLOOPER

From *The Erie* [PA] *Daily Times:* "Some computers — and we don't know what else — is showing up in previously scanned rooms."

Intervening Elements

Groups of words introduced by *as well as, in addition to, such as, including, together with,* and *other than* do *not* contain sentence subjects.

> Our favorite comedian, *in addition to other performers,* is scheduled to appear.

In this sentence the writer has elected to emphasize the subject *comedian* and to deemphasize *other performers.* The writer could have given equal weight to these elements by writing *Our favorite comedian and other performers are scheduled to appear.* Notice that the number (singular or plural) of the verb changes when both *comedian* and *performers* are given equal emphasis. Here are additional examples involving intervening elements:

> Quincy Jones, *together with over 50 other well-known musicians,* was responsible for the success of "We Are the World." (The singular subject *Quincy Jones* agrees with the singular verb *was.*)
>
> Some artists *such as Van Gogh* were penniless during their lives. (The plural subject *artists* agrees with the plural verb *were.*)

The Adverbs *there* and *here*

In sentences beginning with *there* or *here,* look for the true subject *after* the verb. As adverbs, *here* and *there* cannot function as subjects.

> There are many ways to approach the problem. (The subject *ways* follows the verb *are.*)
>
> Here is my application for the position. (The subject *application* follows the verb *is.*)

SPOT THE BLOOPER

Sign above a group of photographs in a Service Merchandise store, Ft. Myers, Florida: "HERE'S OUR STORE MANAGERS."

Inverted Sentence Order

Look for the subject after the verb in inverted sentences and in questions.

On our board of directors are three prominent scientists. (Verb precedes subject.)

Has your tax refund been received? (Subject separates verb phrase.)

How expensive are the books, tuition, and fees? (Verb precedes subjects.)

SPOT THE BLOOPER

From *The Saint John's* [Newfoundland] *Evening Telegram:* "It's important that we have in that position someone who's judgment, integrity, and incompetence is beyond question." [Did you spot three bloopers?]

BASIC RULES FOR VERB–SUBJECT AGREEMENT

Once you have located the sentence subject, decide whether the subject is singular or plural and select a verb that agrees in number.

Subjects Joined by *and*

When one subject is joined to another by the word *and,* the subject is plural and requires a plural verb.

Paul Taylor and Alvin Ailey are two influential choreographers in the world of modern dance

Baking soda and salt work together to make cakes rise.

STUDY TIP

To help you select correct verbs, temporarily substitute *it* for singular subjects or *they* for plural subjects. Then you can more easily make verbs agree with their subjects.

Company Names and Titles

Even though they may appear to be plural, company names and titles of publications are singular; therefore, they require singular verbs.

Road and Track is the only magazine my brother reads.

Procter & Gamble sponsors many charity events each year.

"The Young and the Restless" is my favorite soap opera.

Now complete the reinforcement exercises for Level 1.

LEVEL II

RULES FOR VERB–SUBJECT AGREEMENT

STUDY TIP

Unlike subjects joined by *and,* subjects joined by *or/nor* require a choice between Subject No. 1 and Subject No. 2.

Subjects Joined by *or* or *nor*

When two or more subjects are joined by *or* or *nor,* the verb should agree with the closer subject.

Neither the boys nor their coach wants to compete.

Either the mayor or his constituents were bound to be unhappy with the results.

Madeline or you are responsible for the tickets.

Indefinite Pronouns as Subjects

As you may recall from Chapter 7, some indefinite pronouns are always singular, while other indefinite pronouns are always plural. In addition, some may be singular or plural depending on the words to which they refer.

Always Singular			Always Plural	Singular or Plural
anyone	every	nobody	both	all
anybody	everyone	nothing	few	more
anything	everybody	someone	many	most
each	everything	somebody	several	some
either	many a	something		any
	neither			none

SPOT THE BLOOPER

Headline in *The San Francisco Chronicle:* "One in 11 Have Trouble Speaking California's Official Language"

Either of the candidates *is qualified.*

Anybody who returns merchandise *is reimbursed.*

Many of our friends *are attending* the concert.

Neither of those books *is checked* out.

Indefinite pronouns such as *all, more,* and *most* provide one of the few instances when prepositional phrases become important in determining agreement. Although the prepositional phrase does not contain the subject of the sentence, it does contain the noun to which the indefinite pronoun refers.

All of the women *are* here. (*All* is plural because it refers to *women.*)

All of the cake *was eaten.* (*All* is singular because it refers to *cake.*)

STUDY TIP

This use of a singular verb for two or more subjects joined by *and* is the only exception to the general rule presented in Level I.

If the indefinite pronouns *each, every,* or *many a* are used to describe two or more subjects joined by *and,* the subjects are considered separate. Therefore, the verb is singular.

Many a daughter and mother *has* trouble getting along.

Every man, woman, and child *was evacuated* during the storm.

The indefinite pronouns *anyone, everyone,* and *someone* should be spelled as two words when followed by *of* phrases.

Every one of us should be grateful for the help.

Any one of those greeting cards *is* appropriate.

STUDY TIP

In America collective nouns are almost always considered to be singular (*The staff is . . .*). In Britain, however, collective nouns are usually plural (*The staff are . . .*).

Collective Nouns as Subjects

Words such as *faculty, committee,* and *council* may be singular or plural depending on their mode of operation. When a collective noun operates as a single unit, its verb should be singular. When the elements of a collective noun operate separately, the verb should be plural.

Our staff *has* unanimously *adopted* the board's proposal. (*Staff* is acting as a single unit.)

The jury *were divided* over the testimony of one witness. (*Jury* members were acting separately. While technically correct, the sentence would be less awkward if it read *The jury* members *were divided. . . .*)

SPOT THE BLOOPER

From the *Evansville* (IN) *Press:* "Although a large crowd were gathered . . ."

Now complete the reinforcement exercises for Level II.

LEVEL III

RULES FOR VERB–SUBJECT AGREEMENT

The Distinction Between *the number* and *a number*

When the word *number* is the subject of a sentence, its article (*the* or *a*) becomes significant. *The* is specific and therefore implies *singularity; a* is general and therefore implies *plurality.*

The number of cars on our highways *is increasing.* (Singular)

A number of new cars *are scheduled* to be introduced. (Plural)

Quantities, Measures

When they refer to *total* amounts, quantities and measures are singular. If they refer to *individual units* that can be counted, quantities and measures are plural.

Three days *is* a long time to spend in a car. (Quantity as a total amount.)

Three working days *are* required to obtain a passport. (Quantity as individual units.)

Fractions, Portions

Fractions and portions may be singular or plural depending on the nouns to which they refer.

Three-fourths of the applications *were accepted.*

Half of the eggs *are spoiled.*

The majority of students *live* off-campus.

A minimum of preparation *is required* for this meal.

Part of the problems *were caused* by miscommunication.

A large portion of the pizza *was eaten.*

For sentences with *one of those who* clauses, begin reading with the word *of: Of those people who give 100 percent, Richard is one.* The verb will always be plural. However, if the sentence is limited by *only one,* the verb is always singular.

Who Clauses

Verbs in *who* clauses must agree in number and person with the nouns to which they refer. In *who* clauses introduced by *one of,* the verb is usually plural because it refers to a plural antecedent. In *who* clauses introduced by *the only one of,* the verb is singular.

Richard is *one of* those people who always give 100 percent.

Rachel is *one of* those students who are failing math.

Pamela is *the only one* of the actors who is here on time.

Verbs must agree in person with the nouns or pronouns to which they refer.

It is I who was late for class.

Was it you who were on the phone?

Phrases and Clauses as Subjects

Use a singular verb when the subject of a sentence is a phrase or clause.

To study physics is demanding.

That we will address the invitations is understood.

SPOT THE BLOOPER

From *The Atlanta Journal and Constitution:* "Initiation fee and dues information also is top secret."

Subject Complements

In Chapter 8 you learned that linking verbs are followed by complements. Although a complement may differ from the subject in number, the linking verb should always agree with the subject.

> The most exciting part of our trip was the rafting and hiking.
>
> The reason for her failing was poor study habits.

To avoid awkwardness, it may be better to reconstruct such sentences so that the plural element is first: *The singing and dancing are the best part of the show.*

Now complete the reinforcement exercises for Level III.

HOT LINE QUERIES

QUESTION My uncle insists that *none* is singular. My English book says that it can be plural. Who's right?

ANSWER Times are changing. Thirty years ago *none* was almost always used in a singular sense. Today, through usage, *none* may be singular or plural depending on what you wish to emphasize. For example, *None are more willing than we.* But, *None of the students is* (or *are* if you wish to suggest many students) *failing.*

QUESTION When do you use *all together,* and when do you use *altogether?*

ANSWER *All together* means "collectively" or "all the members of a group" (*we must work all together to reach our goal*). *Altogether* means "entirely" (*he was altogether satisfied*).

QUESTION Please help me with this sentence that I'm transcribing for a medical laboratory: *A copy of our analysis, along with our interpretation of its results,* (*has or have*) *been sent to you.*

ANSWER The subject of your sentence is *copy;* thus the verb must be *has.* Don't let interrupting elements obscure the real sentence subject.

QUESTION After looking in the dictionary, I'm beginning to wonder about this: *We have alot of work yet to do.* I can't find the word *alot* in the dictionary, but it must be there. Everyone uses it.

ANSWER The two-word phrase *a lot* is frequently used in conversation or in very informal writing (*the copier makes a lot of copies*). *Alot* as one word does not exist. Don't confuse it with *allot* meaning "to distribute" (*the company will allot to each department its share of supplies*).

QUESTION Should *reevaluate* be hyphenated?

ANSWER No. It is not necessary to use a hyphen after the prefix *re* unless the resulting word may be confused with another word (*to re-mark the sales ticket, to re-cover the chair*).

QUESTION I'm totally confused by job titles for women today. What do I call a woman who is a *fireman*, a *policeman*, a *chairman*, or a *spokesman?* And what about the word *mankind?*

ANSWER As more and more women enter nontraditional careers, some previous designations are being replaced by neutral, inclusive titles. Here are some substitutes:

firefighter	for fireman
mail carrier	for mailman
police officer	for policeman
flight attendant	for steward or stewardess
reporter or journalist	for newsman

Words like *chairman, spokesman,* and *mankind* traditionally have been used to refer to both men and women. Today, though, sensitive writers strive to use more inclusive language. Possible substitutes are *chair, spokesperson,* and *humanity.*

QUESTION I'm never sure how to handle words that are used to represent quantities and proportions in sentences. For example, what verb is correct in this sentence: *A large proportion of voters (was or were) against the measure.*

ANSWER Words that represent fractional amounts (such as *proportion, fraction, minimum,* and *majority*) may be singular or plural depending on the words they represent. In your sentence *proportion* represents *voters,* which is plural. Therefore, use the plural verb *were.*

11 Verbals

OBJECTIVES When you have completed the materials in this chapter, you will be able to do the following:

Level I
- Recognize gerunds and supply appropriate modifiers of gerunds.
- Identify and remedy split infinitives that result in awkward sentences.

Level II
- Correctly punctuate introductory and other verbal phrases.
- Avoid writing awkward participial phrases.

Level III
- Spot dangling verbal phrases and other misplaced modifiers.
- Rewrite sentences to avoid misplaced verbal phrases and modifiers.

PRETEST

Write the correct letter to describe the following sentences.

a = contains no error
b = contains error in use of verbal form
c = contains error in punctuation of verbal form

1. Closing the door, Paul's sweater was caught in the hinges. ____
2. After arguing intensely the two sisters made up. ____
3. To complete your application, return the enclosed form. ____
4. Experienced in the field, the personnel director chose Jeffrey. ____
5. To visit Disney World was our first priority. ____

As you learned earlier, English is a highly flexible language in which a given word may have more than one grammatical function. In this chapter you will study verbals. Derived from verbs, *verbals* are words that function as nouns, adjectives, or adverbs. Three kinds of verbals are gerunds (verbal nouns), infinitives, and participles (verbal adjectives).

1.b 2.c 3.a 4.b 5.a

LEVEL I

GERUNDS

A verb form ending in *ing* and used as a noun is called a *gerund.*

> *Running* is good exercise. (Gerund used as the subject.)
>
> Chip enjoys *fencing.* (Gerund used as direct object.)

Using Gerunds Correctly

In using gerunds, follow this rule: Make any noun or pronoun modifying a gerund possessive, as in *Karen's typing* or *Dale's computing.* Because we sometimes fail to recognize gerunds as nouns, we fail to make their modifiers possessive:

SPOT THE BLOOPER

From a notice to holders of Exxon credit cards: "We appreciate you choosing Exxon . . ."

> WRONG: We were worried about *Dillon driving.*
>
> RIGHT: We were worried about *Dillon's driving.*

We are not worried about Dillon, as the first version states; we are worried about his driving. If we substitute a more easily recognized noun for *driving*, the possessive form seems more natural: *We were worried about Dillon's behavior. Behavior* is a noun, just as *driving* is a noun; the noun or pronoun modifiers of both must be possessive.

STUDY TIP

To distinguish between *ing* forms used as nouns and those used as adjectives, try the *what?* question approach. In the sentence *I admired Meredith's singing,* say to yourself, "I admired *what?*" Answer: "I admired Meredith's *singing,* not Meredith." Therefore, *singing* is the object and functions as an *ing* noun.

> The manager appreciated *his* working late. (The gerund *working* requires the possessive pronoun *his,* not the objective case pronoun *him.*)
>
> I resent *your* complaining to my boss. (Not *you* complaining.)

Not all verbs ending in *ing* are, of course, gerunds. Some are elements in verb phrases and some act as adjectives.* Compare these three sentences:

> I heard Meredith singing. (The word *singing* functions as an adjective describing Meredith.)
>
> I admired Meredith's singing. (As the object of the verb, *singing* acts as a gerund.)
>
> Meredith is singing. (Here *singing* functions as a verb phrase.)

INFINITIVES

When the present form of a verb is preceded by *to,* the most basic verb form results: the *infinitive.* The sign of the infinitive is the word *to.*

> She tried *to follow* your instructions exactly.
>
> *To play* well requires correct breathing.

SPOT THE BLOOPER

Headline from *The Urbana* [OH] *Daily Citizen:* "Volunteers Use Sandbags to Try and Save Water Plant." [What's wrong with using *and?*]

Using Infinitives Correctly

In certain expressions infinitives may be misused. Observe the use of the word *to* in the following infinitive phrases. Do not substitute the conjunction *and* for the *to* of the infinitive.

> Try *to open* this jar for me. (Not *try and open.*)
>
> Be sure *to lock* the door when you leave. (Not *be sure and lock.*)
>
> Check *to see* when the flight is due to arrive. (Not *check and see.*)

When any word appears between *to* and the verb (*to* carefully *prepare*), an infinitive is said to be split. At one time split infinitives were considered great gram-

*Participles will be discussed in Level II of this chapter.

matical sins. Today most authorities agree that infinitives may be split if necessary for clarity and effect. Avoid, however, split infinitives that result in awkward sentences.

AWKWARD:	The Millers want to, if financing is available, buy a home.
BETTER:	If financing is available, the Millers want to buy a home.
AWKWARD:	Our manager had *to,* when budget cuts were announced, *lay off* several salespeople.
BETTER:	When budget cuts were announced, our manager had to *lay off* several salespeople.
ACCEPTABLE:	*To* honestly *state* the facts is the job of the prosecutor. (No awkwardness results from split infinitive.)
ACCEPTABLE:	Your parents want you *to* really *do* your best. (No awkwardness results from split infinitive.)

Now complete the reinforcement exercises for Level I.

PARTICIPLES

You have already studied the present and past forms of participles functioning as parts of verb phrases. You will recall that in such constructions present and past participles always require helping verbs: *is singing, was seen, had broken.*

In this chapter we will be concerned with a second possible function of participles. Participles can function as adjectives. As adjectives, participles modify nouns or pronouns, and they do not require helping verbs.

Participles used as adjectives have three tenses and two voices:

	PRESENT TENSE	PAST TENSE	PERFECT TENSE
ACTIVE VOICE:	selling	sold	having sold
PASSIVE VOICE:	being sold	sold	having been sold

A participle in the present tense is used to show additional action occurring at the time of the action expressed by the main verb in the sentence (such main verbs may be present, past, or future).

Brenda asked the man *selling* the car for the pink slip. (Present participle.)

A participle in the past or perfect tense is used to show other action completed *before* the action expressed by the main verb in the sentence.

Having run the race, Mitchell was exhausted. (Perfect participle used to show action completed prior to action of main verb *run.*)

The *fallen* leaves had to be raked. (Past participle shows that the leaves had fallen before they were raked.)

Using Participles Correctly

Avoid using participial phrases that sound awkward, such as these:

AWKWARD:	Merrill's having been absent was a coincidence.
BETTER:	Merrill's absence was a coincidence.
AWKWARD:	Being as you live nearby, should we carpool?
BETTER:	Since you live nearby, should we carpool?

PUNCTUATING VERBAL FORMS

Determining whether verbal forms require commas often causes students difficulty. Let's try to clear up this difficulty with explanations and examples.

SPOT THE BLOOPER

From *Country Collectibles:* "Sitting by a blazing fire, reading a good mystery novel, a dog can jump into your lap and beg for a few playful pats on the head."

Punctuating Introductory Verbal Forms

When verbal forms are used in introductory words or expressions, there's no question about punctuating them. A comma should be placed between an introductory verbal form and the main clause of a sentence.

Amazed, we wanted to hear her explanation. (Introductory verbal form.)

To increase productivity, our manager hired a management consultant. (Introductory verbal phrase.)

Changing her spark plugs, Selena discovered another problem. (Introductory verbal phrase.)

Finishing three chapters of the book, Ralph went right to sleep. (Introductory verbal phrase.)

Not all verbal phrases that begin sentences, however, are considered introductory. If the verbal phrase represents the subject or part of the predicate of the sentence, *no* comma should separate it from the rest of the sentence.

"A successful career requires falling in love many times with your work."
— Frank Watson

Opening the mail is the receptionist's job. (Verbal phrase used as subject; no comma.)

To alter the schedule at this point would be difficult. (Verbal phrase used as subject; no comma.)

Offering an incentive is the best way to motivate workers. (Verbal phrase used as subject; no comma.)

Punctuating Nonessential Verbal Phrases*

Essential (restrictive) information is needed for the reader to understand the sentence. Verbal phrases often help identify the subject. These phrases require no commas. Nonessential information could be omitted without altering the basic meaning of the sentence; thus, nonessential phrases are set off by commas.

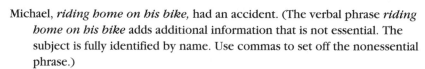

To help you understand the use of commas in dealing with nonessential (nonrestrictive) information, think of a window shade. Use commas to lower the window shade and cover the words enclosed. If words in a verbal phrase are not essential to the meaning of a sentence, use a "comma window shade" to obscure them.

Michael, *riding home on his bike,* had an accident. (The verbal phrase *riding home on his bike* adds additional information that is not essential. The subject is fully identified by name. Use commas to set off the nonessential phrase.)

The man *riding home on his bike* had an accident. (In this sentence the verbal phrase *riding home on his bike* is essential; it is needed to identify the subject. *Which* man had an accident? The man *riding home on his bike.* No commas separate this essential verbal phrase.)

Talleyrand Corporation, *offering services in 50 states,* is a leading real estate firm. (The verbal phrase is not essential because there is only one Talleyrand Corporation, and it has been identified. Commas enclose this nonessential verbal phrase.)

A corporation *offering services in 50 states* would be ideal for our needs. (This verbal phrase is essential to identify which corporation would be ideal. No commas are needed. *Note:* Even though you pause when you reach the end of the verbal phrase, don't be tempted to add a comma.)

*Many students find it easier to work with the words *essential* and *nonessential* than with the more traditional grammatical terms *restrictive* and *nonrestrictive;* therefore, the easier terminology is used here.

Notice in the preceding sentences that whenever a nonessential verbal phrase interrupts the middle of a sentence, *two* commas set it off.

Now complete the reinforcement exercises for Level II.

LEVEL III

SPOT THE BLOOPER

From the *Sun Cities* [AZ] *Independent:* "While pumping gas, an unoccupied car rolled into the victim's car."

AVOIDING MISPLACED VERBAL MODIFIERS

Introductory Verbal Phrases

Introductory verbal phrases must be followed by the words they can logically modify. Such phrases can create confusion or unintended humor when placed incorrectly in a sentence. Consider this sentence: ***Sitting in the car, the mountains were breathtaking.*** The introductory participial phrase in this sentence is said to *dangle* because it is not followed immediately by a word it can logically modify. The sentence could be improved by revising it to read: ***Sitting in the car, we saw the breathtaking mountains.*** Observe how the following illogical sentences have been improved:

STUDY TIP

After reading an introductory verbal phrase, ask the question *who?* The answer to that question must immediately follow the introductory phrase. For example, *Hiking in the hills, who?* Answer: *Hiking in the hills, Lisa suffered . . .*

ILLOGICAL:	Hiking in the hills, her new boots caused several blisters.
LOGICAL:	Hiking in the hills, Lisa suffered several blisters from her new boots.
ILLOGICAL:	Icing the cake, the knife dropped from her hand.
LOGICAL:	Icing the cake, she dropped the knife.
ILLOGICAL:	To receive a free CD, the enclosed card must be returned.
LOGICAL:	To receive a free CD, you must return the enclosed card.
ILLOGICAL:	After leaving the party, Sarah's car wouldn't start.
LOGICAL:	After leaving the party, Sarah found that her car wouldn't start.
BUT:	To master the language, listen carefully to native speakers.
	To master the language, (you) listen carefully. (In commands, the understood subject is *you.* Therefore, this sentence is correctly followed by the word to which it refers.)

SPOT THE BLOOPER

From the *Tri-Cities Herald* [Richland, WA]: "He laid there for 23 hours critically injured. . . . After lingering close to death for many days, newspaper reporters were allowed to visit him." [Did you spot two bloopers?]

Verbal Phrases in Other Positions

In other positions within sentences, verbal phrases must also be placed in logical relation to the words they modify.

ILLOGICAL:	The missing children were found by rangers wandering around dazed and hungry.
LOGICAL:	Rangers found the missing children wandering around dazed and hungry.
ILLOGICAL:	The patient was referred to a psychiatrist with severe emotional problems.
LOGICAL:	The patient with severe emotional problems was referred to a psychiatrist.

SPOT THE BLOOPER

From *The Ft. Lauderdale* [FL] *Sun Sentinel:* "Architect Barry Sugerman of North Miami designed this pergola to divert attention from the garage, which is seen walking up to the house from the motorcourt."

Now complete the reinforcement exercises for Level III.

QUESTION Are there two meanings for the word *discreet?*

ANSWER You are probably confusing the two words *discreet* and *discrete. Discreet* means "showing good judgment" and "prudent" (*the witness gave a discreet answer, avoiding gossip and hearsay*). The word *discrete* means "separate" or "noncontinuous" (*Alpha, Inc., has installed discrete computers rather than a network computer system*). You might find it helpful to remember that the *e*'s are separate in *discrete.*

QUESTION Should I use *complimentary* or *complementary* to describe free tickets?

ANSWER Use *complimentary,* which can mean "containing a compliment, favorable, or free" (*the dinner came with complimentary wine; he made a complimentary remark*). *Complementary* means "completing or making perfect" (*the complementary colors enhanced the room*). An easy way to remember *compliment* is by thinking "*I* like to receive a *compliment.*"

QUESTION I confuse *i.e.* and *e.g.* What's the difference?

ANSWER The abbreviation *i.e.* stands for the Latin *id est,* meaning "that is" (*the package exceeds the weight limit, i.e., 5 pounds*). Notice the use of a comma after *i.e.* The abbreviation *e.g.* stands for the Latin *exempli gratia,* meaning "for the sake of example" or "for example" (*the manufacturer may offer a purchase incentive, e.g., a rebate or discount plan*).

QUESTION We're having an argument in our office about abbreviations. Can *department* be abbreviated *dep't?* How about *manufacturing* as *mf'g?* Where could we find a correct list of such abbreviations?

ANSWER In informal writing or when space is limited, words may be contracted or abbreviated. If a conventional abbreviation for a word exists, use it instead of a contracted form. Abbreviations are simpler to write and easier to read. For example, use *dept.* instead of *dep't;* use *natl.* instead of *nat'l;* use *cont.* instead of *cont'd.* Other accepted abbreviations are *ins.* for *insurance; mfg.* for *manufacturing; mgr.* for *manager;* and *mdse.* for *merchandise.* Notice that all abbreviations end with periods. Some dictionaries show abbreviations of words along with their definitions. Other dictionaries alphabetize abbreviations within the main entries, so that a reader must know how to spell an abbreviation in order to be able to locate it. Reference manuals often have lists of abbreviations that are very helpful.

QUESTION I'm not sure which word to use in this sentence: *They have used all (they're, their, there) resources in combating the disease.*

ANSWER Use *their,* which is the possessive form of *they.* The adverb *there* means "at that place or at that point" (*we have been there before*). *There* is also used as an expletive or filler preceding a linking verb (*there are numerous explanations*). *They're* is a contraction of *they* and *are* (*they're coming this afternoon*).

QUESTION In a letter written by my boss, how should we spell *there: We do not want an open invoice without there being justifiable reasons.*

ANSWER *There* is spelled correctly, but its use creates an awkward verbal form. If your boss agrees, revise the sentence to read: *We do not want an open invoice without justification.*

NAME ______________________________

UNIT 3 REVIEW ■ Chapters 8–11 (Self-Check)

Begin your review by rereading Chapters 8–11. Then test your comprehension of those chapters by completing the exercises that follow. Compare your responses with those provided at the end of this review.

LEVEL I

In the blank provided, write the letter of the word or phrase that correctly completes each of the following sentences.

1. In the sentence *She seems reliable,* the verb *seems* is (a) transitive, (b) intransitive, (c) linking. C

2. In the sentence *Troy is the president,* the word *president* is a(n) (a) object, (b) linking verb, (c) complement. C

3. Our list of customer names and addresses (a) has, (b) have to be updated before the next mailing. B A

4. The college president, together with all the faculty and staff members, (a) hope, (b) hopes to resolve most budget problems before classes begin. B

5. The college president and all the faculty and staff members (a) hope, (b) hopes to resolve the budget problems before classes begin. B A

6. Be sure (a) to record, (b) and record all your trip expenses. A

7. Wilson, Rivers, and Watson, Inc. (a) is, (b) are hiring new employees. A

8. I certainly appreciate (a) you, (b) your picking up my mail while I was gone. B

9. A complete inventory of all books and magazines (a) is, (b) are necessary before we move the library. B A

10. Is there any possibility of (a) Laura, (b) Laura's writing the check in the next two days? A B

LEVEL II

Write the letter of the word or phrase that correctly completes each of the following sentences.

11. When converting a verb from the passive to the active voice, the writer must make the doer of the action the (a) subject, (b) object of the active voice verb. B A

12. In the sentence *Two mistakes were made in our order,* the verb is in the (a) active, (b) passive voice. B

13. Their newspapers have (a) laid, (b) lain, (c) lay in the driveway for the past two weeks. A B

14. Everyone ignores that car's alarm because it has (a) rang, (b) rung too often in the past. B

15. The purse (a) lying, (b) laying on the floor apparently was left by a restaurant patron. A

16. Neither the owner nor the renters (a) is, (b) are willing to pay the damages. B

17. Do you know if (a) anyone, (b) any one of the part-time employees is able to work Saturday night? ______

Insert commas where necessary in the next group of sentences. Indicate the number of commas that you added. Write *0* for none.

18. Parking close to the building Monica was able to carry the packages inside without help. ______

19. Accessing thousands of customer files became much easier when we installed an electronic database. ______

20. Jeremy and Lisa working late to complete their collaborative term paper ordered pizza at 11 p.m. ______

LEVEL III

In the blank provided, write the letter of the word or phrase that correctly completes each sentence.

21. The problem would have been handled differently if I (a) was, (b) were in charge. ______

22. A motion was made that the committee's report (a) is, (b) be, (c) was approved. ______

23. A number of employees (a) has, (b) have complained about drug testing. ______

24. Did you know it is you who (a) is, (b) are to do the driving tomorrow? ______

25. Only one third of the students (a) has, (b) have voted thus far. ______

26. He is one of those people who always (a) keep, (b) keeps a clean desk. ______

For each sentence below, indicate whether (a) the sentence is written correctly or (b) the sentence has a verbal phrase placed illogically. Rewrite illogical sentences. Keep the verbal phrases in their introductory positions.

27. To sleep well, my pillow must be thick but firm. ______

28. Thrilled to see a live TV show, the promoter gave hundreds of tickets to eager Hollywood tourists. ______

29. Driving to Florida, two bad accidents were witnessed by Jeffrey. ______

Hot Line Review

30. One of the (a) principal, (b) principle reasons for becoming a hotel manager is the possibility of a pleasant working environment. ______

31. These new taxes will negatively (a) effect, (b) affect small businesses. ______

32. The President was (a) all together, (b) altogether pleased with the vote of Congress. ______

33. Art students received (a) complimentary, (b) complementary passes to the exhibit. ______

1.c 2.c 3.a 4.b 5.a 6.a 7.a 8.b 9.a 10.b 11.a 12.b 13.b 14.b 15.a 16.b 17.b
18.1 19.0 20.2 21.b 22.b 23.b 24.b 25.b 26.a 27.b 28.b 29.b 30.a 31.b 32.b 33.a

UNIT 4

Modifying and Connecting Words

12 Modifiers: Adjectives and Adverbs

OBJECTIVES When you have completed the materials in this chapter, you will be able to do the following:

Level I
- Form the comparative and superlative degrees of regular and irregular adjectives and adverbs.
- Use articles correctly and avoid double negatives.

Level II
- Use adjectives after linking verbs and use adverbs to modify verbs, adjectives, and other adverbs.
- Punctuate compound and successive independent adjectives correctly.

Level III
- Compare degrees of absolute adjectives and make comparisons within a group.
- Place adverbs and adjectives close to the words they modify.

PRETEST

Underline the correct word.

1. This is the (worse, worst) blizzard we have ever had.
2. It takes over (a, an) hour to complete these exercises.
3. Lori knew she had done (good, well) on the test.
4. Who brought that (two-year-old, two year old) child to the picnic?
5. Our (newly-elected, newly elected) president called the meeting to order.

SPOT THE BLOOPER

Headline in Florida newspaper: "MAN EATING PIRANHA SOLD AS PET FISH"

Both adjectives and adverbs act as modifiers; that is, they describe or limit other words. Since many of the forms and functions of adjectives and adverbs are similar and since faulty usage often results from the confusion of these two parts of speech, adjectives and adverbs will be treated together in this chapter.

1. worst 2. an 3. well 4. two-year-old 5. newly elected

LEVEL I

BASIC FUNCTIONS OF ADJECTIVES AND ADVERBS

NOTABLE QUOTABLE

"The difference between the almost-right word and the right word is . . . [like] the difference between the lightning bug and the lightning."
— Mark Twain

Adjectives describe or limit nouns and pronouns. As you have already learned, they often answer the questions *what kind? how many?* or *which one?* Adjectives in the following sentences are italicized.

Good things come in the *smallest* packages.

Five golden rings were given on the *eighth* day of Christmas.

Adverbs describe or limit verbs, adjectives, or other adverbs. They often answer the questions *when? how? where?* or *to what extent?*

Today we left work *early.*

He won the contest *quite easily.*

Comparative and Superlative Forms

Most adjectives and adverbs have three forms, or degrees: positive, comparative, and superlative. The examples below illustrate how the comparative and superlative degrees of regular adjectives and adverbs are formed.

	POSITIVE	COMPARATIVE	SUPERLATIVE
ADJECTIVE:	soft	softer	softest
ADVERB:	softly	more softly	most softly
ADJECTIVE:	grateful	more grateful	most grateful
ADVERB:	gratefully	more gratefully	most gratefully

The positive degree of an adjective or an adverb is used in merely describing or in limiting another word. The comparative degree is used to compare two persons or things. The superlative degree is used in the comparison of three or more persons or things.

SPOT THE BLOOPER

ABC-TV anchor, quoted in *The San Jose Mercury News:* "They're a lot smarter and a lot savvier in the way they're handling the press now, which means we'll have to be even smarter and a lot more savvier ourselves."

The comparative degree of short adjectives (nearly all one-syllable and most two-syllable adjectives ending in *y*) is formed by adding *r* or *er* (*softer*). The superlative degree of short adjectives is formed by the addition of *st* or *est* (*softest*). Long adjectives, and those difficult to pronounce, form the comparative and superlative degrees, as do adverbs, with the addition of *more* and *most* (*more grateful, most beautiful*). The following sentences illustrate degrees of comparison for adjectives and adverbs.

ADJECTIVES:	She is very *smart.*	(Positive degree)
	She is *smarter* than I.	(Comparative degree)
	She is the *smartest* person in the class.	(Superlative degree)
ADVERBS:	He works *quickly.*	(Positive degree)
	He works *more quickly* than his partner.	(Comparative degree)
	He works *most quickly* under pressure.	(Superlative degree)

Do not create a double comparative form by using *more* and the suffix *er* together (such as *more neater*) or by using *most* and the suffix *est* together (such as *most fastest*).

A few adjectives and adverbs form the comparative and superlative degrees irregularly. Some common irregular adjectives are *good* (*better, best*); *bad* (*worse,*

SPOT THE BLOOPER

From an editorial in *U.S. News & World Report*: "Of two interpretations of conduct, they prefer the worst."

worst); and *little* (*less, least*). Some common irregular adverbs are *well* (*better, best*); *many* (*more, most*); and *much* (*more, most*).

MODIFIERS THAT DESERVE SPECIAL ATTENTION

Adjectives as Articles

The articles *a, an,* and *the* merit special attention. When describing a specific person or thing, use the article *the,* as in *the film.* When describing persons or things in general, use *a* or *an,* as in *a film* (meaning *any* film). The choice of *a* or *an* is determined by the initial sound of the word modified. *A* is used before consonant sounds; *an* is used before vowel sounds.

STUDY TIP

The sound, not the spelling, of a word governs the choice between *a* and *an*. When the letter *u* sounds like a *y,* it is treated as a consonant: a *u*tility, a *u*sed car.

BEFORE VOWEL SOUNDS		BEFORE CONSONANT SOUNDS	
an orange an apple		a pear a grape	
an hour an honor	*h* is not voiced; vowel is heard	a hook a hole	*h* is voiced
an offer an opinion	*o* sounds like a vowel	a one-man band a one-year contract	*o* sounds like the consonant *w*
an ulcer an urgent request	*u* sounds like a vowel	a union a uniform	*u* sounds like the consonant *y*
an X-ray an M.D.	*x* and *m* sound like vowels		

Adverbs and Double Negatives

DID YOU KNOW

At one time in the history of the English language (going back farther than Chaucer), multiple negatives were used to emphasize an idea. (*Don't never say nothing wicked!*) But in the 18th century, grammarians adopted Latin logic and decreed that two negatives created a positive.

When a negative adverb (*no, not, scarcely, hardly, barely*) is used in the same sentence with a negative verb (*didn't, don't, won't*), a substandard construction called a *double negative* results. Such constructions are considered to be illogical and illiterate. In the following examples, notice how eliminating one negative corrects the double negative.

INCORRECT: Hard work *can't do* no harm.
CORRECT: Hard work can do no harm.
CORRECT: Hard work can't do any harm.

INCORRECT: They *couldn't hardly* hear her.
CORRECT: They could hardly hear her.
CORRECT: They couldn't hear her.

INCORRECT: You *can't barely* reach the pedals.
CORRECT: You can barely reach the pedals.
CORRECT: You can't reach the pedals.

The Adjectives *this/that* and *these/those*

SPOT THE BLOOPER

From a Citibank brochure: "Your Citibank card will only access your checking account for these type purchases."

The adjective *this,* and its plural form *these,* indicates something nearby. The adjective *that,* and its plural form *those,* indicates something at a distance. Be careful to use the singular forms of these words with singular nouns and the plural forms with plural nouns: *this shoe, that road, these accounts, those records.* Pay special attention to the nouns *kind, type,* and *sort.* Match singular adjectives to the singular forms of these nouns (for example, *this kind* of question, *that sort* of person; but *these kinds* of questions, *those sorts* of people).

Now complete the reinforcement exercises for Level I.

LEVEL II

SPOT THE BLOOPER

Headline in the *Daily News Tribune* [Tempe, AZ]: "People with 'week' wills can lose weight easy."

PROBLEMS WITH ADJECTIVES AND ADVERBS

Confusion of Adjectives and Adverbs

Because they are closely related, adjectives are sometimes confused with adverbs. Here are guidelines that will help you avoid common adjective-adverb errors.

- Use adjectives to modify nouns and pronouns. Note particularly that adjectives (not adverbs) should follow linking verbs.

This pasta tastes *delicious.* (Not *deliciously.*)

She feels *bad* about your illness. (Not *badly.*)

Does the music sound *loud* to you? (Not *loudly.*)

STUDY TIP

The misuse of *badly* for *bad* is one of the most frequent errors made by educated persons. Following the linking verb *feel,* use the adjective *bad,* not the adverb *badly.*

- Use adverbs to describe verbs, adjectives, or other adverbs.

Time passes *quickly.* (Not *quick.*)

It passes *more quickly* when I am busy. (Not *quicker.*)

Pack those glasses *carefully.* (Not *careful.*)

Our meeting ran *smoothly.* (Not *smooth.*)

It should be noted that a few adverbs have two acceptable forms: *slow, slowly; deep, deeply; direct, directly;* and *close, closely.*

Breathe *deeply.* (Or, less formally, *deep.*)

You may dial us *directly.* (Or, less formally, *direct.*)

Compound Adjectives

Writers may form their own adjectives by joining two or more words. When these words act as a single modifier preceding a noun, they are temporarily hyphenated. If these same words appear after a noun, they are generally not hyphenated.

Words Temporarily Hyphenated Before a Noun	Same Words Not Hyphenated After a Noun
two-story house	house of two stories
government-subsidized loan	loan that is government subsidized
case-by-case evaluation	evaluation that is case by case
high-pressure job	job that is high pressure
duty-free imports	imports that are duty free
six-year-old child	child who is six years old
stress-related illness	illness that is stress related
home-based business	business that is based at home

SPOT THE BLOOPER

Headline in *The Milwaukee Sentinel*: "Police killing suspect to be tried as an adult." [What unintended meaning resulted from the omission of a hyphen?]

Compound adjectives shown in your dictionary with hyphens are considered permanently hyphenated. Regardless of whether the compound appears before or after a noun, it retains the hyphens. Use a current dictionary to determine what expressions are always hyphenated. Be sure that you find the dictionary entry that is marked *adjective.* Here are samples:

Permanent Hyphens Before Nouns	Permanent Hyphens After Nouns
first-class seats	seats that are first-class
up-to-date information	information that is up-to-date

SPOT THE BLOOPER

Under a photograph in *Science* magazine: "Museum staffer Ed Rodley checks out 65 million year-old eggs." [How does the missing hyphen alter the meaning?]

PERMANENT HYPHENS BEFORE NOUNS	PERMANENT HYPHENS AFTER NOUNS
old-fashioned values	values that are old-fashioned
short-term goals	goals that are short-term
well-known expert	expert who is well-known
out-of-pocket expenses	expenses that are out-of-pocket

Don't confuse adverbs ending in *ly* with compound adjectives: *newly appointed judge* and *highly regarded author* would not be hyphenated.

As compound adjectives become more familiar, they are often simplified and the hyphen is dropped. Some familiar compounds that are not hyphenated are *high school teacher, charge account balance, income tax refund, home office equipment* and *data processing center.*

STUDY TIP

To determine whether successive adjectives are independent, mentally insert the word *and* between them. If the insertion makes sense, the adjectives are probably independent and require a comma.

Independent Adjectives

Two or more successive adjectives that independently modify a noun are separated by commas. No comma is needed, however, when the first adjective modifies the combined idea of the second adjective and the noun.

TWO ADJECTIVES INDEPENDENTLY MODIFYING A NOUN	FIRST ADJECTIVE MODIFYING A SECOND ADJECTIVE PLUS A NOUN
productive, reliable employee	assistant deputy director
moving, riveting performance	wicker picnic basket
interesting, educational film	leather cowboy boots

Special Cases

The following adjectives and adverbs cause difficulty for many writers and speakers. With a little study, you can master their correct usage.

farther (adv. — actual distance): Your house is *farther* away than mine.
further (adv. — additionally): Let's discuss this issue *further.*

sure (adj. — certain): She is *sure* of her answers.
surely (adv. — undoubtedly): *Surely* you know how I feel.

later (adv. — after expected time): He postponed the meeting until *later.*
latter (adj. — the second of two things): Of the two options, I prefer the *latter.*

fewer (adj. — refers to numbers): *Fewer* than 50 people applied for the positions.
less (adj. — refers to amounts or quantities): The tour took *less* time than we thought.

real (adj. — actual, genuine): One of the *real* benefits of walking is stress reduction.
really (adv. — actually, truly): Can you *really* run a four-minute mile?

good (adj. — desirable): Kelly had a *good* idea for the graduation party.
well { (adv. — satisfactorily): Jeff did *well* on the exam.
(adj. — healthy): I feel *well* enough to go back to work. }

Now complete the reinforcement exercises for Level II.

LEVEL III

OTHER USES OF ADJECTIVES AND ADVERBS

Absolute Modifiers

Adjectives and adverbs that name perfect or complete (absolute) qualities cannot logically be compared. For example, to say that one ball is more *round* than another ball is illogical. Here are some absolute words that should not be used in comparisons.

SPOT THE BLOOPER

Advertisement in a national magazine: "Quaker Oats is one of nature's most perfect foods."

round	dead	complete
perfect	true	right
unique	correct	straight
perpendicular	endless	unanimous

Authorities suggest, however, that some absolute adjectives may be compared by the use of the words *more nearly* or *most nearly.*

Tia's project is *more nearly complete* than mine. (Not *more complete.*)

Which of the children's drawings shows the *most nearly round* ball? (Not *roundest.*)

SPOT THE BLOOPER

From a radio commercial for The Club, a device to prevent auto theft: "The Club works where other cheap imitations fail." [Does this statement say that The Club is a cheap imitation?]

Comparisons Within a Group

When the word *than* is used to compare a person, place, or thing with other members of a group to which it belongs, be certain to include the words *other* or *else* in the comparison. This inclusion ensures that the person or thing being compared is separated from the group with which it is compared.

ILLOGICAL: Alaska is larger than any state in the U.S. (This sentence suggests that Alaska is larger than itself.)
LOGICAL: Alaska is larger than any other state in the U.S.

ILLOGICAL: The Blackhawks scored more goals than any team in the NHL.
LOGICAL: The Blackhawks scored more goals than any other team in the NHL.

ILLOGICAL: Tori has more experience than anyone in the company.
LOGICAL: Tori has more experience than anyone else in the company.

NOTABLE QUOTABLE

"A determined person is one who, when he or she gets to the end of the rope, ties a knot and hangs on."
— Joe L. Griffith

Placing Adverbs and Adjectives

The position of an adverb or adjective can seriously affect the meaning of a sentence. Study these examples.

Only James can change the password. (No one else can change it.)

James can *only* change the password. (He can't do anything else to it.)

James can change *only* the password. (He can't change anything else.)

To avoid confusion, adverbs and adjectives should be placed close to the words they modify. In this regard, special attention should be given to the words *only, merely, first,* and *last.*

CONFUSING: He *merely* said that the report could be improved.
CLEAR: He said *merely* that the report could be improved.

CONFUSING: Seats in the five *first* rows have been reserved.
CLEAR: Seats in the *first* five rows have been reserved.

Now complete the reinforcement exercises for Level III.

HOT LINE QUERIES

QUESTION One of my favorite words is *hopefully,* but I understand that it's often used improperly. How should it be used?

ANSWER Language purists insist that the word *hopefully* be used to modify a verb (*We looked at the door hopefully, expecting Mr. Gross to return momentarily*). The word *hopefully* should not be used as a substitute for *I hope that* or *We hope that.* Instead of saying *Hopefully, interest rates will decline,* one should say *I hope that interest rates will decline.*

QUESTION Is it necessary to hyphenate a *25 percent* discount?

ANSWER No. Percents are not treated in the same way that numbers appearing in compound adjectives are treated. Thus, you would not hyphenate a *15 percent* loan, but you would hyphenate a *15-year* loan.

QUESTION Should hyphens be used in a *point-by-point analysis?*

ANSWER Yes. When words are combined in order to create a single adjective preceding a noun, these words are temporarily hyphenated (*last-minute decision, two-semester course, step-by-step procedures*).

QUESTION In my writing I want to use *firstly* and *secondly.* Are they acceptable?

ANSWER Both words are acceptable, but most good writers prefer *first* and *second,* because they are more efficient and equally accurate.

QUESTION How many hyphens should I use in this sentence? *The three, four, and five year plans continue to be funded.*

ANSWER Three hyphens are needed: *three-, four-, and five-year plans.* Hyphenate compound adjectives even when the parts of the compound are separated or suspended.

QUESTION Why can't I remember how to spell *already?* I want to use it in this sentence: *Your account has <u>already</u> been credited with your payment.*

ANSWER You—and many others—have difficulty with *already* because two different words (and meanings) are expressed by essentially the same sounds. The adverb *already* means "previously" or "before this time," as in your sentence. The two-word combination *all ready* means "all prepared," as in *The club members are all ready to board the bus.* If you can logically insert the word *completely* between *all* and *ready,* you know the two-word combination is needed.

QUESTION I never know how to write *part time.* Is it always hyphenated?

ANSWER The dictionary shows all of its uses to be hyphenated. *She was a part-time employee* (used as adjective). *He worked part-time* (used as adverb).

QUESTION Here are some expressions that caused us trouble in our business letters. We want to hyphenate all of the following. Right? *Well-produced play, awareness-generation film, decision-making tables, one-paragraph note, swearing-in ceremony, commonly-used book.*

ANSWER All your hyphenated forms are correct except the last one. Don't use a hyphen with an *ly*-ending adverb.

QUESTION Why are these two expressions treated differently: *two-week* vacation and *two weeks'* vacation?

ANSWER Although they express the same idea, they represent two different styles. If you omit the *s, two-week* is hyphenated because it is a compound adjective. If you add the *s,* as in *two weeks' vacation,* the expression becomes possessive and requires an apostrophe. Don't use both styles together (not *two-weeks' vacation*).

13 Prepositions

OBJECTIVES When you have completed the materials in this chapter, you will be able to do the following:

Level I
- Use objective case pronouns as objects of prepositions.
- Avoid using prepositions in place of verbs and adverbs.

Level II
- Use correctly eight troublesome prepositions.
- Omit unnecessary prepositions and retain necessary ones.
- Construct formal sentences that avoid terminal prepositions.

Level III
- Recognize those words and constructions requiring specific prepositions (idioms).

PRETEST

Underline the correct word.

1. Salary is important, but benefits must be considered (to, too).
2. (As, Like) I said, papers must be in before the last day of exams.
3. Are you planning (on taking, to take) a vacation this summer?
4. They were standing (on, in) line for nearly an hour.
5. Who was sitting (besides, beside) you at the theater?

Prepositions are connecting words. They show the relationship of a noun or pronoun to another word in a sentence. This chapter reviews the use of objective case pronouns following prepositions. It also focuses on common problems that communicators have with troublesome prepositions. Finally, it presents many words in our language that require specific prepositions (idiomatic expressions) to sound "right."

LEVEL I

COMMON USES OF PREPOSITIONS

In the following list, notice that prepositions may consist of one word or several.

about	along with	at	beside
according to	among	before	between
after	around	below	but

1. too 2. As 3. to take 4. in 5. beside

by	in	of	to
during	in addition to	off	under
except	in spite of	on	until
for	into	on account of	upon
from	like	over	with

SPOT THE BLOOPER

Photo caption in *The Tribune* [Greeley, CO]: "West's David Shaw hits the winning shot for he and Tom White."

Objective Case Following Prepositions

As you will recall from Chapter 6, pronouns that are objects of prepositions must be in the objective case.

Sean, *along with* Janet and *them,* provided the entertainment.

Recommendations *from* his boss and *her* helped him get the job.

Take that report to Ms. Ng and *him.*

To review further, recall that some prepositions — such as *like, between, but,* and *except* — are particularly likely to lead to confusion in determining pronoun case. Consider the following examples.

SPOT THE BLOOPER

From *The New York Times:* ". . . reflecting on the hardships that pupils like she and Lakesha Perry face in Brownsville, Brooklyn . . ."

Just *between you and me,* the company plans to go public.

Teachers *like Adam and him* provide good role models.

We received offers of help from everyone *but him.*

Fundamental Problems With Prepositions

In even the most casual speech or writing, the following misuses of prepositions should be avoided.

■ **Of *for* have.** The verb phrases *should have* and *could have* should never be written as *should of* or *could of.* The word *of* is a preposition and cannot be used in verb phrases.

You *should have* seen the look on Mara's face.

He *could have* played in the major leagues if he hadn't been injured.

NOTABLE QUOTABLE

"You are the same today that you are going to be five years from now except for two things: the people with whom you associate and the books you read."
— Charles Jones

■ **Off *for* from.** The preposition *from* should never be replaced by *off* or *off of.*

Marsha borrowed the car *from* him. (Not *off of.*)

Did Marty get the money *from* you? (Not *off* or *off of.*)

■ **To *for* too.** The preposition *to* means "in a direction toward." Do not use the word *to* in place of the adverb *too,* which means "additionally," "also," or "excessively."

Give that check *to* the treasurer.

I am *too* tired *to* study any more tonight.

Rich has a green Camaro *too.*

You will recall that the word *to* may also be part of an infinitive construction.

She is hoping *to* obtain a student loan for next semester.

Now complete the reinforcement exercises for Level I.

LEVEL II

TROUBLESOME PREPOSITIONS

Be particularly careful to use the following prepositions properly.

■ **Among, between.** *Among* is usually used to speak of three or more persons or things; *between* is usually used for two.

> This argument is *between* you and me.
>
> Prize money was divided *among* all the winners.

■ **Beside, besides.** *Beside* means "next to"; *besides* means "in addition to."

> The man sitting *beside* me on the plane was a playwright.
>
> No one *besides* Bill has volunteered.

■ **Except.** The preposition *except,* meaning "excluding" or "but," is sometimes confused with the verb *accept,* which means "to receive."

> All of the players *except* Nick were able to practice.
>
> Did you *accept* the job offer from IBM?

■ **In, into.** *In* indicates a position or location. *Into* indicates direction or movement to an interior location.

> The meeting will be held *in* the conference room.
>
> Come *into* my office to see my new monitor.

Some constructions may employ *in* as an adverb preceding an infinitive:

> They went *in* to see the manager. (Adverb *in* precedes infinitive *to see.*)

■ **Like.** The preposition *like* should be used to introduce a noun or pronoun. Do not use *like* to introduce a clause (a group of words with a subject and a predicate). To introduce clauses, use *as, as if,* or *as though.*

STUDY TIP

Look at the word(s) following *like.* If many words follow, chances are they function as a clause; use *as, as if,* or *as though* instead of *like.*

> She sounds *like* Selena. (*Like* used as a preposition to introduce the object, *Selena.*
>
> She sounds *as if* she has had voice lessons. (*As if* used to introduce the clause *she has had voice lessons.*)
>
> *As* I said in my letter, I have experience in this field. (Do not use *like* to introduce the clause *I said in my letter.*)

NECESSARY PREPOSITIONS

NOTABLE QUOTABLE

"Anyone who says the days of opportunity are over is copping out."
— Ann Landers

Don't omit those prepositions necessary to clarify a relationship. Be particularly careful when two prepositions modify a single object.

> What type *of* degree are you working toward? (Do not omit *of.*)
>
> She was sure *of* which college she planned to attend. (Do not omit *of.*)
>
> Benefits are better for exempt employees than *for* nonexempt employees. (Do not omit *for.*)
>
> When will you graduate *from* college? (Do not omit *from.*)*

*See the Hot Line Query on p. 182.

SPOT THE BLOOPER

From an Ann Landers column: ". . . [They] might get their eyes opened up." [Is "up" a needed preposition?]

UNNECESSARY PREPOSITIONS

Omit unnecessary prepositions, particularly the word *of.*

Leave the package *inside* the door. (Not *inside of.*)

Both the books are checked out. (Not *both of.*)

All participants must sign a waiver. (Not *All of the.*)

Where is the party? (Not *party at.*)

Cheryl could not *help* crying. (Not *help from crying.*)

Impulse items are always *near* the cash register. (Not *near to.*)

ENDING A SENTENCE WITH A PREPOSITION

In the past, language authorities warned against ending a sentence (or a clause) with a preposition. In formal writing today most careful authors continue to avoid terminal prepositions. In conversation, however, terminal prepositions are acceptable.

INFORMAL: Which club is she president of?
FORMAL: Of which club is she president?

INFORMAL: What is your term paper about?
FORMAL: About what is your term paper?

INFORMAL: Whom did you talk to?
FORMAL: To whom did you talk?

Now complete the reinforcement exercises for Level II.

LEVEL III

IDIOMATIC USE OF PREPOSITIONS

Every language has idioms (word combinations that are peculiar to that language). These combinations have developed through usage and often cannot be explained rationally. A native speaker usually is unaware of idiom usage until a violation jars his or her ear, such as "He is capable *from* (rather than *of*) violence."

The list below shows words that require specific prepositions to denote precise meanings. This group is just a sampling of the large number of English idioms. Consult a dictionary when you are unsure of the correct preposition to use with a particular word.

acquaint with	Are you *acquainted with* our new manager?
addicted to	Brittany is *addicted to* shopping.
adept in	Lars is *adept in* interior design.
adhere to	You must *adhere to* our personnel policies.
agree to (a proposal)	Can you *agree to* the terms of this contract?
agree with (a person)	I *agree with* you on this issue.
angry at (a thing)	Many employees were *angry at* the change in vacation policy.
angry with (a person)	Are you *angry with* me for being late?
buy from	Did you *buy from* a dealer or from the owner?
capable of	We had no idea he was *capable of* such leadership.

comply with	To receive the prize, you must *comply with* our rules.
concur in (an action)	The directors were able to *concur in* a new business plan.
concur with (a person)	Do you *concur with* the vice president in his analysis?
conform to	Your products do not *conform to* our specifications.
contrast with	The angles *contrast with* the curves in that logo design.
correspond to (match)	A bird's wing *corresponds to* a person's arm.
correspond with (write)	We *correspond with* each other regularly.
desire for	The *desire for* success drives many people.
desirous of	She is *desirous of* a simple lifestyle.
differ from (things)	How does your calling plan *differ from* Sprint's?
differ with (person)	I beg to *differ with* you on that subject.
different from (*not* than)	Our vacation was quite *different from* last year's.
disagree with	Ron *disagrees with* me on just about everything.
expert in	My brother Gary is an *expert in* the stock market.
guard against	We must *guard against* complacency.
identical with *or* to	Our floor plan is *identical with* (or *to*) yours.
independent of	Living alone, the young man was *independent of his parents.*
infer from	I *infer from* your comments that you are unhappy.
interest in	Tiffany has expressed an *interest in* fashion design.
negligent of	Pat was *negligent of* her new puppy's needs.
oblivious of *or* to	He is often *oblivious of* (or *to*) what goes on around him.
plan to (*not* on)	Kathy *plans to* pursue a master's degree.
prefer to	Would you *prefer to* choose your own doctor?
reconcile with (match)	Our expenditures must be *reconciled with* our budget.
reconcile to (accept)	Martin has never become *reconciled to* our decision to move.
responsible for	People are *responsible for* their own actions.
retroactive to	The salary increase is *retroactive to* the first of this year.
sensitive to	Our employer is especially *sensitive to* the needs of employees.
similar to	Your briefcase is *similar to* mine.
standing in (*not* on) line	How long have you been *standing in* line?
talk to (tell something)	Gene will *talk to* us about the reorganization plans.
talk with (exchange remarks)	Let's *talk with* Teresa about our mutual goals.

"Success isn't how far you got, but the distance you traveled from where you started."
— Peter Frame

SPOT THE BLOOPER

From the *Patriot-Ledger* [Quincy, MA]: "Clemens is able to come off the disabled list Sunday, but tests by Dr. Arthur Pappas led to the conclusion that Clemens' groin is still too weak to pitch in a game."

Now complete the reinforcement exercises for Level III.

HOT LINE QUERIES

QUESTION Another employee and I are collaborating on a report. I wanted to write this: *Money was lost due to poor attendance.* She says the sentence should read: *Money was lost because of poor attendance.* My version is more concise. Which of us is right?

ANSWER Most language authorities agree with your coauthor. *Due to* is acceptable when it functions as an adjective, as in *Success was due to proper timing.* In this sense, *due to* is synonymous with *attributable to.* However, when *due to* functions as a preposition, as in your sentence, language experts find fault. Your friend is right; substitute *because of.*

QUESTION What's wrong with saying *Lisa graduated college last year?*

ANSWER The preposition *from* must be inserted for syntactical fluency. Two constructions are permissible: *Lisa graduated from college* or *Lisa was graduated from college.* The first version is more popular; the second is preferred by traditional grammarians.

QUESTION Should *sometime* be one or two words in the following sentence? *Can you come over (some time) soon?*

ANSWER In this sentence you should use the one-word form. *Sometime* means "an indefinite time" (*the convention is sometime in December*). The two-word combination means "a period of time" (*we have some time to spare*).

QUESTION I saw this printed recently: *Some of the personal functions that are being reviewed are job descriptions, job specifications, and job evaluation.* Is *personal* used correctly here?

ANSWER Indeed not! The word *personal* means "private" or "individual" (*your personal letters are being forwarded to you*). The word *personnel* refers to employees (*all company personnel are cordially invited*). The sentence you quote requires *personnel.*

QUESTION Is there any difference between *proved* and *proven?*

ANSWER As a past participle, the verb form *proved* is preferred (*he has proved his point*). However, the word *proven* is preferred as an adjective form (*that company has a proven record*). *Proven* is also commonly used in the expression *not proven.*

QUESTION In my dictionary I found three ways to spell the same word: *life-style, lifestyle,* and *life style.* Which should I use?

ANSWER The first spelling shown is usually the preferred one. In your dictionary a second acceptable form may be introduced by the word *also.* If two spellings appear side by side (*ax, axe*), they are equally acceptable.

QUESTION How should I write *industry wide?* It's not in my dictionary.

ANSWER A word with the suffix *wide* is usually written solid: *industrywide, nationwide, countrywide, statewide, worldwide.*

14 Conjunctions to Join Equals

OBJECTIVES When you have completed the materials in this chapter, you will be able to do the following:

Level I

- Distinguish between simple and compound sentences.
- Punctuate compound sentences joined by *and, or, not,* and *but.*

Level II

- Punctuate compound sentences using conjunctive adverbs such as *therefore, however,* and *consequently.*

Level III

- Recognize correlative conjunctions such as *either . . . or, not only . . . but also,* and *neither . . . nor.*
- Use a parallel construction in composing sentences with correlative conjunctions.

PRETEST

Insert commas and semicolons to punctuate the following sentences correctly.

1. Prices are scheduled to increase on those items therefore we should place our order now.
2. I hope however that you will be able to join us.
3. Marcy is looking for a job in sales but Alice wants to remain in advertising.
4. Lassie is well-trained nevertheless she sometimes chews the furniture.

Underline the letter of the sentence that is more effective.

5. (a) Not only is this course more interesting but it is also more practical than that one.
   (b) This course is not only more interesting but also more practical than that one.

Conjunctions are connecting words. They may be separated into two major groups: those that join grammatically equal words or word groups and those that join grammatically unequal words or word groups. This chapter focuses on those conjunctions that join equals. Recognizing conjunctions and understanding their patterns of usage will, among other things, enable you to use commas and semicolons more appropriately.

1. items; therefore, 2. hope, however, 3. sales, but 4. well-trained; nevertheless, 5. b

LEVEL I

COORDINATING CONJUNCTIONS

Coordinating conjunctions connect words, phrases, and clauses of equal grammatical value or rank. The most common coordinating conjunctions are *and, or, but,* and *nor.* Notice in these sentences that coordinating conjunctions join grammatically equal elements.

"The quality, not the longevity, of one's life is what is important."
— Martin Luther King

The qualities I admire most are *honesty, integrity,* and *reliability.* (Here the word *and* joins equal words.)

Open your mind *to new challenges* and *to new ideas.* (Here *and* joins equal phrases.)

I donated a great deal of money to the cause, but *Mark donated over 40 hours of his time.* (Here *but* joins equal clauses.)

Phrases and Clauses

A group of related words without a subject and a verb is called a *phrase.* You are already familiar with verb phrases and prepositional phrases. It is not important that you be able to identify the other kinds of phrases (infinitive, gerund, participial), but it is very important that you be able to distinguish phrases from clauses.

STUDY TIP

Clauses have subjects and verbs. Phrases do not. Clauses may have phrases within them.

Our hopes were dashed by their announcement of the winning lottery numbers.
(phrase: were dashed; phrase: by their announcement; phrase: of the winning lottery numbers)

A group of related words including a subject and a verb is a *clause.*

We noticed your sign about free refreshments, and we stopped the car to investigate.
(clause: We noticed your sign about free refreshments; clause: we stopped the car to investigate)

Phillip wants some time off, but he can't afford to take it.
(clause: Phillip wants some time off; clause: he can't afford to take it)

The play starts at 8:30, and it should be over by midnight.
(phrase: at 8:30; phrase: by midnight; clause: The play starts at 8:30; clause: it should be over by midnight)

SPOT THE BLOOPER

Advertisement published in the *Los Angeles Times:* "Brother Word Processor with Grammer Check and Word Spell"

Simple and Compound Sentences

A *simple sentence* has one independent clause; that is, it contains a clause that can stand alone. A *compound sentence* has two or more independent clauses.

Lana is leaving town. (Simple sentence.)

Traveling abroad can be very exciting, but I prefer traveling in this country. (Compound sentence.)

Punctuating Compound Sentences

When coordinating conjunctions join clauses in compound sentences, a comma precedes the conjunction unless the clauses are very short (four or fewer words in each clause).

You can close the window, *or* you can put on a sweater.

Close the window or put on a sweater. (Clauses are too short to require a comma.)

Do not use commas when coordinating conjunctions join compound verbs, objects, or phrases.

> You can come with us, *or* you can go with Kevin and Patsy. (Comma used because *or* joins two independent clauses.)
>
> You can come with us *or* go with Kevin and Patsy. (No comma needed because *or* joins the compound verbs of a single independent clause.)
>
> Thomas Edison said that colleges should not have to choose between lighting their buildings *and* enlightening their students. (No comma needed because *and* joins the compound objects of a prepositional phrase.)
>
> Volunteers are asked to be on time *and* to bring their own equipment. (No comma needed because *and* joins two infinitive phrases.)
>
> Eat nutritious foods each day, *and* get exercise at least three times a week. (Comma needed to join two independent clauses; the subject of each clause is understood to be *you.*)

SPOT THE BLOOPER

Headline in *The Orlando* [FL] *Sentinel:* "Women Are Likely to Eat More Than Men Under Stress"

Now complete the reinforcement exercises for Level I.

LEVEL II

CONJUNCTIVE ADVERBS

Conjunctive adverbs may also be used to connect equal sentence elements. Because conjunctive adverbs are used to effect a transition from one thought to another, and because they may consist of more than one word, they have also been called *transitional expressions.* The most common conjunctive adverbs follow.

accordingly	in fact	on the other hand
consequently	in the meantime	that is
furthermore	moreover	then
hence	nevertheless	therefore
however	on the contrary	thus

Some authorities call the conjunctive adverb a "conjunctive joiner." Such a term may help you remember its function.

In the following compound sentences, observe that conjunctive adverbs join clauses of equal grammatical value. Note that semicolons (*not* commas) are used before conjunctive adverbs that join independent clauses. Commas should immediately follow conjunctive adverbs of two or more syllables. Note also that the word following a semicolon is not capitalized — unless, of course, it is a proper noun.

> Sarah did her best; *nevertheless,* she failed to pass the bar exam.
>
> We were unprepared for the storm; *consequently,* we got soaking wet.
>
> A new car is expensive; *on the other hand,* maintenance for an old car can cost more.
>
> They are dedicated to preserving the environment; *thus* they work to educate others.
>
> Demand for this new model is high; *hence* prices may increase sharply.

SPOT THE BLOOPER

From the classified ads in a local newspaper: "Housecleaner with commercial rats."

Generally, no comma is used after one-syllable conjunctive adverbs such as *hence, thus,* and *then* (unless a strong pause is desired).

Use a semicolon only when you are joining two sentences.

DISTINGUISHING CONJUNCTIVE ADVERBS FROM PARENTHETICAL ADVERBS

Many words that function as conjunctive adverbs may also serve as *parenthetical* (interrupting) *adverbs* that are employed to effect transition from one thought to another. Use semicolons *only* with conjunctive adverbs that join independent clauses. Use commas to set off parenthetical adverbs that interrupt the flow of a sentence.

> The credit for our success, *however,* belongs to Rachel.
>
> Rachel deserves credit for our success; *however,* she will not accept it.
>
> The United Nations, *moreover,* works to protect the rights of children throughout the world.
>
> The United Nations works to protect the rights of children; *moreover,* it promotes communication among nations.
>
> I am afraid, *on the other hand,* that we may lose money on our investment.
>
> I am afraid that we may lose money on our investment; *on the other hand,* first-quarter sales were encouraging.

SPOT THE BLOOPER

From the *Sun-Sentinel* [Ft. Lauderdale, FL]: "Weider was a participant on Sunday in a three-hour debate on the question of whether the emperor was poisoned at the 10th annual meeting of the Napoleonic Society of America."

Now complete the reinforcement exercises for Level II.

LEVEL III

OTHER CONJUNCTIONS

We have studied thus far two kinds of conjunctions used to join grammatically equal sentence elements: coordinating conjunctions (used to join equal words, phrases, and clauses) and conjunctive adverbs (used to join grammatically equal clauses in compound sentences). *Correlative conjunctions* form the third and final group of conjunctions that join grammatically equal sentence elements.

Correlative Conjunctions

Correlative conjunctions are always paired: *both . . . and, not only . . . but (also), either . . . or,* and *neither . . . nor.* When greater emphasis is desired, these paired conjunctions are used instead of coordinating conjunctions.

> Your best chances for advancement are in the marketing department *or* in the sales department.
>
> Your best chances for advancement are *either* in the marketing department *or* in the sales department. (More emphatic.)

In using correlative conjunctions, place them so that the words, phrases, or clauses being joined are parallel in construction.

PARALLEL: Molly was flying *either* to Seattle *or* to Portland.
NOT PARALLEL: *Either* Molly was flying to Seattle *or* to Portland.

PARALLEL: She was *not only* talented *but also* bright.
NOT PARALLEL: She was *not only* talented, *but* she was *also* bright.

PARALLEL: I have *neither* the time *nor* the energy for this.
NOT PARALLEL: I *neither* have the time *nor* the energy for this.

Additional Coordinating Conjunctions

At Level I you studied the four most commonly used coordinating conjunctions: *and, or, nor,* and *but.* Three other coordinating conjunctions should also be mentioned: *yet, for,* and *so.*

The words *yet* and *for* may function as coordinating conjunctions, although they are infrequently used as such.

> We have little hope of winning, *yet* we have enjoyed the race.
>
> The young man was proud of his diploma, *for* he had overcome many obstacles to obtain it.

NOTABLE QUOTABLE

"Great minds have purposes; others have wishes."
— Washington Irving

The word *so* is sometimes informally used as a coordinating conjunction. In more formal contexts the conjunctive adverbs *therefore* and *consequently* should be substituted for the conjunction *so.*

> INFORMAL: We live near the lake, *so* we often fish on weekends.
>
> FORMAL: We live near the lake; *therefore,* we often fish on weekends.

Now complete the reinforcement exercises for Level III.

HOT LINE QUERIES

QUESTION Please help me decide which *maybe* to use in this sentence: *He said that he (maybe, may be) able to help us.*

ANSWER Use the two-word *may be,* which is the verb form. *Maybe* is an adverb that means "perhaps" (*maybe she will call*).

QUESTION At the end of a printed line, is it acceptable to type part of an individual's name on one line and carry the rest to the next line?

ANSWER Full names may be divided between the first and last names or after the middle initial. For example, you could type *John R.* on one line and *Williamson* on the next line. Do not, however, separate a short title and a surname (such as *Mr./Williamson*), and do not divide a name (such as *William/son*). By the way, many computer programs make unacceptable line-ending decisions. Be sure to inspect your copy, either on the screen or on the printout, so that you can correct poor hyphenation and unacceptable word separations.

QUESTION What should the verb in this sentence be? *There (has, have) to be good reasons. . . .*

ANSWER Use the plural verb *have,* which agrees with the subject *reasons.* In sentences that begin with the word *there,* look for the subject after the verb.

QUESTION Does *Ms.* have a period after it? Should I use this title for all women in business today?

ANSWER *Ms.* is probably a blend of *Miss* and *Mrs.* It is written with a period following it. Some women in business prefer to use *Ms.,* presumably because it is a title equal to *Mr.* Neither title reveals one's marital status. Many other women, however, prefer to use *Miss* or *Mrs.* as a title. It's always wise, if possible, to determine the preference of the individual.

QUESTION I just typed this sentence: *He was given a new title in lieu of a salary increase.* I went to my dictionary to check the spelling of *in lieu of,* but I can't find it. How is it spelled and what does it mean?

ANSWER The listing in the dictionary is under *lieu,* and it means "instead of." Many authorities today are recommending that such phrases be avoided. It's easier and clearer to say "instead of."

QUESTION Can you help me with the words *averse* and *adverse?* I've never been able to straighten them out in my mind.

ANSWER *Averse* is an adjective meaning "disinclined" and generally is used with the preposition *to* (*the little boy was averse to bathing; she is averse to statistical typing*). *Adverse* is also an adjective, but it means "hostile" or "unfavorable" (*adverse economic conditions halted the company's growth; the picnic was postponed because of adverse weather conditions*). In distinguishing between these two very similar words, it might help you to know that the word *averse* is usually used to describe animate (living) objects.

QUESTION What should I write: *You are our No. 1 account,* or *You are our number one account?* Should anything be hyphenated?

ANSWER Either is correct, but I prefer *No. 1* because it is more easily recognizable. No hyphen is required.

15 Conjunctions to Join Unequals

OBJECTIVES When you have completed the materials in this chapter, you will be able to do the following:

Level I
- Distinguish among phrases, dependent clauses, and independent clauses.
- Expand dependent clauses into complete sentences.

Level II
- Punctuate correctly introductory and terminal dependent clauses.
- Punctuate parenthetical, essential, and nonessential dependent clauses.

Level III
- Recognize simple, compound, complex, and compound-complex sentences.
- Convert simple sentences into a variety of more complex patterns.

PRETEST

Insert appropriate commas in the following sentences. Mark *C* if correct.

1. When we arrive at the hotel we will call your room.
2. If possible leave a key for us at the front desk.
3. The woman who left her purse will surely be back.
4. I believe that Ingrid who is good with computers will help you.
5. Although we waited for several hours Michael never arrived.

In Chapter 14 you learned about conjunctions that joined equal sentence elements such as words, phrases, and clauses. These equal sentence parts were joined by coordinate conjunctions (*and, or, nor, but*), conjunctive adverbs (such as *therefore, however, consequently*), and correlative conjunctions (*either . . . or*). Now let's look at a special group of conjunctions that join unequal sentence parts.

LEVEL I

SUBORDINATING CONJUNCTIONS

To join unequal sentence elements, such as independent and dependent clauses, use *subordinating conjunctions.* A list of the most common subordinating conjunctions follows.

1. hotel, 2. possible, 3. C 4. Ingrid, computers, 5. hours,

after	because	since	when
although	before	so that	where
as	if	that	whether
as if	in order that	unless	while
as though	provided	until	

SPOT THE BLOOPER

From *The San Francisco Chronicle*: "He [Burt Reynolds] describes himself growing up tough and brash as the part-Indian son of a Florida police chief and a football hero who thought he was destined for stardom until a knee injury sidelined him."

You should become familiar with this list of conjunctions, but do not feel that you must at all times be able to recall every subordinating conjunction. Generally, you can recognize a subordinating conjunction by the way it limits, or subordinates, the clause it introduces. In the clause *because he always paid with cash,* the subordinating conjunction *because* limits the meaning of the clause it introduces. The clause is incomplete and could not stand alone as a sentence.

INDEPENDENT AND DEPENDENT CLAUSES

Main clauses that can stand alone are said to be *independent.* They have subjects and verbs and make sense by themselves.

Kelli was an intern at the White House. (One main clause.)

Kelli scheduled appointments, and she worked with the First Lady's staff. (Two main clauses.)

She loved the internship, but her appointment lasted only five months. (Two main clauses.)

Dependent clauses should never be written or punctuated as if they were complete sentences.

Clauses that cannot stand alone are said to be *dependent.* They have subjects and verbs, but they depend on other clauses for the completion of their meaning. Dependent clauses are often introduced by subordinating conjunctions.

When this project is completed, we will take a vacation. (Dependent clause precedes the main clause.)

Since I am the president, my participation is expected. (Dependent clause precedes the main clause.)

Experience is required because this is a high-level position. (Dependent clause, *because this is a high-level position,* comes after the main clause.)

RELATIVE PRONOUNS

Although classified as pronouns, the words *who, whom, whose, which,* and *that* actually function as conjunctions when they introduce dependent clauses. *Who* and *whom* are used to refer to human antecedents. *Which* is used to refer to nonhuman antecedents, and *whose* and *that* may refer to either human or nonhuman antecedents.

Blaine is the person *who* can answer your questions.

This software, *which* helps with personal finances, is due out soon.

The course *that* you need is offered in the spring.

Now complete the reinforcement exercises for Level I.

LEVEL II

PUNCTUATION OF SENTENCES WITH DEPENDENT CLAUSES

NOTABLE QUOTABLE

"You can have brilliant ideas, but if you can't get them across, your ideas won't get you anywhere."
— Lee Iacocca

Business writers are especially concerned with clarity and accuracy. A misplaced or omitted punctuation mark can confuse a reader by altering the meaning of a sentence. The following guidelines for using commas help ensure clarity and consistency in writing. Some professional writers, however, take liberties with accepted conventions of punctuation, particularly in regard to comma usage. These experienced writers may omit a comma when they feel that such an omission will not affect the reader's understanding of a sentence. Beginning writers, though, are well advised to first develop skill in punctuating sentences by following traditional guidelines.

Introductory Dependent Clauses

Use a comma after a dependent (subordinate) clause that precedes an independent clause.

Before winter arrives, we must finish roofing the house.

Until I receive your records, I cannot complete your tax return.

When he gets here, we can start the meeting.

Use a comma after an introductory dependent clause even though the subject and verb may not be stated.

As [it is] expected, the opening was delayed.

If [it is] possible, send your application today.

When [it is] completed, it will be the tallest building in town.

Terminal Dependent Clauses

Generally, a dependent clause introduced by a subordinating conjunction does not require a comma when the dependent clause falls at the end of a sentence.

We must finish the research *before* we write the report.

They cannot leave *until* the manager returns.

Be prepared to distribute brochures and annual reports *when* the clients arrive.

SPOT THE BLOOPER

From classified ads in local newspapers: "LAWNMORE SHOP" and a house for sale with "walking closets"

If, however, the dependent clause at the end of a sentence interrupts the flow of the sentence and sounds as if it were an afterthought, a comma should be used.

I am sure I paid the bill, *although* I cannot find my receipt.

We will begin immediately, *if* the materials are available.

Parenthetical Clauses

Within a sentence, dependent clauses that interrupt the flow of a sentence and are unnecessary for the grammatical completeness of the sentence are set off by commas.

Our trip, *unless* we can raise more money, will be postponed.

At our next conference, *provided* our members show interest, we will address that topic.

Relative Clauses

Dependent clauses introduced by relative pronouns such as *who, that,* and *which* may be essential (restrictive) or nonessential (nonrestrictive).

An *essential clause* is needed to identify the noun to which it refers; therefore, no commas should separate this clause from its antecedent.

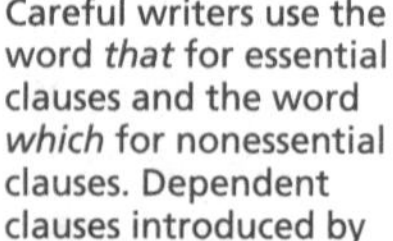

Careful writers use the word *that* for essential clauses and the word *which* for nonessential clauses. Dependent clauses introduced by *which* require commas.

All employees *who have been here more than five years* are eligible for the program.

Seat belts *that are faulty* will be replaced at no charge.

A *nonessential clause* supplies additional information that is not needed to identify its antecedent; therefore, commas are used to separate the nonessential information from the rest of the sentence. Notice that *two* commas are used to set off internal nonessential dependent clauses.

Melissa, *who has been here more than five years,* is eligible for the program.

New seat-belt legislation, *which was recently enacted by Congress,* goes into effect January 1.

Punctuation Review

Let's briefly review three common sentence patterns and their proper punctuation.

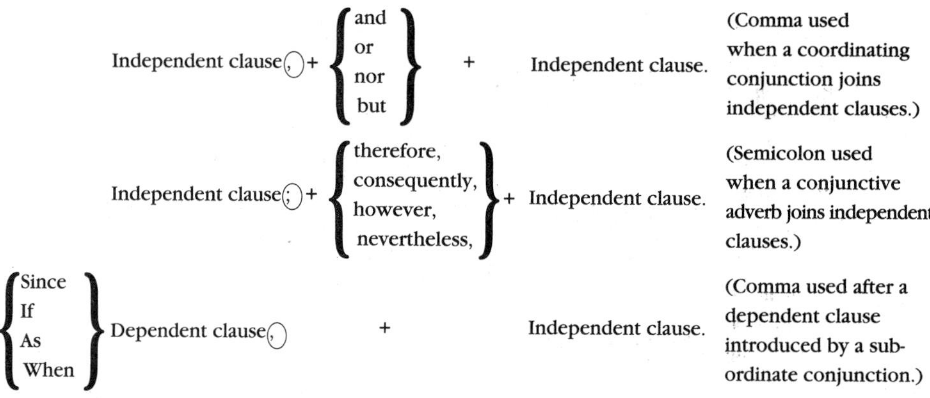

Independent clause , + { and / or / nor / but } + Independent clause.
(Comma used when a coordinating conjunction joins independent clauses.)
Independent clause ; + { therefore, / consequently, / however, / nevertheless, } + Independent clause.
(Semicolon used when a conjunctive adverb joins independent clauses.)
{ Since / If / As / When } Dependent clause , + Independent clause.
(Comma used after a dependent clause introduced by a subordinate conjunction.)

Now complete the reinforcement exercises for Level II.

An advertisement from *Patient Information & News* [Edmonds, WA]: "Dentistry at it's best."

SENTENCE VARIETY

To make messages more interesting, good writers strive for variety in sentence structure. Notice the monotony and choppiness of a paragraph made up entirely of simple sentences:

The *Titanic* was the world's largest passenger ship in 1912. It struck an iceberg in the North Atlantic on its maiden voyage. It began to sink. It was believed to be unsinkable. Some people refused to leave on the lifeboats. Over 700 survivors were picked up by rescue ships. Over 1,500 people went down with the ship.

Compare the following version of this paragraph, which uses dependent clauses and other structures to achieve greater sentence variety:

> On its maiden voyage in 1912, the *Titanic,* the world's largest passenger ship, struck an iceberg in the North Atlantic. When the ship began to sink, some passengers, believing the ship to be unsinkable, refused to leave on the lifeboats. Over 700 survivors were rescued, while 1,500 passengers went down with the ship.

Recognizing the kinds of sentence structures available to writers and speakers is an important step in achieving effective expression. Let's review the three kinds of sentence structures that you have been studying and include a fourth category as well.

SPOT THE BLOOPER

From a local newspaper: "Two cycles belonging to girls that had been left leaning against lamp posts were badly damaged."

KIND OF SENTENCE	MINIMUM REQUIREMENT	EXAMPLE
Simple	One independent clause	The *Titanic* was the world's largest passenger ship in 1912.
Compound	Two independent clauses	The *Titanic* was the world's largest passenger ship in 1912, and it struck an iceberg in the North Atlantic.
Complex	One independent clause and one dependent clause	The *Titanic,* which was the world's largest passenger ship in 1912, struck an iceberg in the North Atlantic.
Compound-complex	Two independent clauses and one dependent clause	The *Titanic,* which was the world's largest passenger ship in 1912, struck an iceberg in the North Atlantic; hence it sank.

Developing the ability to use a variety of sentence structures to facilitate effective communication takes practice and writing experience.

Now complete the reinforcement exercises for Level III.

HOT LINE QUERIES

QUESTION Can the word *that* be omitted from sentences? For example, *She said [that] she would come.*

ANSWER The relative pronoun *that* is frequently omitted in conversation and casual writing. For absolute clarity, however, skilled writers include it.

QUESTION Is there some rule about putting periods in organization names that are abbreviated? For example, does *IBM* have periods?

ANSWER When the names of well-known business, educational, governmental, labor, and other organizations or agencies are abbreviated, periods are normally not used to separate the letters. Thus, no periods would appear in IBM, ITT, UCLA, AFL-CIO, YWCA, AMA. The names of radio and television stations and networks are also written without periods: Station WJR, KNX-FM, PBS, WABC-TV. Geographical abbreviations, however, generally do require periods: U.S.A., U.S.S.R., S.A. The two-letter state abbreviations recommended by the U.S. Postal Service require no periods: NY, OH, CA, MI, NJ, OR, MA, and so on.

QUESTION As a command, which is correct: *lay down* or *lie down?*

ANSWER Commands are given in the present tense. You would never tell someone to *closed the door,* because commands are not given in the past tense. To say *lay down* (which is the past tense form of *lie*) is the same as saying *closed the door.* Therefore, use the present tense: *lie down.*

QUESTION In this sentence which word should I use? *Your order will be sent to you in the (later* or *latter) part of the week.*

ANSWER Use *latter.* The word *latter* designates the second of two persons or things. In addition, *latter* can be used to mean "further advanced in time or sequence," or *latter* can be used to contrast with *former.* In your sentence, the *latter* part of the week contrasts with the *former* part of the week.

QUESTION We're having a sale on *nonChristmas* items. Should a hyphen follow *non?* In my dictionary the prefix *non* is not hyphenated when it is joined to other words.

ANSWER A hyphen is not used when a prefix is joined to most words: *nonessential, prewar, unwelcome, anticlimax.* A hyphen is used, however, when a prefix is joined to a proper (capitalized) noun: *non-Christmas, pre-Columbian, un-Christian, anti-American.*

QUESTION I have a lot of trouble with verbs in sentences like this: *He is one of the 8 million Americans who (has* or *have) a drinking problem.*

ANSWER You're not alone. Make your verb agree with its antecedent (*Americans*). One easy way to work with sentences like this is to concentrate on the clause that contains the verb: *Of the 8 million Americans who have a drinking problem, he is one.*

NAME ______________________________

UNIT 4 REVIEW ■ Chapters 12–15 (Self-Check)

Begin your review by rereading Chapters 12–15. Then test your comprehension of those chapters by completing the exercises that follow. Compare your responses with those provided at the end of this review.

LEVEL I

In the blanks provided, write the letter of the word or phrase that correctly completes each of the following sentences.

1. Our fair has never had a (a) worse (b) worst turnout than this year. ____
2. We could not decide if Pizza Hut or Domino's pizza was (a) better, (b) best. ____
3. Enclosed is (a) a, (b) an example of a typical report. ____
4. With only three more credits, she (a) could of (b) could have graduated a semester early. ____
5. It's (a) to, (b) too hot to go running at noon. ____
6. Friends like Thomas and (a) he, (b) him are hard to find ____
7. Our company is seeking a recent graduate (a)whom, (b) which we can train. ____
8. The group of words *when you find it* is a(n) (a) phrase, (b) independent clause, (c) dependent clause. ____

Insert appropriate commas and semicolons in the following sentences. In the space provided, indicate the number of punctuation marks you added. Write *0* if you add none.

9. Rich accepted the position in May but took a leave of absence in July. ____
10. Billy may take a Caribbean cruise this year or he may vacation in Europe. ____
11. Drink plenty of liquids and get adequate rest. ____
12. Marsha drives a Porsche but Yvonne prefers the roominess of her BMW. ____
13. Charlie was our guide for the trip and we followed his directions carefully. ____

LEVEL II

Write the letter of the word or phrase that correctly completes each sentence.

14. Let's not discuss this matter any (a) further, (b) farther until the mediator arrives. ____
15. MGM's talent search was launched (a) coast-to-coast, (b) coast to coast. ____
16. These cookies have (a) less, (b) fewer fat than the leading brand. ____
17. Because he was personally involved, Robert read the report (a) cynical, (b) cynically. ____
18. We must divide the candy equally (a) among, (b) between the four children. ____
19. Can you help me move this desk (a) in, (b) into my office? ____

Insert appropriate commas and semicolons in the following sentences. In the space provided, indicate the number of marks you added.

20. Andy suffered a back injury consequently he was out for the season. _____

21. Before she agreed to serve on the committee Sheila asked for a list of responsibilities. _____

22. The student who spent last semester in France will be the guest speaker. _____

23. Direct your questions to Mr. Ceglia who is responsible for quality control. _____

24. As expected sales have declined this quarter. _____

25. We believe however that we are entitled to a refund. _____

26. Mai refused to pay the bill until her order had arrived. _____

LEVEL III

Write the letter of the word or phrase that correctly completes each sentence.

27. New York is larger than (a) any city, (b) any other city in the United States. _____

28. Check carefully the (a) ten first, (b) first ten pages in your book. _____

29. She worked only part-time, yet she remained independent (a) of, (b) from her parents. _____

30. Although our backgrounds are quite different, your values are not very different (a) than, (b) from mine. _____

31. Will our salary increases be retroactive (a) to, (b) from January 1? _____

Insert appropriate commas and semicolons in the following sentences. In the space provided, indicate the number of marks you added.

32. If you want to remove that red wine from your shirt try using mineral water on the stain. _____

33. When you offered your resignation last week I did not think you were serious. _____

34. I did not think you were serious when you offered your resignation last week. _____

35. Sales in your district have really increased moreover requests for service have decreased. _____

36. Although Brooke did not have the money for a private school she hoped to receive a scholarship. _____

37. It has been said that the meek will inherit the earth however the strong will retain the mineral rights. _____

38. Because the weather was wet the paint took a long time to dry. _____

39. Life can only be understood backwards but it must be lived forwards. _____

Check your answers below.

1. a 2. a 3. b 4. b 5. b 6. b 7. a 8. c 9. (0) 10. (1) year, 11. (0) 12. (1) Porsche, 13. (1) guide, 14. a 15. b 16. a 17. b 18. a 19. b 20. (2) injury; consequently, 21. (1) committee, 22. (0) 23. (1) Ceglia, 24. (1) expected, 25. (2) believe, however, 26. (0) 27. b 28. b 29. a 30. b 31. a 32. (1) shirt, 33. (1) week, 34. (0) 35. increased; moreover, 36. (1) school, 37. (2) earth; however, 38. (1) wet, 39. (1) backwards,

UNIT

5 Punctuating Sentences

16

Commas

OBJECTIVES When you have completed the materials in this chapter, you will be able to do the following:

Level I

- Correctly place commas in series, direct address, and parenthetical expressions.
- Use commas correctly in punctuating dates, addresses, geographical items, and appositives.

Level II

- Place commas correctly in punctuating independent adjectives, verbal phrases, and prepositional phrases.
- Use commas correctly in punctuating independent, introductory, terminal, and nonessential clauses.

Level III

- Use commas correctly in punctuating degrees, abbreviations, and numerals.
- Use commas to indicate omitted words, contrasting statements, clarity, and short quotations.

PRETEST

Insert appropriate commas in the following sentences.

1. Can you tell us Mr. Nguyen your version of the story?
2. Their office has branches in Anchorage Alaska and Portland Oregon.
3. Our natural history museum has by the way one of the best fossil collections in the country.
4. No more deliveries are due today but we are expecting more tomorrow.
5. Although long this year's speeches not last year's were preferred by the attendees.

DID YOU KNOW

Some writers in other languages envy English. Our systematic use of commas and other punctuation makes it easy to signal pauses, to emphasize ideas, and to enhance readability.

When you talk with a friend, you are probably unaware of the "invisible" commas, periods, and other punctuation marks that you are using. In conversation your pauses and voice inflections punctuate your thoughts and clarify your meaning. In writing, however, you must use a conventional set of symbols—called punctuation marks—to help your reader understand your meaning.

Over the years we have gradually developed a standardized pattern of usage for all punctuation marks. This usage has been codified (set down) in rules that are

1. us, Nguyen, 2. Anchorage, Alaska, Portland, 3. has, way, 4. today, 5. long, speeches, year's,

observed by writers who wish to make their writing as precise as possible. As noted earlier, some professional writers may deviate from conventional punctuation practices. In addition, some organizations, particularly newspapers and publishing houses, maintain their own style manuals to establish a consistent "in-house" style.

The punctuation guidelines presented in this book represent a consensus of punctuation styles that are acceptable in most writing. Following these guidelines will enable you to write with clarity, consistency, and accuracy.

LEVEL I

BASIC COMMA GUIDELINES

As you begin to learn about commas, try to name a rule or guideline for every comma you insert. For example, *comma/series, comma/parenthetical,* and so forth.

The most used and misused punctuation mark, the comma, indicates a pause in the flow of a sentence. *Not all sentence pauses, however, require commas.* It is important for you to learn the standard rules for the use of commas so that you will not be tempted to clutter your sentences with needless, distracting commas. Here are the guidelines for basic comma usage.

Series

Commas are used to separate three or more equally ranked (coordinate) elements (words, phrases, or short clauses) in a series. A comma before the conjunction ensures separation of the last two items. No commas are used when conjunctions join all the items in a series.

SPOT THE BLOOPER

Poster for a university departmental event: "Door prizes will include lab equipment, books written by members of the biology department and a fruitcake.

Lava, Crystal, and Hance are three of the largest rapids on the Colorado River. (Series of words. Notice that a comma precedes *and,* but no comma follows the last item, *Hance.*)

Gino cultivated the soil, planted the vines, and harvested the grapes. (Series of phrases.)

Terry brought apples, Amanda brought peaches, and Lila brought pears. (Series of clauses.)

All swimmers and runners and bicyclists should sign up for the triathlon. (No commas needed when conjunctions are repeated.)

Direct Address

Words and phrases of direct address are set off with commas.

I do believe, *Daphne,* that you have outdone yourself.

May we ask, *sir,* that you repeat the question?

Parenthetical Expressions

Parenthetical words, phrases, and clauses may be used to create transitions between thoughts. These expressions interrupt the flow of a sentence and are unessential to its grammatical completeness. These commonly used expressions, some of which are listed below, are considered unessential because they do not answer specifically questions such as *when? where? why?* or *how?* Set off these expressions with commas.

accordingly
all things considered
as a matter of fact
as a result
as a rule
at the same time
by the way
consequently
for example
furthermore

hence
however
in addition
incidentally
in fact
in my opinion
in other words
in the first place
in the meantime
moreover

namely
needless to say
nevertheless
no doubt
of course
on the contrary
on the other hand
otherwise
therefore
under the circumstances

SPOT THE BLOOPER

An article in the *Enterprise* [Brockton, MA] referred to "the Massachusetts Society for the Prevention of Animals."

Under the circumstances, I will allow you to repeat the quiz. (At beginning of sentence.)

You will, *however,* be required to make an oral presentation. (Inside sentence.)

You are prepared for the presentation, *no doubt.* (At end of sentence.)

The words in question are set off by commas only when they are used parenthetically and actually interrupt the flow of a sentence.

However things turn out, you are always welcome here. (No comma needed after *however.*)

I have *no doubt* about her competence. (No commas needed to set off *no doubt.*)

Phrases are essential (no commas) when they answer the questions *when? where? why?* or *how?*

Don't confuse short, introductory, essential, prepositional phrases for parenthetical expressions. Notice that the following phrases are essential and, therefore, require no commas.

In the spring more rental units become available. (No comma is needed because the short prepositional phrase answers the question *when?*)

At the seminar we will discuss goals and objectives. (No comma is needed because the short prepositional phrase answers the question *where?*)

For this reason we must be at the meeting. (No comma is needed because the short prepositional phrase answers the question *why?*)

With your help I'm sure I can improve my backhand. (No comma is needed because the short prepositional phrase answers the question *how?*)

Dates, Addresses, and Geographical Items

When dates, addresses, and geographical items contain more than one element, the second and succeeding elements are normally set off by commas. Study the following illustrations.

■ Dates

STUDY TIP

In separating cities and states and dates and years, many writers remember the initial comma but forget the final one (my friend from Albany, New York, called).

On July 4 we celebrate Independence Day. (No comma needed for one element.)

On July 4, 1776, the Declaration of Independence was adopted. (Two commas set off second element.)

On Monday, July 4, 1776, the Declaration of Independence was adopted. (Commas set off second and third elements.)

In July, 1776, the frustration of the colonists was at a breaking point. (Commas set off second element.)

Note: In July 1776 the frustration of the colonists was at a breaking point. (This alternate style is acceptable in writing the month and year only.)

- *Addresses*

Please send an application to Ms. Pamela Richards, 1913 Piazza Court, Baton Rouge, Louisiana 70817, as soon as possible. (Commas are used between all elements except the state and zip code, which are considered a single unit in this special instance.)

SPOT THE BLOOPER

From *The Union-Leader* [Manchester, NH]: "Prince Louis Ferdinand of Prussia, a grandson of Germany's last emperor who worked in a Detroit auto plant in the 1930s and later opposed Nazi dictator Adolf Hitler, has died at age 86." [Could a comma help clarify who worked in the auto plant? Would the idea be better expressed in two sentences?]

- *Geographical items*

Their tour began in Santa Cruz, California, and ended in Asheville, North Carolina. (Two commas set off the state unless it appears at the end of the sentence.)

Appositives

You will recall that appositives rename or explain preceding nouns or pronouns. An appositive that provides information not essential to the identification of its antecedent should be set off by commas.

Ann Landers, *the advice columnist,* is the twin sister of Abigail Van Buren, *author of "Dear Abby."* (The appositives add nonessential information; commas set them off.)

The advice columnist *Ann Landers* is the twin sister of Abigail Van Buren. (The appositive is needed to identify which columnist you are speaking about; therefore, no commas are used.)

One-word appositives do not require commas.

My brother *Max* is a golf pro at the club.

Now complete the reinforcement exercises for Level I.

LEVEL II

COMMA GUIDELINES

At this level we will review comma usage guidelines that you studied in previous chapters, and we will add one new guideline.

NOTABLE QUOTABLE

"When one door of opportunity closes, another opens; however, we often look so long at the closed door that we do not see the one that has been opened for us."
— Helen Keller

Independent Adjectives

Separate two or more adjectives that equally modify a noun (see Chapter 12).

An *industrious, ambitious* student came to see me.

Introductory Verbal Phrases

Verbal phrases (see Chapter 11) that precede main clauses should be followed by commas.

To master a musical instrument, you must practice every day.

Working steadily, we built the fence in one day.

Prepositional Phrases

One or more introductory prepositional phrases totaling five or more words should be followed by a comma.

On the third Tuesday of each month, we hold a steering committee meeting.

In a company of this size, standards and procedures are necessary.

Introductory prepositional phrases of fewer than five words require *no* commas.

In September the county fair is held.

In this case I believe we can waive the filing fee.

Prepositional phrases in other positions do not require commas when they are essential and do not interrupt the flow of the sentence.

She has included *in her monthly report* a summary of her findings.

You may *at your convenience* stop by to pick up your check.

Independent Clauses

When a coordinating conjunction (see Chapter 14) joins independent clauses, use a comma before the coordinating conjunction, unless the clauses are very short.

Sandra may study French, *or* she may choose to study Spanish.

The comma after an introductory clause is probably the most frequently missed comma in student writing. Be sure to insert a comma after a clause beginning with *If, When, As, Since,* and so forth.

Introductory Clauses

Dependent clauses that precede independent clauses are followed by commas.

When you have finished dinner, please wash the dishes.

If you need help, call me at my office.

Since I am the project leader, I will attend all meetings.

Terminal Dependent Clauses

Use a comma before a dependent clause at the end of a sentence only if the dependent clause is an afterthought.

Please wash the dishes *when you have finished dinner.*

I will submit my term paper next week, *if that meets with your approval.*

SPOT THE BLOOPER

From a sports column in *The Atlanta Constitution:* [The teams] "were tied, thanks to Smith, who had spent Saturday night at the hospital witnessing the birth of his daughter, who on Sunday had lofted a pinch-hit home run."

Nonessential Clauses

Use commas to set off clauses that are used parenthetically or that supply information unneeded for the grammatical completeness of a sentence.

Her first priority, *as you can understand,* must be her studies.

We received a reply from Senator Moore, *who will be speaking here next week.*

Do *not* use commas to set off clauses that contain essential information.

Students *who made the dean's list* will be recognized at the luncheon. (No commas are necessary because the italicized clause is essential; it tells which students will be recognized.)

Now complete the reinforcement exercises for Level II.

LEVEL III

COMMA GUIDELINES

Degrees and Abbreviations

Degrees following individuals' names are set off by commas. Abbreviations such as *Jr.* and *Sr.* are not set off by commas unless the individual prefers to use the commas.

> Robert Payne, D.D.S., has been my dentist for years.
>
> Perry Mason, Esq., never lost a case.
>
> John D. Rockefeller Jr. had five sons. (Individual prefers to omit commas.)
>
> Martin Luther King, Sr., was also a minister. (Individual prefers to use commas.)

The abbreviations *Inc.* and *Ltd.* are set off by commas if the company's legal name includes the commas.

> Blackstone & Smythe, Inc., exports goods worldwide. (Notice that two commas are used if *Inc.* appears in the middle of a sentence.)
>
> Shoes Inc. operates at three locations in Tampa. (Legal name does not include comma before *Inc.*)

Numerals

Unrelated figures appearing side by side should be separated by commas.

> A total of 150, 1994 graduates attended the reception.

Numbers of more than three digits require commas.

> 1,760 47,950 6,500,000

However, calendar years and zip codes are written without commas within the numerals.

CALENDAR YEARS:	1776	1995	2001
ZIP CODES:	02116	45327	90265

"Both tears and sweat are salty, but they render a different result. Tears will get you sympathy; sweat will get you change."
— Jesse Jackson

Telephone numbers, house numbers, decimals, page numbers, serial numbers, and contract numbers are also written without commas within the numerals.

TELEPHONE NUMBER:	(212) 555-4432
HOUSE NUMBER:	20586 Victory Avenue
DECIMAL NUMBER	.98651, .0050
PAGE NUMBER:	page 3561
SERIAL NUMBER:	36-5710-1693285763
CONTRACT NUMBER:	No. 359063420

Omitted Words

A comma is used to show the omission of words that are understood.

> This year our theater company produced four plays; last year, three plays. (Comma shows omission of *our theater company produced* after *year.*)

Contrasting Statements

Commas are used to set off contrasting or opposing expressions. These expressions are often introduced by such words as *not, never, but,* and *yet.*

We chose Luigi's, not Stoddard's, to cater our reception. (Two commas set off contrasting statement that appears in the middle of a sentence.)

SPOT THE BLOOPER

From *The Boston Globe*: "Then her hair caught fire while sitting in a front seat during a fireworks display."

Our earnings this year have been lower, yet quite adequate. (One comma sets off contrasting statement that appears at the end of a sentence.)

The more he protests, the less we believe. (One comma sets off contrasting statement that appears at the end of a sentence.)

Clarity

Commas are used to separate words repeated for emphasis and words that may be misread if not separated.

War and Peace is a very, very long book.

Whatever happens, happens for a reason.

No matter what, we will always be friends.

Here's a good rule to follow in relation to the comma: *When in doubt, leave it out!*

Short Quotations

A comma is used to separate a short quotation from the rest of a sentence. If the quotation is divided into two parts, two commas are used.

John Paul Jones said, "I have not yet begun to fight."

"Give me liberty," said Patrick Henry, "or give me death."

Now complete the reinforcement exercises for Level III.

HOT LINE QUERIES

QUESTION My boss always leaves out the comma before the word *and* when it precedes the final word in a series of words. Should the comma be used?

ANSWER Although some writers omit that comma, present practice favors its use so that the last two items in the series cannot be misread as one item. For example, *The departments participating are Engineering, Accounting, Personnel, and Human Resources.* Without that final comma, the last two items might be confused as one item.

QUESTION Should I use a comma after the year in this sentence: *In 1992 we began operations?*

ANSWER No. Commas are not required after short introductory prepositional phrases unless confusion might result without them. If two numbers, for example, appear consecutively, a comma would be necessary to prevent confusion: *In 1992, 156 companies used our services.*

QUESTION Are these three words interchangeable: *assure, ensure,* and *insure?*

ANSWER Although all three words mean "to make secure or certain," they are not interchangeable. *Assure* refers to persons and may suggest setting someone's mind at rest (*let me assure you that we are making every effort to locate it*). *Ensure* and *insure* both mean "to make secure from loss," but only *insure* is now used in the sense of protecting or indemnifying against loss (*the building and its contents are insured*).

QUESTION It seems to me that the word *explanation* should be spelled as *explain* is spelled. Isn't this unusual?

ANSWER Many words derived from root words change their grammatical form and spelling. Consider these: *maintain, maintenance; repeat, repetition; despair, desperate, desperation; pronounce, pronunciation.*

QUESTION Is *appraise* used correctly in this sentence? *We will appraise stockholders of the potential loss.*

ANSWER No. Your sentence requires *apprise,* which means "to inform or notify." The word *appraise* means "to estimate" (*he will appraise your home before you set its selling price*).

QUESTION Is an apostrophe needed in this sentence: *The supervisor('s) leaving early on Thursday prevented us from finishing the job by Friday?*

ANSWER The apostrophe is needed: *the supervisor's leaving*. . . . The word *leaving* is a verbal noun (a gerund), and its modifier must be possessive. Other examples are: *the boy's whistling, the lion's roaring, my friend's driving.*

QUESTION Which word is correct in this sentence? *The officer (cited, sited, sighted) me for speeding.*

ANSWER Your sentence requires *cited,* which means "to summon" or "to quote." *Site* means "a location," as in *a building site. Sight* means "a view" or "to take aim," as in *the building was in sight.*

17 Semicolons and Colons

OBJECTIVES When you have completed the materials in this chapter, you will be able to do the following:

Level I

- Use semicolons correctly in punctuating compound sentences.
- Use semicolons when necessary to separate items in a series.

Level II

- Distinguish between the proper and improper use of colons to introduce listed items.
- Correctly use colons to introduce quotations and explanatory sentences.

Level III

- Distinguish between the use of commas and semicolons preceding expressions such as *namely, that is,* and *for instance.*
- Understand why semicolons are sometimes necessary to separate independent clauses joined by *and, or, nor,* or *but.*
- Use colons appropriately and be able to capitalize words following colons when necessary.

PRETEST

Insert appropriate semicolons, colons, and commas in the following sentences.

1. We often need people to help on weekends consequently I keep a list of available volunteers on file.
2. The following people were honored Jimmy Carter former President Henry Kissinger former Secretary of State and Walter Cronkite journalist.
3. Our spring schedule is set the fall schedule has not yet been finalized.
4. You must therefore continue your efforts on our behalf.
5. Although we had offers from many cities, we have decided to hold conferences in the following namely Birmingham, Providence, and Cleveland.

1. weekends; consequently, 2. seminar: Carter, President; Kissinger, State; Cronkite, 3. set; 4. , must, therefore, 5. following: namely,

Skilled writers use semicolons and colons to signal readers about the ideas that will follow. Semicolons tell readers that two closely related ideas should be thought of together. The semicolon is a stronger punctuation mark than a comma, which signifies a pause; but the semicolon is not as strong as a period, which signifies a complete stop. Understanding the use of semicolons will help you avoid fundamental writing errors, such as the *comma splice* and the *run-on sentence.* This chapter presents basic uses and advanced applications of semicolons and colons.

LEVEL I

BASIC USES OF THE SEMICOLON

Remember that a comma is used only after a two-syllable conjunctive adverb. And don't capitalize the word following a semicolon unless it's a proper noun.

Independent Clauses Separated by Conjunctive Adverbs

Semicolons are used primarily when two independent clauses are separated by a conjunctive adverb or a transitional expression. You studied this basic semicolon use in Chapter 14. Here are some review examples.

> Lauren had never ridden a horse before; *therefore,* she chose the most gentle pony. (Semicolon separates two independent clauses joined by the conjunctive adverb *therefore.*)
>
> Mariette worked for the company for over 20 years; *thus* she had witnessed many changes. (Semicolon separates two independent clauses joined by the conjunctive adverb *thus.*)

In addition to the application shown here, semicolons may be used in other constructions, as we'll discuss next.

Independent Clauses Without a Coordinating Conjunction or a Conjunctive Adverb

SPOT THE BLOOPER

Advertisement for a car wash: "We do not scratch your paint finish with machinery; we do it by hand."

Two or more closely related independent clauses not separated by a conjunctive adverb or a coordinating conjunction (*and, or, nor, but*) require a semicolon.

> The contract was delivered on Monday; it was not signed until Thursday.
>
> Jake provided the business experience; Marian provided the capital.

As you learned in Chapter 3, a serious punctuation error results when separate independent clauses are joined by only a comma (a comma splice) or without any punctuation whatever (a run-on sentence).

COMMA SPLICE:	Jake provided the business experience, Marian provided the capital.
RUN-ON SENTENCE:	Jake provided the business experience Marian provided the capital.

Series Containing Internal Commas or Complete Thoughts

Semicolons are used to separate items in a series when one or more of the items contain internal commas.

> Our company has branches in Austin, Texas; San Jose, California; and São Paulo, Brazil.

Representing us at the meeting were Ross, student body president; Annette, student body secretary; and Daniel, head of the student union.

Semicolons are used to separate three or more serial independent clauses.

SPOT THE BLOOPER

Sign in a craft shop in Buxton, MA: "Her's and Mine."

The first step consists of surveying all available information related to the company objective so that an understanding of all problems can be reached; the second step involves interviewing consumers, wholesalers, and retailers; and the third step consists of developing a research design in which the actual methods and procedures to be used are indicated.

A series of short independent clauses, however, may be separated by commas.

The monitor size is satisfactory, the keyboard action is excellent, and the processing speed is more than adequate for our needs.

LEVEL II

BASIC USES OF THE COLON

NOTABLE QUOTABLE

"There are but two powers in the world: the sword and the mind. In the long run the sword is always beaten by the mind."
— Napoleon

Formally Listed Items

Use a colon after an independent clause introducing a formal list of items—whether listed vertically or horizontally. A formal list is usually introduced by such words as *the following, as follows, these,* or *thus.* A colon is also used when words like these are implied but not stated.

Some of the most commonly used household appliances are *the following:* the toaster, the blender, and the microwave oven. (Formal list with introductory expression stated.)

Our company uses several delivery services for our important packages: United Parcel Service, Federal Express, and Airborne. (Formal list with introductory expression only implied.)

These are just a few of the services our advertising agency will provide for you:

1. Developing long-term advertising strategies and budgets
2. Designing memorable and effective ads
3. Analyzing sales to determine the value of the campaign

SPOT THE BLOOPER

From a student paper: "The three kinds of blood vessels are: arteries, vanes, and caterpillars." [Check spelling, word use, and punctuation.]

Do not use a colon unless the list is introduced by an independent clause. Often, lists function as sentence complements or objects. Because the statement introducing the list is not complete, no colon should be used. It might be easiest to remember that lists introduced by verbs or prepositions require no colons (because the introductory statement is incomplete).

Three plants that grow well in shady gardens are inpatiens, azaleas, and camellias. (No colon is used because the introductory statement is not complete; the list is introduced by a *to be* verb and functions as a complement to the sentence.)

Awards were given to the accounts payable, human resources, and sales departments for increased productivity. (No colon is used because the introductory statement is not an independent clause; the list functions as an object of the preposition *to.*)

SPOT THE BLOOPER

From *The Milwaukee Sentinel* in an article describing a restaurant called Twins Cafe: "There are two bathrooms and two sets of silverware at most tables."

Do not use a colon when an intervening sentence falls between the introductory statement and the list.

> I am considering attending the following universities. I must make my final decision by April 1.
>
> | | |
> |---|---|
> | Duke University | Auburn University |
> | Tulane University | Louisiana State University |
>
> (No colon appears after *colleges* because an intervening sentence comes between the introductory statement and the list.)

Quotations

Use a colon to introduce long one-sentence quotations and quotations of two or more sentences.

> Consumer advocate Lorraine Fairfield said: "Historically, in our private-enterprise economy, consumers determine what and how much is to be produced through their purchases in the marketplace; hence the needs of consumers are carefully monitored by producers."

Incomplete quotations not interrupting the flow of a sentence require no colon, no comma, and no initial capital letter.

> I took her seriously when she said to "be on time."

Explanatory Sentences

Use a colon to separate two independent clauses if the second clause explains, illustrates, or supplements the first.

> We were faced with a difficult problem: we could continue to fund the program in the hopes that it would become self-supporting, or we could redirect the funds to a program that showed more promise.
>
> One of the traits of highly successful people is this: they never give up on themselves.

Now complete the reinforcement exercises for Level II.

LEVEL III

SPECIAL CONSIDERATIONS IN USING SEMICOLONS AND COLONS

Introductory Expressions Such as *namely, for instance,* and *that is*

When introductory expressions (such as *namely, for instance, that is,* and *for example*) are used immediately following independent clauses, they may be preceded by either commas or semicolons. Generally, if the words following the introductory expression appear at the end of the sentence and form a series or an independent clause, use a semicolon before the introductory expression. If not, use a comma.

Notice that a comma follows *namely, for instance, that is,* and *for example* when these words are used as introductory expressions.

> A number of services are available to help you in your studies; *namely*, group study sessions, private tutoring, and review classes with the instructor. (A semicolon is used because *namely* introduces a series at the end of the sentence.)
>
> Several books give additional information you may find useful when opening your own business; *for example,* Johnson's *Tax Tips for the Self-Employed*

is an excellent resource. (A semicolon is used because *for example* introduces an independent clause.)

We are proposing many new additions to the the health care package, for example, vision and dental benefits. (A comma is used because *for example* introduces neither a series nor an independent clause.)

SPOT THE BLOOPER

From a column in *The Chicago Tribune*: "[A] letter from her mother, written in Polish, for example, has the date (for we dummies in the audience) written in English."

These same introductory expressions may introduce parenthetical words within sentences. Usually, commas punctuate parenthetical words within sentences. If the parenthetical words thus introduced are punctuated by internal commas, however, use dashes or parentheses. (Dashes and parentheses will be treated in detail in Chapter 18.)

The biggest health problems facing workers, *namely,* drug abuse and alcoholism, cost American industry over $10 billion a year. (Commas are used because the parenthetical words contain only two items joined by *and.*)

The pursuit of basic job issues — *for instance,* wages, job security, and working conditions — has been the main concern of American workers. (Dashes are used because the parenthetical words are punctuated with commas.)

Independent Clauses With Coordinating Conjunctions

Normally, a comma precedes a coordinating conjunction (*and, or, nor, but*) when it joins two independent clauses. If either of the independent clauses contains an additional comma, however, the reader might be confused as to where the second independent clause begins. For this reason many writers prefer to use a semicolon, instead of the normally expected comma, to separate independent clauses when either independent clause contains a comma.

We have forwarded your suggestions to our product manager, and he will consider them in future product-design decisions. (Comma separates independent clauses joined by *and.*)

At the recommendation of our Customer Service Department, we have forwarded your suggestions to our product manager; and he will consider them in future product-design decisions. (Because one clause contains a comma, a semicolon is used before *and.*)

We are born naked, wet, and hungry; and then things get worse. (Because one clause contains internal commas, a semicolon separates the independent clauses.)

SPOT THE BLOOPER

Headline in *Parade* magazine: "What Our Children Need Is Adults Who Care."

Other Uses of the Colon

- After the salutation of a business letter.

Dear Mr. Tarson:　　Dear Personnel Director:　　Dear Allen:

- In expressions of time to separate hours from minutes.

10:15 a.m.　　9:45 p.m.

- Between titles and subtitles.

Twilight Zone: The Movie

- Between place of publication and name of publisher.

Guffey, Mary Ellen. *Essentials of College English.* Cincinnati: South-Western College Publishing, 1996.

Capitalization Following Colons

Do not capitalize the initial letter of words or of phrases listed following a colon unless the words so listed are proper nouns or appear as a vertical array.

STUDY TIP

Generally, no punctuation follows incomplete statements listed vertically.

The qualities we are looking for in a manager are the following: experience, demonstrated management ability, product knowledge, and good communication skills.

These countries have no armed forces: Iceland, Liechtenstein, and Costa Rica.

For your application to be considered, it must include the following items:

1. A completed application form
2. A current résumé
3. A list of three business references

Do not capitalize the first letter of an independent clause following a colon if that clause explains or supplements the first one (unless, of course, the first word is a proper noun).

We have chosen your bid for one reason: it encompasses all our needs for half the cost of the next lowest bidder.

Capitalize the first letter of an independent clause following a colon if that clause states a formal rule or principle.

In business the Golden Rule is often stated in the following way: He with the gold rules.

For a quotation following a colon, capitalize the initial letter of each complete sentence.

In his book *The Age of Unreason,* John Handy says: "Less than half the workforce in the industrial world will be holding conventional full-time jobs in organizations by the beginning of the 21st century. Those full-timers or insiders will be the new minority."

A FINAL WORD

SPOT THE BLOOPER

From a Hewlett-Packard contest form: "If you would like the name of the winner . . . send a elf-addressed stamped envelope."

Semicolons are wonderful punctuation marks when used carefully and knowingly. After reading this chapter, though, some students are guilty of semicolon overkill. They begin to string together two — and sometimes even three — independent clauses with semicolons. Remember to use semicolons in compound sentences *only* when two ideas are better presented together. Forget about joining three independent clauses with semicolons — too unconventional and too difficult to read. In most instances, independent clauses should end with periods.

Now complete the reinforcement exercises for Level III.

HOT LINE QUERIES

QUESTION Here's a sentence we need help with: *We plan to present the contract to whoever makes the lowest bid.* My supervisor recommends *whoever* and I suggest *whomever.* Which of us is right?

ANSWER Your supervisor. The preposition *to* has as its object the entire clause (*whoever makes the lowest bid*). Within that clause *whoever* functions as the subject of the verb *makes;* therefore, the nominative case form *whoever* should be used.

Question When I list items vertically, should I use a comma or semicolon after each item? Should a period be used after the final item? For example,

Please inspect the following rooms and equipment:

1. *The control room*
2. *The power transformer and its standby*
3. *The auxiliary switchover equipment*

Answer Do not use commas or semicolons after items listed vertically, and do not use a period after the last item in such a list. However, if the listed items are complete sentences or if they are long phrases that complete the meaning of the introductory comment, periods may be used after each item.

Question Is there a plural form of *plus and minus?*

Answer The plural form is *pluses* (or *plusses*) *and minuses* (*consider all the pluses and minuses before you make a decision*).

Question I'm setting up advertising copy, and this sentence doesn't look right to me: *This line of fishing reels are now priced . . .*

Answer Your suspicion is correct. The subject of the verb in this sentence is *line;* it requires the singular verb *is.*

Question I wonder if the possessive is correctly expressed in this sentence that I'm transcribing: *I appreciate the candor of both you and Neil in our conversation.* Shouldn't both *you* and *Neil* be made possessive?

Answer No. It would be very awkward to say *your and Neil's candor.* It's much better to use the *of* construction, thus avoiding the awkward double possessive.

Question Is this a double negative: *We <u>can't</u> schedule the meeting because we have <u>no</u> room available?*

Answer No, this is not regarded as a double negative. In grammar a double negative is created when two negative adverbs modify a verb, such as *can't hardly, won't barely, didn't do nothing,* or *can't help but.* Avoid such constructions.

18 Other Punctuation

OBJECTIVES When you have completed the materials in this chapter, you will be able to do the following:

Level I
- Use periods to correctly punctuate statements, commands, indirect questions, and polite requests.
- Use periods to correctly punctuate abbreviations, initials, and numerals.
- Use question marks and exclamation points correctly.

Level II
- Recognize acceptable applications of the dash.
- Use parentheses to deemphasize material.
- Explain when to use commas, dashes, or parentheses to set off nonessential material.
- Correctly punctuate and capitalize material set off by parentheses and dashes.

Level III
- Correctly use double and single quotation marks.
- Correctly place other punctuation marks in relation to quotation marks.
- Use brackets, underscores, and italics appropriately.

PRETEST

Insert appropriate punctuation in the following sentences.

1. Please send invitations to Ellen Farmer and Nolan Rao
2. Sam Tony and Liz have all taken jobs with the EPA in Washington
3. London Paris and Berlin these are the only cities on our tour
4. The chapter entitled Frequently Asked Questions was the most valuable one in the book Desktop Publishing Made Easy
5. Was it John Kennedy who said Ask not what your country can do for you

This chapter teaches you how to use periods, question marks, and exclamation points correctly. It also includes suggestions for punctuating with dashes, parentheses, single quotation marks, double quotation marks, brackets, and underscores (italics).

1. Rao. 2. Sam, Tony, 3. London, Paris, Berlin— 4. "Frequently Asked Questions" Desktop Publishing Made Easy 5. said, "Ask you"?

LEVEL I

USES FOR THE PERIOD

NOTABLE QUOTABLE

"There's not so much to be said about the period except that most people don't reach it soon enough."
— William Zinsser, writing expert

To Punctuate Sentences

Use a period at the end of a statement, a command, an indirect question, or a polite request. Although it may have the same structure as a question, a polite request ends with a period.

Sabrina received the highest grade in the class on her midterm. (Statement.)

Send an E-mail message to all employees immediately. (Command.)

Martin asked if he could go with us to the game. (Indirect question.)

Will you please send me a copy of your latest brochure. (Polite request.)

To Punctuate Abbreviations

Because of their inconsistencies, abbreviations present problems to writers. The following suggestions will help you organize certain groups of abbreviations and provide many models. In studying these models, note the spacing, capitalization, and use of periods. Always consult a good dictionary or style manual when in doubt.

Use periods after most abbreviations beginning with lowercase letters.

a.m. (ante meridiem)
e.g. (for example)
c.o.d. (cash on delivery)
i.e. (that is)
ft. (foot or feet)
f.o.b. (free on board)

Exceptions: mph (miles per hour), wpm (words per minute), mm (millimeter), and kg (kilogram).

Use periods for most abbreviations containing capital and lowercase letters.

Dr. (Doctor)
Esq. (Esquire)
Mon. (Monday)
Ms. (blend of Miss and Mrs.)
Mr. (Mister)
No. (number)
Sat. (Saturday)

Use periods with abbreviations that represent academic degrees, geographical expressions, and initials of a person's first and middle names.

B.A. (bachelor of arts)
M.B.A. (master of business administration)
M.D. (doctor of medicine)
Ph.D. (doctor of philosophy)
S.A. (South America)
U.K. (United Kingdom)
U.S.A. (United States of America)
Mr. J. A. Jones (initials of name)

Do *not* use periods for most capitalized abbreviations.

Most abbreviations fall in this group. Note capitalized letters, lack of periods, and tight spacing.

CEO (chief executive officer)
CFO (chief financial officer)
CPA (certified public accountant)
CPU (central processing unit)
EPA (Environmental Protection Agency)
EST (Eastern Standard time)
IBM (International Business Machines)
ID (identification)
OCR (optical character reader)
RAM (random-access memory)
SEC (Securities and Exchange Commission)

FYI (for your information)

GDP (gross domestic product)

SASE (self-addressed, stamped envelope)

SOP (standard operating procedure)

ZIP (zone improvement plan)

To Punctuate Numerals

For a monetary sum use a period (decimal point) to separate dollars from cents.

> We spent $14.46 for paper products and $75 for food.

Use a period (decimal point) to mark a decimal fraction.

> Only 35.3 percent of eligible voters are registered in this precinct.

USES FOR THE QUESTION MARK

To Punctuate Direct Questions

Use a question mark at the end of a direct question.

> When is your manager scheduled to return?
>
> Have you received a response from the software company?

Use a period after a polite request if you expect an action rather than a yes-or-no answer.

Do not punctuate polite requests as questions. These are considered to be commands or "please do" statements. A polite request asks the reader to perform a specific action and is usually answered by an action rather than a verbal response.

> Will you please take a moment to complete this survey.

To Punctuate Questions Appended to Statements

Place a question mark after a question that is appended to a statement. Use a comma to separate the statement from the question.

> You have all the credits needed to graduate, haven't you?
>
> Announcements should be posted at all locations, don't you think?

To Indicate Doubt

A question mark within parentheses may be used to indicate a degree of doubt about some aspect of a statement.

> Each application should be accompanied by two(?) letters of recommendation.
>
> A starting salary of $2,500(?) per month is expected.

USES FOR THE EXCLAMATION POINT

SPOT THE BLOOPER

Ad for an electronics store published in the *Journal-News* [Rockland, NY]: "Bring in any competitor's ad and we will beat the price plus 10% of the difference in price or it's your's free!"

To Express Strong Emotion

After a word, phrase, or clause expressing strong emotion, use an exclamation point. In business writing, however, exclamation points should be used sparingly.

> Ridiculous! I will never be able to meet such a tight deadline.
>
> Unbelievable! Have you seen these sales figures?
>
> It is amazing that the copier has not broken down after all this abuse!

Do not use an exclamation point after mild interjections, such as *oh* and *well.*

> Well, I was expecting something like this.

Now complete the reinforcement exercises for Level I.

LEVEL II

USES FOR THE DASH

The dash is a legitimate and effective punctuation mark when used according to accepted conventions. As an emphatic punctuation mark, however, the dash loses effectiveness when it is overused. In typewritten or simple word processing-generated material, a dash is formed by typing two hyphens with no space before, between, or after the hyphens. In printed or desktop publishing-generated material, a dash appears as a solid line (an *em* dash). Study the following suggestions for and illustrations of appropriate uses of the dash.

"In the Information Age, flexibility is the critical foundation for success. Future generations will need more than just mastery of subject matter. They will need mastery of learning."
— Morris Weeks

To Set Off Parenthetical Elements

Within a sentence parenthetical elements are usually set off by commas. If, however, the parenthetical element itself contains internal commas, use dashes (or parentheses) to set it off.

> Some of my required classes—math, science, composition, and foreign language—are not being offered this semester.
>
> Three famous modern dancers—Martha Graham, Daniel Nagrin, and Merce Cunningham—are featured in the film.

To Indicate an Interruption

An interruption or abrupt change of thought may be separated from the rest of a sentence by a dash.

> We will refund your money—you have my guarantee—if you are not satisfied.
>
> You can submit your report on Friday—no, we must have it by Thursday at the latest.

Sentences with abrupt changes of thought or with appended afterthoughts can usually be improved through rewriting.

To Set Off a Summarizing Statement

Use a dash (not a colon) to separate an introductory list from a summarizing statement.

> Experience, communication skills, patience—these are the qualities I appreciate most in a manager.
>
> Kayaking, canoeing, and rafting—these are Matt's favorite sports.

To Attribute a Quotation

Place a dash between a quotation and its source.

> "Courage is the price that life exacts for granting peace."—Amelia Earhart
>
> "There's no limit to how complicated things can get, on account of one thing always leading to another."—E. B. White

USES FOR PARENTHESES

To Set Off Nonessential Sentence Elements

Generally, nonessential sentence elements may be punctuated as follows: (a) with commas, to make the lightest possible break in the normal flow of a sentence; (b) with dashes, to emphasize the enclosed material; and (c) with parentheses, to deemphasize the enclosed material.

Figure 17, which appears on page 9, clearly illustrates the process involved. (Normal punctuation.)

Figure 17—which appears on page 9—clearly illustrates the process involved. (Dashes emphasize enclosed material.)

Figure 17 (which appears on page 9) clearly illustrates the process involved. (Parentheses deemphasize enclosed material.)

Explanations, references, and directions are often enclosed in parentheses.

My days off (Friday and Saturday) are when I study most.

I recommend we direct more funds (see the budget on page 14) to research and development.

Additional Considerations

If the material enclosed by parentheses is embedded within another sentence, a question mark or exclamation point may be used where normally expected. Do not, however, use a period after a statement embedded within another sentence.

I bought the latest Grafton mystery (have you read it?) last week at the book sale. (A question mark concludes a question enclosed in parentheses and embedded in another sentence.)

We held a special meeting (but no one attended it!) to discuss these policy issues. (An exclamation mark concludes an exclamation enclosed by parentheses and embedded in another sentence.)

The program's AutoCorrect feature (this will be described in a later chapter) corrects misspelled words as soon as you type them. (A period is not used at the end of a statement that is enclosed by parentheses and embedded in another sentence.)

If the material enclosed by parentheses is not embedded in another sentence, use whatever punctuation is required.

Our proposal is to hire eight new employees immediately to keep the project on track. (See Appendix A for job descriptions and associated costs.)

An estimated two-thirds of U.S. employees work in the services sector. (This represents quite a change from the 1960s when almost half of all jobs were in manufacturing.)

SPOT THE BLOOPER

From an ad for PageMaker, a computer program: "It is still the most easiest program to learn yet the most powerful."

In sentences involving expressions within parentheses, a comma, semicolon, or colon that would normally occupy the position occupied by the second parenthesis is then placed after that parenthesis.

When we deliver the product (in mid-June), we can begin testing on site. (Comma follows parenthesis.)

Your tax return was received before the deadline (April 15); however, you did not include a payment. (Semicolon follows parenthesis.)

Now complete the reinforcement exercises for Level II.

LEVEL III

USES FOR QUOTATION MARKS

SPOT THE BLOOPER

From *The Press* [Atlantic City, NJ]: "John Merrill of Dorchester in Cumberland County called to say he'd seen an immature [rattlesnake] crossing a dirt road while out running for exercise."

To Enclose Direct Quotations

Double quotation marks are used to enclose direct quotations. Unless the exact words of a writer or speaker are being repeated, however, quotation marks are not employed.

"Many students today must be able to balance studies with full-time jobs," said Dean Alice Mills. (Direct quotation enclosed.)

Tracy said that she would provide the location for our party if we would provide the refreshments. (Indirect quotation requires no quotation marks.)

Capitalize only the first word of a direct quotation.

"Our funds for this project," said Mr. Thomas, "are in jeopardy." (Do not capitalize *are.*)

To Enclose Quotations Within Quotations

Single quotation marks (apostrophes on most keyboards) are used to enclose quoted passages cited within quoted passages.

My professor said, "I agree with Helen Keller, who said, 'We could never learn to be brave and patient if there were only joy in the world.'" (Single quotation marks within double quotation marks.)

SPOT THE BLOOPER

From *The Journal-American* [Bellevue, WA]: "Youths caught breaking the law or their parents could face a $250 fine or community service."

To Enclose Short Expressions

Slang, words used in a special sense, and words following *stamped* or *marked* are often enclosed within quotation marks.

Evan called the lecture a "snooze." (Slang.)

Computer buffs are called "hackers." (Words used in a special sense.)

In hockey a "hat trick" is when one player scores three goals in a single game. (Words used in a special sense.)

The letter was stamped "Return to Sender." (Words following *stamped.*)

To Enclose Definitions

Quotation marks are used to enclose definitions of words or expressions. The word or expression being defined should be underscored or set in italics.

The French term *fait accompli* means "an accomplished deed or fact."

A *vanishing point* is a "point in a drawing at which parallel lines converge or seem to converge."

SPOT THE BLOOPER

From *The Times & Record News* [Wichita Falls, TX]: "Do not sweep an area where there have been rodents with a broom."

To Enclose Titles

Quotation marks are used to enclose titles of literary and artistic works, such as magazine and newspaper articles, chapters of books, movies, television shows, poems, lectures, and songs. Names of books, magazines, pamphlets, and newspapers, however, are set in italics, underscored, or typed in all capital letters.

You will find the article "Writing Travel Articles That Pay" in last month's *Writer's Digest* very interesting.

The chapter "Effective Memos" in Brown's book on business writing is particularly helpful.

Additional Punctuation Considerations

Periods and commas are always placed inside closing quotation marks, whether single or double. Semicolons and colons are, on the other hand, always placed outside quotation marks.

SPOT THE BLOOPER

From an invitation to a dinner honoring newly elected Board of Education members [Scarborough, MA]: "Your Invited."

Angie said, "I'm sure the package was stamped 'First Class.'"

The article is entitled "Making Use of Your Imagination," but I don't have a copy.

Her letter stated that "refunds will be issued within the week"; however, we haven't received ours.

Three dates have been scheduled for the seminar "Fearless Freelancing": May 23, June 1, and July 5.

Question marks and exclamation points may go inside or outside closing quotation marks, as determined by the form of the quotation.

Lynn said, "Will you be at our rehearsal on Tuesday night?" (Quotation is a question.)

"If your pager beeps again," fumed Ms. Henshaw, "we will ask you to leave!" (Quotation is an exclamation.)

Do you know who said, "Beauty is in the eye of the beholder"? (Incorporating sentence asks question; quotation does not.)

I can't believe that package was marked "Fragile"! (Incorporating sentence is an exclamation; quotation is not.)

When did you say, "Who will give me a ride?" (Both incorporating sentence and quotation are questions. Use only one question mark inside the quotation marks.)

USES FOR BRACKETS

SPOT THE BLOOPER

Sign on I-75 in Florida: "Speed Limit Strickly Enforced"

Within quotations, brackets are used by writers to enclose their own inserted remarks. Such remarks may be corrective, illustrative, or explanatory. Brackets are also used within quotations to enclose the word *sic,* which means "thus" or "so." This Latin form is used to emphasize the fact that an error obvious to all actually appears *thus* in the quoted material.

"A British imperial gallon," reported Miss Hardwick, "is equal to 1.2 U.S. gallons [4.54 liters]."

"The company's reorganization program," wrote President Ian James, "will have its greatest affect [*sic*] on our immediate sales."

USES FOR THE UNDERSCORE AND ITALICS

With today's sophisticated software programs and printers, you can, like professional printers, use italics instead of underscoring for titles and special words.

The underscore or italics are normally used for titles of books, magazines, newspapers, and other complete works published separately. In addition, words under discussion in the sentence and used as nouns are italicized or underscored.

Your Money or Your Life, the book on personal finance by Dominguez and Robin, received a favorable review in *The New York Times.*

Two of the most frequently misused words are *affect* and *effect.* (Words used as nouns.)

Now complete the reinforcement exercises for Level III.

HOT LINE QUERIES

QUESTION We can't decide whether the period should go inside quotation marks or outside. At the end of a sentence, I have typed the title "Positive Vs. Negative Values." The author of the document I'm typing wants the period outside because she says the title does not have a period in it.

ANSWER In the U.S., typists and printers have adopted a uniform style: when a period or comma falls at the same place quotation marks would normally fall, the period or comma is always placed inside the quotation marks—regardless of the content of the quotation. In Britain a different style is observed.

QUESTION I'm not sure where to place the question mark in this sentence: *His topic will be "What Is a Good Health Plan (?)"* Does the question mark go inside the quotation marks? Too, should a comma precede the title of the talk?

ANSWER First, a question mark goes inside the quotation mark because the quoted material is in the form of a question. Be sure that you do not use another end punctuation mark after the quotation mark. Second, do not use a comma preceding the title of the topic because the sentence follows normal subject-verb-complement order. No comma is needed to separate the verb and the complement.

QUESTION Is it correct to say *Brad and myself were chosen* . . . ?

ANSWER No. Use the nominative case pronoun *I* instead of *myself.*

QUESTION What salutation should I use when addressing a letter to Sister Mary Elizabeth?

ANSWER The salutation of your letter should be *Dear Sister Mary Elizabeth.* For more information on forms of address, consult a good dictionary or reference manual.

QUESTION Is anything wrong with saying *someone else's car?*

ANSWER Although it sounds somewhat awkward, the possessive form is acceptable. The apostrophe is correctly placed in *else's.*

QUESTION I have looked in the dictionary but I am still unsure about whether to hyphenate *copilot.*

ANSWER The hyphen is no longer used in most words beginning with the prefix *co* (*coauthor, cocounsel, codesign, cofeature, cohead, copilot, costar, cowrite*). Only a few words retain the hyphen (*co-anchor, co-edition, co-official*). Check your dictionary for usage. In reading your dictionary, notice that centered periods are used to indicate syllables (*co•work•er*); hyphens are used to show hyphenated syllables (*co-own*).

QUESTION Can you tell me what sounds strange in this sentence and why? *The building looks like it was redesigned.*

ANSWER The word *like* should not be used as a conjunction, as has been done in your sentence. Substitute *as if* (*the building looks as if it was redesigned*).

NAME ______________________________

UNIT 5 REVIEW ■ Chapters 16–18 (Self-Check)

First, review Chapters 16–18. Then, test your comprehension of those chapters by completing the exercises that follow and comparing your responses with those shown at the end of the review.

LEVEL I

Insert necessary punctuation in the following sentences. Write C if the sentence is correct.

1. Because of your many years of service Ms. Welch we are presenting you with this plaque. ____

2. However the verdict comes out, we will always believe she is innocent. ____

3. Our Human Resources Department is concerned with recruiting hiring and training new employees. ____

4. All students who attend each class and do all the work will receive passing grades. ____

5. I feel on the other hand that I must do some independent research. ____

6. The field technician Janice Maxwell knows the equipment thoroughly. ____

Select (a), (b), or (c) to indicate the correctly punctuated sentence.

7. (a) Reports have arrived from our offices in Bonn, Switzerland, Munich, Germany, and Vienna, Austria.
(b) Reports have arrived from our offices in Bonn, Switzerland; Munich, Germany; and Vienna, Austria.
(c) Reports have arrived from our offices in Bonn; Switzerland; Munich; Germany; and Vienna; Austria. ____

8. (a) Most of your order was shipped Thursday the rest will be shipped today.
(b) Most of your order was shipped Thursday, the rest will be shipped today.
(c) Most of your order was shipped Thursday; the rest will be shipped today. ____

9. (a) His proposal arrived after the deadline; therefore, we could not consider it.
(b) His proposal arrived after the deadline, therefore, we could not consider it.
(c) His proposal arrived after the deadline; therefore we could not consider it. ____

10. (a) Would you please send the shipment c.o.d.
(b) Would you please send the shipment c.o.d.?
(c) Would you please send the shipment cod? ____

LEVEL II

Select (a), (b), or (c) to indicate the correctly punctuated sentence.

11. (a) Molly holds both BS and MS degrees doesn't she?
(b) Molly holds both B.S. and M.S. degrees, doesn't she?
(c) Molly holds both BS and MS degrees, doesn't she? ____

12. (a) Wow, sales increased by over 15 point five percent.
(b) Wow! Sales increased by over 15.5 percent!
(c) Wow. Sales increased by over 15.5%. ____

13. (a) We are looking for three qualities in an employee: honesty, intelligence, and experience.
    (b) We are looking for three qualities in an employee, honesty, intelligence, and experience.
    (c) We are looking for three qualities in an employee; honesty, intelligence, and experience. _____

14. (a) So far we have narrowed the candidate list to: Amy, Walter, or John.
    (b) So far we have narrowed the candidate list to Amy, Walter, or John.
    (c) So far we have narrowed the candidate list to, Amy, Walter, or John. _____

15. (a) Tom said, "That is not my area of responsibility."
    (b) Tom said: "That is not my area of responsibility."
    (c) Tom said; "That is not my area of responsibility." _____

16. (a) Three of our students: Laurel, Michael, and Timothy, will receive scholarships for next year.
    (b) Three of our students, Laurel, Michael, and Timothy, will receive scholarships for next year.
    (c) Three of our students—Laurel, Michael, and Timothy—will receive scholarships for next year. _____

17. (a) October, November, and December—these are our busiest months.
    (b) October, November, and December; these are our busiest months.
    (c) October, November, and December: these are our busiest months. _____

18. (Emphasize.)
    (a) In only three months, October, November, and December, our store does 80 percent of its yearly business.
    (b) In only three months: October, November, and December, our store does 80 percent of its yearly business.
    (c) In only three months—October, November, and December—our store does 80 percent of its yearly business. _____

19. (a) The three Alaskan towns selected are Nome, Anchorage, and Juneau.
    (b) The three Alaskan towns selected are: Nome, Anchorage, and Juneau.
    (c) The three Alaskan towns selected are—Nome, Anchorage, and Juneau. _____

20. (Deemphasize.)
    (a) Recent statistics—refer to page 4 of this study—show a decrease in population.
    (b) Recent statistics (refer to page 4 of this study) show a decrease in population.
    (c) Recent statistics, refer to page 4 of this study, show a decrease in population. _____

LEVEL III

Select (a), (b), or (c) to indicate the correctly punctuated sentence.

21. (a) In summary reports of a hostile takeover are exaggerated.
    (b) In summary, reports of a hostile takeover are exaggerated.
    (c) In summary—reports of a hostile takeover are exaggerated _____

22. (a) Our goal is to encourage, not hamper good communication.
    (b) Our goal is to encourage: not hamper good communication.
    (c) Our goal is to encourage, not hamper, good communication. _____

23. (a) Only one source can be used to format reports, namely, our company style guide.
    (b) Only one source can be used to format reports; namely, our company style guide.
    (c) Only one source can be used to format reports: namely, our company style guide. _____

24. (a) The time for the meeting has been narrowed to three days; that is, Monday, Tuesday, or Friday.
(b) The time for the meeting has been narrowed to three days, that is, Monday, Tuesday, or Friday.
(c) The time for the meeting has been narrowed to three days: that is, Monday, Tuesday, or Friday. ____

25. (a) The output we received was “garbage,” that is, the printout showed only indecipherable characters.
(b) The output we received was “garbage”; that is, the printout showed only indecipherable characters.
(c) The output we received was “garbage;” that is, the printout showed only indecipherable characters. ____

26. (a) A buffer is defined as a “section of memory set aside for temporary storage.”
(b) A “buffer” is defined as a ‘section of memory set aside for temporary storage.’
(c) A buffer is defined as a “section of memory set aside for temporary storage.” ____

27. (a) MacWeek, a weekly magazine for Macintosh users, features an article called “Mac the Knife.”
(b) *MacWeek,* a weekly magazine for Macintosh users, features an article called “Mac the Knife.”
(c) “MacWeek,” a weekly magazine for Macintosh users, features an article called *Mac the Knife.* ____

28. (a) “Our strategy,” said Mr. Nichols, “is to take the competition by surprise.”
(b) “Our strategy,” said Mr. Nichols, “Is to take the competition by surprise.”
(c) “Our strategy, said Mr. Nichols, “is to take the competition by surprise.” ____

29. (a) Do you know who said, “Time is our most precious commodity.”?
(b) Do you know who said, “Time is our most precious commodity?”
(c) Do you know who said, “Time is our most precious commodity”? ____

30. (a) Did Richard really say, “Stamp this package ‘Fragile’?”
(b) Did Richard really say, “Stamp this package ‘Fragile’”?
(c) Did Richard really say, “Stamp this package ‘Fragile”? ____

Hot Line Review

Write the letter of the word or phrase that correctly completes each sentence.

31. Following directions carefully will (a) ensure, (b) insure a smooth installation. ____

32. Has the value of your home been (a) appraised, (b) apprised in the last five years? ____

33. Direct your inquiries to the manager and (a) I, (b) me, (c) myself. ____

34. This restaurant was (a) cited, (b) sited, (c) sighted for health code violations last year. ____

35. Offer the extra clothing to (a) whoever, (b) whomever needs it most. ____

1. (2) service, Ms. Welch, 2. C 3. (2) recruiting, hiring, 4. C 5. (2) feel, hand, 6. C 7. b 8. c 9. a 10. a 11. b 12. b 13. a 14. b 15. a 16. c 17. a 18. c 19. a 20. b 21. b 22. c 23. a 24. a 25. b 26. c 27. b 28. a 29. c 30. b 31. a 32. a 33. b 34. a 35. a

UNIT

6

Writing With Style

19 Capitalization

OBJECTIVES When you have completed the materials in this chapter, you will be able to do the following:

Level I
- Distinguish between common and proper nouns for purposes of capitalization.
- Decide when to capitalize proper adjectives and when not to.

Level II
- Understand when to capitalize personal titles, numbered items, and points of the compass.
- Correctly capitalize departments, divisions, committees, government terms, product names, and literary titles.

Level III
- Capitalize beginning words, celestial bodies, and ethnic references.
- Apply special rules in capitalizing personal titles and terms.

PRETEST

Use three short lines to underscore any letters that should be capitalized below.

1. This fall I plan to take classes in english composition, computer science, and psychology.
2. My mother's family reunion will be held in the bayview room at the sheraton hotel in new york city.
3. After receiving a master's degree from michigan state university, bill became assistant marketing director at the sony corporation.
4. Jeff arrives this afternoon at 3 p.m. at gate 32 on american airlines flight no. 421.
5. The department of housing and urban development has several internships open for the summer.

Rules governing capitalization reflect conventional practices; that is, they have been established by custom and usage. By following these conventions, a writer tells a reader, among other things, what words are important. In earlier times writers capitalized most nouns and many adjectives at will; few conventions of capitalization or punctuation were then consistently observed. Today most capitalization fol-

1. English 2. Bayview Room Sheraton Hotel New York City 3. Michigan State University Bill Sony Corporation 4. Gate American Airlines Flight No. 5. Department of Housing and Urban Development

lows definite rules that are fully accepted and practiced at all times. Dictionaries are helpful in determining capitalization practices, but they do not show all capitalized words. To develop skill in controlling capitals, study the rules and examples shown in this chapter.

LEVEL I

BASIC RULES OF CAPITALIZATION

Proper Nouns

Capitalize proper nouns, including the *specific* names of persons, places, schools, streets, parks, buildings, religions, holidays, months, nicknames, agreements, and so forth. Do *not* capitalize common nouns that make *general* reference.

"Find a job you love, and you'll never have to work a day in your life."
— Anonymous

PROPER NOUNS	COMMON NOUNS
Nathan Jackson	a young man on the debating team
Alaska, Hawaii	two states in the U.S.
Foothill College, Temple University	a community college and a university
Wrigley Field	a baseball park
Episcopalian, Methodist	representatives of two religions
Sycamore Room, Empire Hotel	a room in the hotel
Labor Day, Thanksgiving	two holidays
Golden Gate Bridge	a bridge over the bay
Empire State Building	a building in the city
Supreme Court, Congress	components of government
October, November, December	three last months of the year
the City of Angels, the Big Apple	nicknames of cities
North America Free Trade Agreement	an agreement between countries

Most proper nouns retain their capital letters when they become adjectives — for example, French toast, Russian roulette, Persian cat, Spanish moss, Italian marble, and Swedish massage.

Proper Adjectives

Capitalize most adjectives that are derived from proper nouns.

Renaissance art	Trojan horse
Danish pastry	Belgian waffle
Freudian slip	Roman numeral
Heimlich maneuver	Swiss cheese

Do not capitalize those adjectives originally derived from proper nouns that have become common adjectives (without capitals) through usage. Consult your dictionary when in doubt.

venetian blinds	epicurean feast
plaster of paris	french fries
india ink	diesel engine
manila folder	china dishes

Beginning of Sentence

Capitalize the first letter of a word beginning a sentence.

One of Benjamin Franklin's many inventions was the rocking chair.

Geographic Locations

Capitalize the names of *specific* places such as states, cities, mountains, valleys, lakes, rivers, oceans, and geographic regions. Capitalize *county* and *state* when they follow the proper nouns.

Maine, New Hampshire, Vermont
Kansas City, Nashville
Death Valley
Lake Ontario, Dead Sea
Dade County, Montgomery County (but the city of Miami, the county of Dade, the state of Missouri)
Salmon River, Columbia River
Atlantic Ocean, Arctic Ocean
Pacific Northwest, Texas Panhandle
European Community (EC)
Washington State

Organization Names

Capitalize the principal words in the names of all business, civic, educational, governmental, labor, military, philanthropic, political, professional, religious, and social organizations.

United States Air Force
Society for Technical Communication
Humane Society of the United States
National Academy of Recording Arts and Sciences
Screen Actors Guild
American Heart Association
San Jose Unified School District
Microsoft Corporation
Federal Reserve Board
The Boeing Company*

"A genius is a talented person who does his homework."
— Thomas Edison

Generally, do *not* capitalize *company, association, board,* and other shortened name forms when they are used to replace full organization names. If these shortened names, however, are preceded by the word *the* and are used in formal or legal documents (contracts, bylaws, minutes, etc.), they may be capitalized.

The company is moving its headquarters to Carbondale, Illinois. (Informal document.)

The Treasurer of the Association is herein authorized to disburse funds. (Formal document.)

Academic Courses and Degrees

Capitalize the names of numbered courses and specific course titles. Do not capitalize the names of academic subject areas unless they contain a proper noun.

Course titles with numbers are usually capitalized (*Marketing 101*). Those without numbers usually are not capitalized (*marketing*).

Peter plans to take American history, French, and Chemistry 101 next semester.

Natalie's best subjects were marketing, business administration, and accounting.

This quarter I am taking English composition and computer science.

Capitalize abbreviations of academic degrees whether they stand alone or follow individuals' names. Do not capitalize general references to degrees.

Bob Mitchell earned B.S., M.S., and Ph.D. degrees before his thirtieth birthday. (Bachelor of Science, Master of Science, and Doctor of Philosophy degrees.)

*Capitalize *the* only when it is part of an organization's official name (as it would appear on the organization's stationery).

SPOT THE BLOOPER

Headline in *The Washington Times*: "Threat of espionage hinder Paris air show."

Anthony hoped to earn bachelor's and master's degrees in environmental studies. (General reference to degrees.)

Darren Webster, Ph.D., is my academic counselor.

New employees include Teresa Wang, M.S., and John Young, B.S.

Seasons

Do not capitalize seasons unless they are personified (spoken of as if alive).

Our annual sales meeting is held each spring.

"Come, Winter, with thine angry howl. . ."—Burns

Now complete the reinforcement exercises for Level I.

LEVEL II

SPECIAL RULES OF CAPITALIZATION

Titles of People

Capitalize personal titles when they precede names.

Uncle Martin	Chief of Staff Walters
Senator Blake	Mayor Lindsay
Commander Harry Reynolds	President Perez

Capitalize only the first word in salutations (*My dear Ms. Jones*) and complimentary closes (*Very truly yours*).

Capitalize titles in addresses and closing lines.

Ms. Carla Watson	Yours truly,
Marketing Manager	
Technology Communications, Inc.	
303 Madison Avenue	John R. Jacobson
New York, NY 10022	Budget Director

Notice that titles of high rank are capitalized whether they precede, follow, or replace a name.

Capitalize titles of high government rank or religious office.

the President of the U.S.	our Governor, Ronald Forbes
the Pope's announcement	John Hughes, Prime Minister
the Senator from North Carolina	an audience with the Queen
the Chief Justice	the Secretary of Defense

Do not capitalize titles following names.

Rachel Stone, president of Innovative Designs, Inc.

Mickey Cavanaugh, supervisor, Data Processing Center

Rick Mills, personnel manager

SPOT THE BLOOPER

From a student paper: "The difference between a King and a President is that a King is the son of his father, but a President isn't."

Do not capitalize titles appearing alone.

Our president and vice president held a meeting for all sales managers.

Will the marketing manager or the customer services manager be there?

Do not capitalize titles that precede or follow appositives (unless they represent high rank). You will recall that appositives rename or explain previously mentioned nouns or pronouns.

SPOT THE BLOOPER

From a Wendy's International poster: "Be Cool in School! Good Grades Has Its Rewards!" [See any problem with subject-verb agreement? How about pronoun-antecedent agreement?]

Our research director, John Clarke, prepared the proposal.

Miriam Wallace, vice president of finance, oversees the budget.

The capitalization of business titles can be summarized in one rule: Capitalize business titles only when they precede personal names and replace courtesy titles, such as *Research Director Clarke* or *Vice President Wallace.*

Do not capitalize family titles used with possessive pronouns.

my mother	our uncle
his father	your nephew

But do capitalize titles of close relatives when they are used without pronouns.

Everyone knows Mother for her green thumb.

Numbered and Lettered Items

Capitalize nouns followed by numbers or letters (except in page, paragraph, line, size, and verse references).

Gate 15, Flight 167	IRS Form 321-B	Building A-31
Invoice No. 1314	Volume I, Appendix B	Medicare Form 23B
page 4, line 10	Interstate 85	Supplement No. 2

A clue to the capitalization of a region is the use of *the* preceding it: *the East Coast, the West, the Pacific Northwest.*

Points of the Compass

Capitalize *north, south, east, west,* and their derivatives when they represent *specific* regions. Do not capitalize the points of the compass when they are used in directions or in general references.

the Middle East, the Far East	turn east on Central Expressway
the Midwest, the Pacific Northwest	west of town
the East Coast, the West Coast	eastern Washington, western Wyoming
Easterners, Southerners	southern Michigan
Northern Hemisphere	in the northern Rockies

Departments, Divisions, and Committees

Capitalize the names of departments, divisions, or committees within your own organization. Outside your organization capitalize only *specific* department, division, or committee names.

Contact our Client Support Department for more information.

He works with the International Division of Apple.

Address your request to their public relations department.

You have been appointed to our Process Improvement Committee.

The recreation committee has not met yet.

SPOT THE BLOOPER

From *The San Francisco Chronicle*: "Keenan has just awoken from a nap."

Governmental Terms

Do not capitalize the words *federal, government, nation,* or *state* unless they are part of a specific title.

We studied both state and federal government structure in political science.

The Federal Communications Commission regulates broadcasting in all states.

Product Names

Capitalize product names only when they represent trademarked items. Except in advertising, common names following manufacturers' names are not capitalized.

Coca-Cola	DuPont Teflon	Polaroid camera
Kleenex tissues	Xerox copier	NordicTrack Walkfit
Magic Marker	Maytag washer	Styrofoam cup
Amana Radarange	Macintosh computer	Jeep Cherokee
Q-Tip	Frigidaire refrigerator	Formica counter

Literary Titles

Capitalize the principal words in the titles of books, magazines, newspapers, articles, movies, plays, songs, poems, and reports. Do *not* capitalize articles (*a, an, the*), conjunctions (*and, but, or, nor*), and prepositions with three or fewer letters (*in, to, by, for,* etc.) unless they begin or end the title.

By the way, the titles of published works that contain subdivisions—such as books, magazines, pamphlets, newspapers, plays, and musicals—are italicized or underscored. Titles of literary or artistic works without subdivisions (such as articles, poems, and movies) are placed in quotation marks.

Kenneth C. Davis's *Don't Know Much About History* (Book.)

Smith's *Easy WordPerfect—Worth Waiting For* (Book with preposition at end of title.)

Panati's *Extraordinary Origins of Everyday Things* (Book.)

"Visualization: Another Tool to Help You Reach Your Goals" (Magazine article.)

Frost's "Stopping by Woods on a Snowy Evening" (Poem.)

MGM's classic "Gone With the Wind" (Movie.)

Now complete the reinforcement exercises for Level II.

ADDITIONAL RULES OF CAPITALIZATION

Beginning Words

In addition to capitalizing the first word of a complete sentence, capitalize the first words in quoted sentences, independent phrases, enumerated items, and formal rules or principles following colons.

Calvin Coolidge said, "The business of America is business." (Quoted sentence.)

No, not at the present time. (Independent phrase.)

We chose these options with our new car:

1. Sunroof
2. Air conditioning
3. Dual airbags

The fire department recommends the following home-safety rule: Install smoke detectors in every room. (Rule following colon.)

Celestial Bodies

Capitalize the names of celestial bodies such as Jupiter, Saturn, and Neptune. Do not capitalize the terms *earth, sun,* or *moon* unless they appear in a context with other celestial bodies.

> Columbus believed that the earth was round, not flat.
>
> The planets closest to the Sun are Mercury, Mars, and Earth.

Ethnic References

Terms that relate to a particular culture, language, or race are capitalized.

> In Hawaii, Asian and Western cultures merge.
>
> Both English and Hebrew are spoken by Jews in Israel.

"Most of the things worth doing in the world had been declared impossible before they were done."
— Louis D. Brandeis

Words Following *marked* and *stamped*

Capitalize words that follow the words *marked* and *stamped.*

> My check came back marked "Insufficient Funds."
>
> Please make sure the package is stamped "First Class."

Special Uses of Personal Titles and Terms

Generally, titles are capitalized according to the specifications set forth earlier. However, when a title of an official appears in that organization's minutes, bylaws, or other official document, it may be capitalized.

> The Controller will have authority over college budgets. (Appearing in bylaws.)
>
> By vote of the stockholders, the President is empowered to implement a stock split. (Appearing in annual report.)

When the words *ex, elect, late,* and *former* are used with capitalized titles, they are not capitalized.

> We went to hear ex-President Bush speak at the symposium.
>
> Mayor-elect Brown proposed a city council meeting for next week.
>
> I have just learned that former Secretary of Transportation Dole will attend our conference.

Titles other than *sir, ladies,* and *gentlemen* are capitalized when used in direct address.

> I hope, Doctor, that you will be able to see me today.
>
> Welcome, ladies and gentlemen, to our grand opening.

Now complete the reinforcement exercises for Level III.

HOT LINE QUERIES

QUESTION I don't know how to describe the copies made from our copy machine. Should I call them *Xerox* copies or something else?

ANSWER They are *Xerox* copies only if made on a Xerox copier. Copies made on other machines may be called *xerographic* copies, *machine* copies, or *photocopies.*

QUESTION In the doctor's office where I work, I see the word *medicine* capitalized, as in *the field of Medicine.* Is this correct?

ANSWER No. General references should not be capitalized. If it were part of a title, as in the Northwestern College of *Medicine,* it would be capitalized.

QUESTION I work for the National Therapy Association. When I talk about *the association* in a letter, should I capitalize it?

ANSWER No. When a shortened form of an organization name is used alone, it is generally not capitalized. In formal or legal documents (contracts, bylaws, printed announcements), it may be capitalized.

QUESTION I work for a state agency, and I'm not sure what to capitalize or hyphenate in this sentence: *State agencies must make forms available to <u>non-English speaking</u> applicants.*

ANSWER Words with the prefix *non* are usually not hyphenated (*nonexistent, nontoxic*). But when *non* is joined to a word that must be capitalized, it is followed by a hyphen. Because the word *speaking* combines with *English* to form a single-unit adjective, it should be hyphenated. Thus, the expression should be typed *non-English-speaking applicants.*

QUESTION When we use a person's title, such as *business manager,* in place of a person's name, shouldn't the title always be capitalized?

ANSWER No. Business titles are capitalized only when they precede an individual's name, as in *Business Manager Smith.* Do not capitalize titles when they replace an individual's name: *Our business manager will direct the transaction.*

QUESTION How do you spell *marshal,* as used in *the Grand Marshal of the Rose Parade?*

ANSWER The preferred spelling is with a single *l: marshal.* In addition to describing an individual who directs a ceremony, the noun *marshal* refers to a high military officer or a city law officer who carries out court orders (*the marshal served papers on the defendant*). As a verb, *marshal* means "to bring together" or "to order in an effective way" (*the attorney marshaled convincing arguments*). The similar-sounding word *martial* is an adjective and means "warlike" or "military" (*martial law was declared after the riot*).

NAME ______________________________

19 REINFORCEMENT EXERCISES

LEVEL I

A. (Self-check) In the following sentences, use standard proofreading marks to correct errors you find in capitalization. Use three short lines (≡) under a lowercase letter to indicate that it is to be changed to a capital letter. Draw a diagonal (/) through a capital letter you wish to change to a lowercase letter. Indicate at the right the total number of changes you have made in each sentence.

EXAMPLE: Does the President of your company have a Master's degree? 2

1. The Brennan corporation is holding its annual picnic at Serra park. ____
2. Born in Harlan county, Bryce grew up in the state of Kentucky. ____
3. Every Sony Stereo comes with a one-year Warranty. ____
4. This semester Ed is taking courses in french, Computer Science, and accounting. ____
5. Brenda studied Victorian literature in her english class last quarter. ____
6. The Country of Bhutan is located in the Himalaya mountains. ____
7. Salt lake city, in the State of Utah, was founded by Brigham Young and a small Party of Mormons in 1847. ____
8. Our County's welfare system was praised by the Department of Health and Human Services. ____
9. Vicki and Lyle held their wedding reception in the Redwood Room of the Ahwahnee hotel in Yosemite national park. ____
10. Deficit-reduction bills were passed by both the Senate and the house. ____

Check your answers below.

B. Use proofreading marks to correct any capitalization errors in these sentences. Indicate the total number of changes at the right. If no changes are needed, write *0*.

1. For a Bachelor's degree in business, you must complete the following courses: accounting 30, management 105, and computer science 37. ____
2. Presbyterian, methodist, and baptist ministers met to discuss community issues last week. ____
3. Kevin was transferred to the company's Sioux city office for the Months of October, November, and December. ____
4. Global economics seriously affect business at The Boeing Company. (The word *the* is part of the company name.) ____
5. Brad Chin, ph.d., is the keynote speaker for tonight's banquet. ____
6. How does your word processing program handle greek symbols and roman numerals? ____
7. Is the napa room at the holiday inn available for our labor day celebration? ____

1. (2) president master's 2. (1) County 3. (2) stereo warranty 4. (3) French computer science 5. (1) English 6. (2) country Mountains 7. (4) Lake City state party 8. (1) county's 9. (3) Hotel National Park 10. (1) House

8. Mitchell received his m.s. from Virginia polytechnic institute in Blacksburg. _____

9. At last year's spring fair, french fries, candy apples, and cotton candy were available. _____

10. I hope to spend a few days in the windy city on my trip through the State of Illinois. _____

11. Victoria Peak is the highest point on the island of Hong Kong. _____

12. American Rivers, a leading Conservation Organization, identified the Yellowstone river as this country's most endangered river. _____

13. The Pacific ocean is larger than all the land in the world. _____

14. Montreal, Canada, is second only to Paris as the largest french-Speaking City in the world. _____

15. Please use only india ink on those manila envelopes. _____

16. After Randy received his Bachelor's Degree from Boston college, he obtained his M.S. from Rutgers university. _____

17. His case, first tried in the State of New York, will now be sent to the Supreme court. _____

18. My business math class was canceled last Monday for veteran's day. _____

19. Hells Canyon on the Idaho-Oregon border, the deepest chasm in North America, is over 2,000 feet deeper than the Grand Canyon. _____

20. Our reunion was held last Fall at the Coconut Grove ballroom in Atlantic City. _____

NAME ______________________________

LEVEL II

A. **(Self-check)** Use proofreading marks to correct errors you find in capitalization. Indicate at the right the total number of changes you make.

EXAMPLE: Project manager James Willis was promoted to Vice President. ___3___

1. Nicole Scott, a member of our marketing research department, will be our new Far East representative. ______
2. Additional information on the features of this program is available on Page 41 in appendix B. ______
3. Personnel director Rosenburg will head the new steering committee. ______
4. My cousin and my aunt from the east will visit this week. ______
5. The exhibit features the work of many artists from the southwest. ______
6. Our human resources department and computer sales division are sponsoring a conference on recruiting strategies. ______
7. Eric's Father is from the Northern part of Illinois. ______
8. Address your inquiries to Mr. David Martin, manager, customer services, Atlas Fitness Equipment, 213 Summit Drive, Spokane, Washington. ______
9. The president met with the secretary of state to discuss the pope's upcoming visit to the U.S. ______
10. Brazil, Australia, and Argentina are the three largest countries in the southern hemisphere. ______

Check your answers below.

B. Use proofreading marks to correct errors in the sentences below. Indicate the number of changes you make for each sentence.

1. Jasmine Lee, President of Manning Corporation, offered the position of Budget Director to Jim Reynolds. ______
2. I am planning a trip to the west coast to visit my Mother, brother, and Uncle Arnold. ______
3. Our research and development division is moving to Houston, Texas. ______
4. When the president met with the secretary of agriculture, they discussed crop subsidies for the midwest. ______
5. Turn to volume 2, page 16 for detailed installation instructions. ______
6. The Sales Manager will be arriving on Alaska Airlines flight 341 at gate 12B. ______
7. I have just read a magazine article entitled "America's 10 best cities to live in." ______
8. For further information, write to John Golden, technical publications manager, Educational Software Company, 211 Sand Hill Road, Menlo Park, California 94022. ______
9. Memorial Day is a federal holiday; therefore, banks will be closed. ______
10. Mindy asked me to make a photocopy of the article entitled "The 100 best companies to work for." ______

1. (3) Marketing Research Department 2. (2) page Appendix 3. (1) Director 4. (1) East 5. (1) Southwest 6. (6) Human Resources Department Computer Sales Division 7. (2) father northern 8. (3) Manager, Customer Services 9. (4) President Secretary of State Pope's 10. (2) Southern Hemisphere

11. For lunch Ahmal ordered a big mac, french fries, and a coca-cola. _____

12. The Vice President and Marketing Director were called to the President's office for a meeting. _____

13. Our personnel department will submit an IRS Form No. 1099 for your consultant. _____

14. My cousins and your niece and nephew loved their trip to Disneyland. _____

15. Karen shopped for play-doh and a slinky at toy world. _____

16. The Southern part of the state is subject to extreme temperatures in the summer. _____

17. Susan searched for levi 501 jeans at the westside pavilion. _____

18. Did you meet marketing director Martin Evans at the company meeting? _____

19. Please refer to our invoice no. 37421 dated January 10. _____

20. A temporary state called "Franklin" existed in the western part of North Carolina (now part of eastern Tennessee) from 1784 to 1788. _____

21. She went to wal-mart for kodak film and kleenex tissues. _____

22. Ms. White suggested I read Strunk and White's book, *The Elements Of Style.* _____

23. Although he was a Southerner, he preferred the cooler weather of the San Francisco Bay Area. _____

24. I would rather play monopoly, but scrabble takes less time. _____

25. We read Eugene O'Neil's *Desire under the elms* in my literature class. _____

NAME ____________________

LEVEL III

A. (Self-check) Use standard proofreading marks to indicate necessary changes. Write the total number of changes at the right.

EXAMPLE: Where on Earth did you find that ancient camera? 1

1. Because the package was marked "fragile," we handled it carefully. ____
2. The guiding principle of capitalization is this: capitalize *specific* names and references, but do not capitalize *general* references. ____
3. Since 1960 the greatest number of asian immigrants in the U.S. has come from the Philippines. ____
4. Heading the negotiations was Former Secretary of State Cyrus Vance. ____
5. Large tracts of the Amazon tropical rain forest have been cleared for the following: ____
   1. cattle ranches
   2. lumber
   3. tax incentives
6. An eclipse occurs when the earth passes between the sun and the moon. ____
7. Southern Louisiana is famous for its cajun and creole cuisine. ____
8. You, Sir, may be held in contempt of court. ____
9. My manager said, "you must submit your timecards by Friday afternoon." ____
10. Only Ex-President Bush and Mayor-Elect Brown have responded to our invitations. ____

Check your answers below.

B. Use proofreading marks to indicate necessary changes. Write the total number of changes at the right.

1. As the Sun beat down on the crowd, the Vice Chancellor continued his graduation address. ____
2. Would you like a ride home? yes, thank you very much. ____
3. Our Advertising Agency operates according to this rule: you must spend money to make money. ____
4. Most Brazilians speak portuguese, most Surinamese speak dutch, and most Guyanese speak english. In all other South American countries, the official language is spanish. ____
5. Please take this fax marked "confidential" to our human resources department. ____
6. She said she would move Heaven and Earth to meet her deadline. ____
7. Mexico's Ex-President Salinas met with the President-Elect. ____
8. Tell me, doctor, how dangerous this procedure really is. ____
9. Three important factors to consider in purchasing a personal computer are the following: ____
   1. processing speed
   2. memory
   3. cost
10. It was Thomas Paine who said, "these are the times that try men's souls." ____

1. (1) Fragile 2. (1) Capitalize 3. (1) Asian 4. (1) former 5. (3) Cattle Lumber Tax 6. (3) Earth Sun Moon 7. (2) Cajun Creole
8. (1) sir 9. (1) You 10. (2) ex-President Mayor-elect

C. *Review.* Select (a) or (b) to indicate correct capitalization.

1.	(a) our personnel director	(b) our Personnel Director	_____
2.	(a) the Empire State building	(b) the Empire State Building	_____
3.	(a) obtained a master's degree	(b) obtained a Master's Degree	_____
4.	(a) courses in Spanish and literature	(b) courses in spanish and literature	_____
5.	(a) the Tiki Room at the Ritz	(b) the Tiki room at the Ritz	_____
6.	(a) French Fries and a Dr. Pepper	(b) french fries and a Dr. Pepper	_____
7.	(a) a file stamped "top secret"	(b) a file stamped "Top Secret"	_____
8.	(a) danced by the light of the moon	(b) danced by the light of the Moon	_____
9.	(a) the president's address to Congress	(b) the President's address to Congress	_____
10.	(a) go south on Highway 101	(b) go South on highway 101	_____

D. *Proofreading Alert!* Use proofreading marks to correct errors in the following meeting minutes. Your instructor may ask you to revise these minutes on a computer. Consider adding an item to the new business section. As Randolph Reagan, suggest that a committee investigate the possibility of new staff computers. Be sure to use your spell checker when you finish.

INTERNATIONAL DESIGN INSTITUTE

MINUTES, MONTHLY MEETING OF MANAGEMENT COUNCIL

Febuary 15, 1996, 10 a.m.

Room 1315, Trade and Merchantile Center

Members Present: Stephanie Andrews-Wilson
Dennis Caldwell
Deborah L. Helms
Anastasia Perez
Randolph R. Reagan
Elizabeth Stoneman

Member Absent: Nicholas Tomasini

The meeting was call to order at 10:05 a.m., by Deborah Helms. Minutes from the previous' meeting was read and approved.

Announcements

1. New copy equipment and software has been purchased for our reprographics department. This additions will facilitate mailings and document production.
2. Effective March 1 Michelle Yarmo will assume the position of Executive Assistant to the Vice President of our Residential interior design department.

Progress on Showcase Home

Anastasia Perez reported on the progress of our showcase home in cheviot hills. Renovation and remodeling of the home is progressing on schedule, the house should be ready for the photographers from metropolitan home magazine june 1.

During the Fall work crews completed the following tasks; removal of all wood shingles, repair of the plywood roof base, and installation of an permawear tile roof. In december damaged window facings were replaced, the plumbing in two baths and the kitchen were also repaired. Anastasia reported that she was investigating italian marble for the entry, and spanish tiles for the patio.

One work crew have concentrated on the Living Room which required ceiling repair and electrical rewiring. A pyramid skylight has been install in the libary, however, two bookcases had to be altared in doing so. Consulting the President and General Manager of the contractors company, a decision was made by Anastasia to proceed. Anastasia concluded her report by saying that she expected the showcase home to exceed it's budget by $15,500. She moved that the council authorize $15,500 to complete the cheviot hills showcase project. Elizabeth Stoneman seconded the motion.

In the discussion that followed Randolph Reagan called the project a "Money Pit," and recomended that it is abandoned. Elizabeth Stoneman disagreed, stating that to much had all ready been invested to quite now. Dennis Caldwell anticipated that the showcase home would generate considerable income when completed. Most of the council agreed with this position the motion passed 5-1-0.

New Business

Stephanie Andrews-Wilson suggested that the management council investigate expanded Health benefits for employees and managers. She volunteered to head a Exploratory Committee. Dennis Caldwell moved that such a committee be formed, Elizabeth Stoneman seconded the motion. The motion passed 6-0-0.

The meeting was adjourn at 11 a.m. by Deborah Helms. The next meeting of the management council is scheduled for march 14 at 10 a.m.

Respectfully submited,

Vanessa Toliver, Secretary

E. *Optional Composition.* Your instructor may ask you to complete this exercise on a separate sheet. Write six original sentences that contain at least 20 properly capitalized words.

POSTTEST

Use three short lines to underline any letter that should be capitalized.

1. Mother and father are both fluent in spanish and english.
2. I am taking french literature, sociology, and anthropology in the spring semester.
3. Our sales department is holding its sales meeting in the cypress room at the westin hotel.
4. Do you know that the xerox model 4200 copier in room 321 has not worked all week?
5. The personnel director is considering adding easter to our list of company holidays.

1. Father Spanish English 2. French 3. Sales Department Cypress Room Westin Hotel 4. Xerox Model Room 5. Easter

20

Numbers

OBJECTIVES When you have completed the materials in this chapter, you will be able to do the following:

Level I
- Correctly choose between figure and word forms to express general numbers, money, and numbers beginning sentences.
- Express dates, clock time, addresses, and telephone numbers appropriately.

Level II
- Use the correct form in writing related numbers, consecutive numbers, periods of time, and ages.
- Use the correct form in expressing numbers in conventional phrases, with abbreviations and symbols, and as round numbers.

Level III
- Express correctly weights, measures, and fractions.
- Use the correct form in expressing percentages, decimals, and ordinals.

PRETEST

Examine the expression of numbers in the following sentences. Should word or figure form be used? Underline any incorrect form and write an improved form in the blank provided. For example, which is preferred: *$10* or *ten dollars?*

1. On the sixth of March at four a.m., our 1st child was born. ____________
2. By the time he was 17, Joe was six feet eleven inches tall. ____________
3. Michelle donated thirty dollars to the housing project to purchase one thousand four-inch nails. ____________
4. We had over twenty requests for information on June 3rd, but we had only nine requests today. ____________
5. Almost ninety-five percent of Egypt's fifty-three million people live within twelve miles of the Nile River. ____________

Just as capitalization is governed by convention, so is the expression of numbers. Usage and custom determine whether numbers are to be expressed in the form of a

1. 6th 4 a.m. first 2. seventeen, 6 feet 11 inches 3. $30 1,000 4. 20 June 3 9 5. 95 53 million 12

figure (for example, *5*) or in the form of a word (for example, *five*). Numbers expressed as figures are shorter and more easily comprehended, yet numbers used as words are necessary in certain instances. The following guidelines are observed in expressing numbers that appear in written *sentences.* Numbers that appear in business communications—such as invoices, statements, and purchase orders—are always expressed as figures.

LEVEL I

BASIC GUIDELINES FOR EXPRESSING NUMBERS

To remember it better, some people call this the "Rule of Ten": Words for one through ten; figures for 11 and above.

General Rules

The numbers *one* through *ten* are generally written out as words. Numbers above *ten* are written as figures.

A basketball team consists of *two* guards, *two* forwards, and *one* center.

The continent of Africa contains *51* independent countries.

Numbers that begin sentences are written as words. If a number involves more than two words, however, the sentence should be rewritten so that the number no longer falls at the beginning.

Thirty-four people applied for the programmer position.

A total of 340 citizens signed the petition. (Not *Three hundred forty* citizens signed the petition.)

Money

Sums of money $1 or greater are expressed as figures. If a sum is a whole dollar amount, most business writers omit the decimal and zeros (whether or not the amount appears with fractional dollar amounts).

Sarah planned to spend under *$50* for running shoes, but the ones she wanted cost *$67.50.*

My credit card statement showed purchases of *$10.49, $30, $51.55, $81.99, and $237.62.*

Sums less than $1 are written as figures that are followed by the word *cents.* If they are part of sums greater than $1, use a dollar sign and a decimal instead of the word *cents.*

I went to the market with only *45 cents* in my pocket.
Wendy paid $1.35, $.75, $2.40, and $.95 for the four postage-due envelopes.

Dates

In dates, numbers that appear after the name of the month are written in cardinal figures (*1, 2, 3,* etc.). Those that stand alone or appear before the name of a month are written in ordinal figures (*1st, 2d, 3d,* etc.*).

My birthday party will be held on *November 23* at Steve's house.
On the *3d* Thursday of each month, we hold a team project meeting.

In business documents dates generally take the following form: month, day, year. An alternative form, used primarily in military and international correspondence, begins with the day of the month.

Our lease expires on *31 July 1996.*

*Many writers today are using the more efficient *2d* and *3d* instead of *2nd* and *3rd.*

Some business organizations also prefer the international date style for its clarity, since it separates the numerical date of the month from the year.

Clock Time

Figures are used when clock time is expressed with *a.m.* or *p.m.* Omit the colon and zeros with whole hours. When exact clock time is expressed with *o'clock,* either figures or words may be used.

> The first showing of the movie is at *7 p.m.,* and the second is at *9:30 p.m.*
>
> Department mail is usually distributed at *four* (or *4*) *o'clock.*

Addresses and Telephone Numbers

Except for the number *One,* house numbers are expressed as figures.

805 Fiske Avenue	27321 Riverside Drive
One Wilshire Boulevard	1762 Cone Street

SPOT THE BLOOPER

From *The Suburban & Wayne Times*: "Cases of Lyme disease, which is transmitted by deer-carrying ticks, are on the rise." [What unintended meaning resulted from the unneeded hyphen?]

Street names that involve the number *ten* or a lower number are written entirely as words. In street names involving numbers greater than *ten,* the numeral portion is written as figures. If no compass direction (*North, South, East, West*) separates a house number from a street number, the street number is expressed in ordinal form (*-st, -d, -th*).

> 201 Third Street
>
> 958 Eighth Avenue
>
> 201 West 53 Street
>
> 3261 South 105 Avenue
>
> 901 34th Avenue (Use *th* when no compass direction separates house number and numerical portion of street name.)

Telephone numbers are expressed with figures. When used, the area code is placed in parentheses preceding the telephone number.

> Please call *(415) 941-7682* for further information.
>
> You may reach me at *(704) 289-3766, Ext. 231,* after 8 a.m.

Now complete the reinforcement exercises for Level I.

SPOT THE BLOOPER

Classified advertisement: "For Sale. 8 puppies from a German Shepherd and an Alaskan Hussy."

LEVEL II

SPECIAL GUIDELINES FOR EXPRESSING NUMBERS

Related Numbers

Numbers used similarly in the same document are considered related and should be expressed as the largest number is expressed. Thus, if the largest number is greater than *ten,* all the numbers should be expressed as figures.

> In March *four* orders were placed, in April *eight* orders were placed, and in May an additional *nine* orders were placed.
>
> Only *7* students out of *35* failed to complete the course.
>
> Of the *46* jobs in the print queue, only *4* reports and *3* letters printed.

Unrelated numbers within the same reference are written as words or figures according to the general guidelines presented earlier in this chapter.

Only *two* women were included in the *12* people interviewed for the *four* open positions.

The *three* tornadoes, with speeds up to 200 mph, destroyed *five* houses.

Consecutive Numbers

When two numbers appear consecutively and both modify a following noun, readers may misread the numbers because of their closeness. The writer should (a) rewrite the expression or (b) express one number in word form and the other in figure form. Use word form for the number that may be expressed in the fewest words. If both numbers have an equal word count, spell out the first number and place the second one in figures.

Our Publications Department printed *150 twenty-page* reports.

The historian divided the era into *four 25-year* periods.

They will need *thirty 4-inch* nails to finish the bookcases. (Use word form for the first number since both have an equal word count.)

"Everyone must row with the oars he or she has."
— English proverb

Periods of Time

Periods of time are generally expressed in word form. However, figures may be used to achieve special emphasis in expressing business concepts such as discount rates, interest rates, warranty periods, credit terms, loan periods, and payment terms.

- ***Word form.***

These tariffs have been regulated for over *thirty-five years.*

Hiking the full length of that trail usually takes *fifteen days.*

- ***Figure form for business concept.***

The warranty period on parts is limited to *2 years.*

After *30 days* your account is considered past due.

SPOT THE BLOOPER

From *The Times Union* [Albany, NY] featuring an advertisement with the following 2-inch headline: "On Thursday morning, I found the car of my dreams in my pajamas."

Ages

Ages are generally expressed in word form unless the age appears immediately after a name or is expressed in exact years and months.

Mr. Montross made his first million dollars before he was *seventeen.*

Lillian Withers, *75,* has just written her first novel.

Our son is *2 years* and *6 months* old.

Numbers Used in Conventional Phrases, With Abbreviations, and With Symbols

Numbers used in conventional phrases are expressed as figures.

page 6	Policy 651040	Area Code 408
Room 232	Volume 2	Section 8
Option 2	Form 1040	Assembly Bill 109

Numbers used with abbreviations are expressed as figures.

Apt. 19	Serial No. 2198675	Nos. 203 and 301
Ext. 167	Account No. 08166-05741	Social Security No. 250-93-6749

Notice that the word *number* is capitalized and abbreviated when it precedes a number. Notice, too, that no commas are used in serial, account, and policy numbers.

Symbols (such as #, %, ¢) are usually avoided in contextual writing (sentences). In other documents where space is limited, however, symbols are frequently used. Numbers appearing with symbols are expressed as figures.

50% 34¢ #2 can 2/10, n/60

Round Numbers

Round numbers are approximations. They may be expressed in word or figure form, although figure form is shorter and easier to comprehend.

SPOT THE BLOOPER

From *The Denver Post*: "The Allied Jewish Federation, which overseas the fund drive, hopes to raise $5.5 million."

Almost *300* (or *three hundred*) people attended the rally.

So far we have received about *20* (or *twenty*) donations.

For ease of reading, round numbers in the millions or billions should be expressed with a combination of figures and words.

The population of the Dominican Republic is *6.5 million.*

As of 1991, between *5.2 billion* and *5.5 billion* people populated the world.

To make just one pound of honey, bees must collect nectar from over *2 million* flowers.

Now complete the reinforcement exercises for Level II.

LEVEL III

ADDITIONAL GUIDELINES FOR EXPRESSING NUMBERS

Weights and Measurements

Weights and measurements are expressed as figures.

A typical index card measures *3 by 5 inches.*

At birth the baby weighed *7 pounds 8 ounces.*

Add *3 tablespoons* of oil and *1 tablespoon* of vinegar.

In sentences the nouns following weights and measurements should be spelled out (for example, *21 gallons* instead of *21 gal.*). In business forms or in statistical presentations, however, such nouns may be abbreviated.

5″ × 17″ #10 16 oz. 20 sq. yds. 4 lb. 3 qt.

Fractions

A fraction immediately followed by an *of* phrase usually functions as a noun (*one third of the cars*). Therefore, it is not hyphenated.

Simple fractions are expressed as words. If a fraction functions as a noun, no hyphen is used. If it functions as an adjective, a hyphen separates its parts.

Almost *three fourths* of the surface of the earth is ocean. (Fraction used as a noun.)

A *two-thirds* majority is needed to carry the measure. (Fraction used as an adjective.)

Complex fractions appearing in sentences may be written either as figures or as a combination of figures and words.

The microcomputer will execute a command in *1 millionth* of a second. (Combination of words and figures is easier to comprehend.)

Flight records revealed that the emergency system was activated *13/200* of a second after the pilot was notified. (Figure form is easier to comprehend.)

"Patience is the greatest of all shock absorbers. The only thing you can get in a hurry is trouble."
— Lord Thomas R. Dewar

Mixed fractions (whole numbers with fractions) are always expressed by figures.

The shelves were ordered to be 36 1/4 inches wide, not 36 1/2 inches. (Notice that no space follows a whole number and a key fraction.)

My window measures 46 5/8 inches by 54 1/2 inches. (Notice that fractions that must be constructed with slashes are separated from their related whole numbers.)

When fractions that are constructed with slashes appear with key fractions, be consistent by using the slash construction for all the fractions involved.

Percentages and Decimals

Percentages are expressed with figures followed by the word *percent.* The percent sign (%) is used only on business forms or in statistical presentations.

Did the dealer say that you could get a car loan with *5.9 percent* financing?

Seafood accounts for a mere *1 percent* of the human diet.

Decimals are expressed with figures. If a decimal does not contain a whole number (an integer) and does not begin with a zero, a zero should be placed before the decimal.

SPOT THE BLOOPER

From a newspaper ad for an attorney in Winter Park, FL: "For your family's protection . . . and piece of mind."

In the bantam weight championships, Mitchell was knocked out in *10.33* seconds. (Contains a whole number.)

For this experiment, the settings must be accurate to within *.005 inch.* (Begins with a zero.)

Only about *0.4 percent* of the costs will be passed on to consumers. (Zero placed before decimal that neither contains a whole number nor begins with a zero).

Ordinals

Although ordinal numbers are generally expressed in word form (*first, second, third,* etc.), three exceptions should be noted: (a) figure form is used for dates appearing before a month or appearing alone, (b) figure form is used for street names involving numbers greater than *ten,* and (c) figure form is used when the ordinal would require more than two words.

- ***Most ordinals.***

My parents just celebrated their *thirtieth* wedding anniversary.

Before the *twentieth century,* child labor laws were almost nonexistent.

Jane ranked *third* in her nursing school class of 250.

Ms. Blackmon represents the *Twenty-fifth Congressional District.*

- ***Dates.***

Classes start on the *15th* of September this year.

If rent is not paid by the *3d* of each month, you must pay a late fee.

- ***Streets.***

She lives at the corner of *Second Street* and Broadway.

The bank's new offices will be on *45th Avenue.*

- ***Larger ordinals.***

  Our firm ranks *102d* in the world in terms of number of accounts.

Now complete the reinforcement exercises for Level III.

HOT LINE QUERIES

QUESTION I'm never sure when to hyphenate numbers, such as *thirty-one.* Is there some rule to follow?

ANSWER When writtern in word form, the numbers *twenty-one* through *ninety-nine* are hyphenated. Numbers are also hyphenated when they form compound adjectives and precede nouns (*ten-year-old* child, *16-story* building, *four-year* term, *30-day* lease).

QUESTION I've always been confused by *imply* and *infer.* Which is correct in this sentence: *We (imply* or *infer) from your letter that the goods are lost.*

ANSWER In your sentence use *infer. Imply* means "to state indirectly." *Infer* means "to draw a conclusion" or "to make a deduction based on facts." A listener or reader *infers.* A speaker or writer *implies.*

QUESTION When fractions are written as words, why are they hyphenated sometimes and not hyphenated other times?

ANSWER Most writers do not hyphenate a fraction when it functions as a noun (*one fourth of the letters*). When a fraction functions as an adjective, it is hyphenated (*a one-third gain in profits*).

QUESTION Should I put quotation marks around figures to emphasize them? For example, *Your account has a balance of "$2,136.18."*

ANSWER Certainly not! Quotation marks are properly used to indicate an exact quotation, or they may be used to enclose the definition of a word. They should not be used as a mechanical device for added emphasis.

QUESTION I'm an engineer, and we have just had a discussion in our office concerning spelling. I have checked the dictionary, and it shows *usage.* Isn't this word ever spelled *useage?*

ANSWER No. The only spelling of *usage* is without the internal *e.* You are probably thinking of the word *usable,* which does have a variant spelling—*useable.* Both forms are correct, but *usable* is recommended for its simplicity. Incidentally, if the word *usage* can be replaced by the word *use,* the latter is preferred (*the use* [*not usage*] *of ink pens is declining*).

QUESTION How should I spell the word *lose* in this sentence: *The employee tripped over a (lose* or *loose) cord.*

ANSWER In your sentence use the adjective *loose,* which means "not fastened," "not tight," or "having freedom of movement." Perhaps you can remember it by thinking of the common expression *loose change,* which suggests unattached, free coins jingling in your pocket. If you *lose* (*mislay*) some of those coins, you have less money and fewer *o's.*

NAME ______________________________

20 REINFORCEMENT EXERCISES

LEVEL I

A. (Self-check) Choose (a) or (b) to complete the following sentences.

1. Travis counted (a) 12, (b) twelve hummingbirds at our feeder today. ______
2. (a) 14, (b) Fourteen rooms are available on that floor for our guests. ______
3. A grand-opening sale is scheduled for the (a) 16th, (b) sixteenth of October. ______
4. This direct mail piece will cost about (a) 2 cents, (b) two cents per unit. ______
5. Robin paid only (a) $50.00, (b) $50 for the stereo at the garage sale. ______
6. My address is (a) Two, (b) 2 Susquehanna Court. ______
7. The parade route follows three blocks of (a) Fifth, (b) 5th Avenue. ______
8. A branch of your bank is located at (a) 260 34th Street, (b) 260 34 Street. ______
9. I'm afraid it will cost over (a) $6, (b) six dollars to replace that battery. ______
10. Tomorrow's meeting is scheduled for (a) 10:00 a.m., (b) 10 a.m. ______

Check your answers below.

B. Assume that the following phrases appear in business correspondence. Write the preferred forms in the spaces provided. If a phrase is correct as shown, write C.

EXAMPLE: 4210 32 Avenue ______ 4210 32d Avenue

1. fifteen orders ______
2. Twelfth Avenue ______
3. $.09 per package ______
4. 6 letters ______
5. May fifth ______
6. 4th Street ______
7. $3.20, 53 cents, and $20.00 ______
8. the nineteenth of January ______
9. 8:00 p.m. ______
10. seven o'clock ______
11. twenty-four disks ______
12. March 23d ______
13. 134 23d Street ______
14. 134 North 23d Street ______
15. four applicants ______

1.a 2.b 3.a 4.a 5.b 6.b 7.a 8.a 9.a 10.b

16. thirty-six dollars ______________

17. 8 Shattuck Square ______________

18. 1 Shattuck Square ______________

19. forty-three cartons ______________

20. 5 o'clock ______________

21. (military style) June 23, 1996 ______________

22. 928 6th Street ______________

23. four thirty p.m. ______________

24. the fifth of August ______________

25. two hundred dollars ______________

26. fifty cents ______________

27. 3402 Eleventh Street ______________

28. 3402 West Eleventh Street ______________

29. 48 accounts ______________

30. 3 books ______________

C. Rewrite these sentences correcting any errors you note.

1. On March fifteenth we received a bill for the following amounts: $1.54, 98 cents, $5.00, and 16 cents. ______________

2. Our offices have moved from one hundred twenty-four Barkley Drive to 1 Oakmead Parkway. ______________

3. 29 kinds of rattlesnakes are found in North America. ______________

4. As of the 31 of June, you were 2 months behind on your payments. ______________

5. I have only twenty dollars to spend on Katie's gift, but I know she would like this pen for $39.99. ______________

6. If you came in at 7:30 a.m., you should be able to leave by 5:00 p.m. ______________

7. The play starts on the twenty-fifth, but Allison will not be able to come until the thirtieth. ______________

8. 374 new accounts were opened this year alone. ______________

NAME ________________________

LEVEL II

A. (Self-check) Select (a) or (b) to complete each of the following sentences.

1. The documentation group has prepared (a) four 20-page, (b) 4 twenty-page brochures to introduce our products. ______
2. We do not plan to move for at least (a) 15, (b) fifteen years. ______
3. Your class is being held in (a) Room Five, (b) Room 5. ______
4. Of the 45 people on the bus, only (a) four, (b) 4 had correct change for the fare. ______
5. Although he is over (a) 65, (b) sixty-five, Mr. Lawrence has no plans to retire. ______
6. In the United States (a) 20 million, (b) 20,000,000 acres are planted in wheat. ______
7. Have you completed your IRS Form (a) Ten Forty, (b) 1040? ______
8. About (a) 750, (b) seven hundred fifty orders were processed in our warehouse this week. ______
9. For a discount, your payment must be received within (a) 60, (b) sixty days. ______
10. You must tell the representative that our model number is (a) 45,678,901, (b) 45678901. ______

Check your answers below.

B. For the following sentences underscore any numbers or words that are expressed inappropriately. For sentences with inappropriate forms, write the correct forms in the spaces provided. If a sentence is correct as written, write *C.*

EXAMPLE: Only <u>2</u> 32-cent stamps are required for that letter. two

1. Our Board of Directors is composed of 15 members, of whom three are doctors, four are nurses, and eight are other health-care professionals. ______
2. We plan to print one thousand four-page brochures. ______
3. After a period of sixteen years, ownership reverts to the state. ______
4. The entire domestic bee population of 70,000,000 is at risk to killer bees. ______
5. These policy Nos. are affected by the change in coverage: No. 12434–12575. ______
6. Serial No. 1,245,679 is registered to Pon Electronics. ______
7. More than 12,000,000 people live in Shanghai, the most populous city in China. ______
8. Of the 75 students in Martha's class, nine went to medical school, seven received master's degrees, and four received teaching credentials. ______
9. Peter Dillon, thirty-three, and Barbara Marney, thirty-five, have recently been chosen for the astronaut training program. ______
10. Look on page fifteen of Volume three for the latest job placement statistics. ______
11. The warranties on our new monitors are limited to ninety days. ______
12. In the golden age of Greece, Athens had a population of about one hundred fifty thousand. ______

1. a 2. b 3. b 4. b 5. b 6. a 7. b 8. a (preferred) 9. a 10. b

13. More than half of our 47 students attended the two orientation sessions. ______

14. About fifty people will be laid off from our Atlanta office. ______

15. In most states you must be 16 years old to drive a car. ______

16. The square mileage of Washington, DC, is 67; and its population is about 650,000. ______

17. Her mother is now 63 years old, but she looks as though she is forty-three. ______

18. With 9 flights daily, United Airlines flies eighteen hundred people between San Francisco and Los Angeles each day. ______

19. Ms. Brown's art history lecture is being held in Building Forty-One. ______

20. The Pacific Ocean covers about 70,000,000 square miles. ______

C. Assume that the following phrases appear in business correspondence. Write the preferred forms in the spaces provided. If a phrase is correct as shown, write *C*.

1. three disks with eleven directories and nineteen files ______
2. nine sixty-five page reports ______
3. loan period of thirty days ______
4. Donna Wright, fifty-one, and her son, twenty-two ______
5. Model No. 456,781,876 ______
6. five point one million dollars ______
7. Room Three ______
8. nineteen days ______
9. fifty-two cards ______
10. about three hundred requests ______
11. four point five million people ______
12. Section six point one ______
13. five hundred one-inch binders ______
14. thirteen years ______
15. warranty period of two years ______
16. approximately 250 guests ______
17. three houses with 12 rooms ______
18. page nineteen of Volume Four ______
19. 2,000,000 units sold ______
20. IRS Form 1,040 ______

NAME ______________________

LEVEL III

A. (Self-check) Choose (a) or (b) to complete the following sentences.

1. This copier can make copies up to (a) 11″ x 17″, (b) 11 by 17 inches. ____
2. About (a) one third, (b) 1/3 of the world's population lives in the tropics. ____
3. The tropics encompass (a) 36%, (b) 36 percent of the world's land. ____
4. Next year marks my (a) 15th, (b) fifteenth anniversary with this company. ____
5. The ten most populous countries in the world account for (a) two thirds, (b) two-thirds of the world's population. ____
6. Ellison Furniture has just moved into warehouses on (a) 52d, (b) Fifty-second Street. ____
7. Sherry needs a frame measuring (a) 9 by 12 inches, (b) nine by twelve inches. ____
8. This year's office expenses are up by only (a) 0.5, (b) .5 percent over last year's. ____
9. A fence (a) one thousand miles (b)1,000 miles long was put up in the middle of Australia to keep rabbits from overrunning the country. ____
10. Did you know that many buildings have no (a) 13th, (b) thirteenth floor? ____

Check your answers below.

B. Rewrite the following sentences with special attention to appropriate number usage.

1. The box is ten and three-quarters inches long, four and one-half inches wide, and nine inches high.

____

____

2. It is expected that the population of the world will be six billion by the end of this century. ______

____

____

3. Even our most precise instrument cannot measure more closely than 0.005 inch. ______

____

____

4. My new laptop weighs less than five pounds and is twelve inches long and two inches deep. ______

____

____

5. About 4/5 of the world's reindeer live in Siberia. ______

____

____

6. In the 23d Congressional District, only 1/3 of the potential voters are registered. ______

____

____

1.b 2.a 3.b 4.b 5.a 6.a 7.a 8.a 9.b 10.b

7. Our bank ranks one hundred fifth in the world in terms of number of accounts. ______________

____

____

8. Invoices paid before the tenth will receive a two percent cash discount. ______________

____

____

9. A two thirds majority vote is required to pass this new budget of eighty-five thousand dollars. ______

____

____

10. In the year 2,001 our nation will celebrate its two hundred twenty-fifth anniversary. ______________

____

____

11. Our retail price of four dollars is nine percent lower than our nearest competitor's. ______________

____

____

POSTTEST

Underline numbers that are expressed inappropriately. Write corrected forms in the space provided.

1. Over twelve million dollars was contributed by the 8 participating countries. ______________
2. On the second of each month we hold a payday party for our nineteen employees and two consultants. ______________
3. Larry collected thirty insects, including four beetles, six flies, and twenty mosquitoes. ______________
4. The Sales Department reports sales of four hundred units, an increase of eleven percent over last month. ______________
5. Our customer requested that two hundred six-page brochures be delivered before June 1st. ______________

1. $12 eight 2. 2d 19 3. 30 4 6 20 4. 400 11 5. 200 June 1

21 Effective Sentences

OBJECTIVES When you have completed the materials in this chapter, you will be able to do the following:

Level I
- Eliminate wordy phrases and redundant words.
- Use the active voice in writing efficient sentences.
- Compose unified sentences by avoiding excessive detail and extraneous ideas.

Level II
- Write clear sentences using parallel construction for similar ideas.
- Place words, phrases, and clauses close to the words they modify.
- Avoid ambiguous pronoun references such as *this, that,* and *which.*

Level III
- Achieve emphasis by subordinating secondary ideas to primary ideas.
- Recognize and use concrete words instead of abstract words.
- Use transitional expressions (such as *therefore, however,* and *for example*) to develop coherency between thoughts.

PRETEST

Rewrite the following sentences to rectify problems in parallelism, redundancy, modification, reference, conciseness, and coherence.

1. In view of the fact that the sun's rays are dangerous, you must protect your skin and eyes. ____________________
2. Angered at the slowness of the computer program, complaints were called in by hundreds of disgruntled users. ____________________
3. Orange juice lovers can squeeze their own, buy freshly made juice, or the new extended-shelf-life packaged juice can be tried. ____________________
4. Nike did not wish to repeat again its advertising blunder. ____________________
5. After the death of his mother at the age of four, William went to live with his grandparents ____________________

1. Because the sun's rays are dangerous, you must protect your skin and eyes. 2. Angered at the slowness of the computer program, disgruntled users called in hundreds of complaints. 3. Orange juice lovers can squeeze their own, buy freshly made juice, or try the new extended-shelf-life packaged juice. 4. Nike did not wish to repeat its advertising blunder. 5. At the age of four, after the death of his mother, William went to live with his grandparents.

Business and professional people value efficient, economical writing that is meaningful and coherent. Wordy communication wastes the reader's time; unclear messages confuse the reader and are counterproductive. In the business world, where time is valuable, efficient writing is demanded. You can improve your writing skills by emulating the practices of good writers. Most good writers begin with a rough draft that they revise to produce a final version. This chapter shows you how to revise your rough draft sentences to make them more efficient, clear, emphatic, and coherent.

LEVEL I

"I write as I walk because I want to get somewhere; and I write as straight as I can, just as I walk as straight as I can, because that is the best way to get there."
— H. G. Wells

WRITING EFFICIENT SENTENCES

Revising Wordy Phrases

Sentences are efficient when they convey a thought directly and economically—that is, in the fewest possible words. Good writers excise all useless verbiage from their writing. Some of our most common and comfortable phrases are actually full of "word fat"; when examined carefully, these phrases can be pared down considerably.

Wordy Phrases	Efficient Substitutes
as per your suggestion	as you suggested
at the present time	now
due in large part to	because, since
give consideration to	consider
in addition to the above	also
in all probability	probably
in spite of the fact that	even though
in the amount of	for
in the event that	if
in the near future	soon
in the neighborhood of	about
in view of the fact that	since
it is recommended that	we suggest that
under date of	on, dated
until such time as	until

SPOT THE BLOOPER

From a company newsletter: "Our next issue will present an article that will allow you to understand the elements necessary to a better comprehension."

Notice that the revised versions of the following wordy sentences are more efficient.

WORDY: *As per your suggestion,* we will change the meeting.
MORE EFFICIENT: *As you suggested,* we will change the meeting.

WORDY: *Until such time* as we receive the contract, we cannot proceed.
MORE EFFICIENT: *When* we receive the contract, we can proceed.

WORDY: He will *in all probability* run for reelection.
MORE EFFICIENT: He will *probably* run for reelection.

SPOT THE BLOOPER

Announcer's voice on a TV ad for Ford: "What is it about Ford cars that makes it the best-selling car in America?"

Eliminating Redundant Words

Words that are needlessly repetitive are said to be "redundant." Writers can achieve greater efficiency (and thus more effective sentences) by eliminating redundant words or phrases.

REDUNDANT: Have you *assembled together* all the pages?
MORE EFFICIENT: Have you *assembled* all the pages?

REDUNDANT: This paragraph is *exactly identical* to that one.
MORE EFFICIENT: This paragraph is *identical* to that one.

REDUNDANT: *First and foremost,* we must balance the budget.
MORE EFFICIENT: *First,* we must balance the budget.

REDUNDANT: The examples shown in Figure 3 illustrate truck bodies.
MORE EFFICIENT: Figure 3 illustrates truck bodies.

Using the Active Voice

Sentences that use active verbs are more economical—and, of course, more direct—than those using passive verbs. (See Chapter 8 for a review of passive and active voices.)

PASSIVE: A discrepancy in the bank balance was detected by auditors.
ACTIVE: Auditors detected a discrepancy in the bank balance.

PASSIVE: In the April issue your article will be published by us.
ACTIVE: In the April issue we will publish your article.

PASSIVE: The coach was informed by the trainer of the athlete's injury.
ACTIVE: The trainer informed the coach of the athlete's injury.

SPOT THE BLOOPER

From *The Northern Star,* student newspaper of Northern Illinois University: "Never pet, play with, or give commands to a person using a guide dog without permission."

Writing Unified Sentences

A sentence is unified if it contains only closely related ideas. When extraneous or unrelated ideas appear in a sentence, they confuse the reader. Sentences lacking unity can be improved by excising the extraneous ideas or by shifting the unrelated ideas to separate sentences.

LACKS UNITY: I am appreciative of the time you spent interviewing me last week, and I plan to enroll in a computer application course immediately.
IMPROVED: I appreciate the time you spent with me last week. Because of our interview, I plan to enroll in a computer application course immediately.

LACKS UNITY: It is easy for you to do your Christmas shopping, and we offer three unique catalogs.
IMPROVED: Because we offer three unique catalogs, it is easy for you to do your Christmas shopping.

"I have never thought of myself as a good writer. Anyone who wants reassurance of this should read one of my first drafts. But I'm one of the world's greatest rewriters."
— James Michener

LACKS UNITY: Last spring the Treasury Department asked Americans to circulate pennies, and many people toss these coins in a junk drawer or hoard them in mayonnaise jars, creating a shortage, and some people just throw them away.
IMPROVED: Last spring the Treasury Department asked Americans to circulate pennies. Many people toss these coins in a junk drawer or hoard them in mayonnaise jars. Some people even throw them away, thus creating a shortage.

The inclusion of excessive detail can also damage sentence unity. If many details are necessary for overall clarity, put them in an additional sentence.

EXCESSIVE DETAIL: Germany is preparing to auction 20 castles that formerly belonged to the Communist government, although hundreds of bidders have submitted offers and price is not the determining factor because the government is looking for responsible investors who can protect the cultural values of the monuments as well as preserve the structures.

IMPROVED:	Germany will auction 20 castles that formerly belonged to the Communist government. Price is not as important as finding responsible investors who can protect and preserve the monuments.
EXCESSIVE DETAIL:	A report can be important, but it may not be effective or be read because it is too long and bulky, which will also make it more difficult to distribute, to store, and to handle, as well as increasing its overall cost.
IMPROVED:	An important report may be ineffective because it is too long. Its bulk may increase its costs and make it difficult to read, handle, distribute, and store.

Now complete the reinforcement exercises for Level I.

The language of the Information Age is English. More than 80 percent of all the information stored in the more than 100 million computers around the world is stored in English. And 85 percent of all international telephone conversations are conducted in English.

LEVEL II

WRITING CLEAR SENTENCES

Clear sentences are those that immediately convey their central thought. Good writers achieve sentence clarity by the use of parallel construction, the avoidance of misplaced modifiers, and the use of unambiguous pronoun references.

Developing Parallel Construction

Sentence clarity can be improved by expressing similar ideas with similar grammatical structures. For example, if you are listing three ideas, do not use *ing* words for two of the ideas and a *to* verb for the third idea: *buying, trading, and selling* (not *to sell*). Use nouns with nouns, verbs with verbs, phrases with phrases, and clauses with clauses. In the following list, use all verbs: *the machine sorted, stamped, and counted* (not *and had a counter*). For phrases, the wording for all parts of the list should be matched: *Stopping distances were checked on concrete pavement, over winding roads, and on wet surfaces* (not *when it rains*).

FAULTY:	Improving the stability of the car resulted in less passenger comfort, reduced visibility, and the car weighed more.
IMPROVED:	Improving the stability of the car resulted in less passenger comfort, reduced visibility, and added weight. (Matches nouns)
FAULTY:	The new laser printer helped us improve quality, save money, and we got our work done faster.
IMPROVED:	The new laser printer helped us improve quality, save money, and work faster. (Matches verb-noun construction.)
FAULTY:	Collecting, organizing, and documentation—these are important steps in researching a problem.
IMPROVED:	Collecting, organizing, and documenting—these are important steps in researching a problem. (Matches *ing* nouns.)

SPOT THE BLOOPER

From *The Daily Camera* [Boulder, CO]: "A dog bit a man in the face, who walked into the dog's residence on Pheasant Run on August 15."

Avoiding Misplaced Modifiers

As you will recall, modifiers are words, phrases, or clauses that limit or restrict other words, phrases, or clauses. To be clear, modifiers must be placed carefully so that the words modified by them are obvious. When a modifier is placed so that it does not appear to be modifying the word or words intended to be modified, that modifier is said to be *misplaced.* In Chapter 11 introductory verbal modifiers were discussed. An introductory verbal modifier is sometimes misplaced simply by being at the beginning of the sentence. Consider how the introductory verbal modifier makes the following sentence nonsensical: *While pumping gas, an unoccupied car rolled into mine.* After all, the unoccupied car is not pumping gas. In positions other than the beginning of a sentence, misplaced modifiers may also damage sentence clarity.

SPOT THE BLOOPER

From *The Florida Times-Union* [Jacksonville]: "The club was closed in 1947 after A.L. Lewis died and was eventually sold."

FAULTY: Please take time to examine the brochure *that is enclosed with your family.*

IMPROVED: Please take time to examine with your family the enclosed brochure.

FAULTY: We provide a map for all *visitors reduced to a one-inch scale.*

IMPROVED: For all visitors we provide a *map reduced to a one-inch scale.*

FAULTY: A 30-year-old St. Petersburg man was found murdered by his parents in his home late Tuesday.

IMPROVED: Murdered in his home, a 30-year-old St. Petersburg man was found by his parents late Tuesday.

SPOT THE BLOOPER

From *The Murray* [KY] *Ledger & Times:* "The car was reported stolen by the police."

Improving Pronoun References

Sentence confusion results from the use of pronouns without clear antecedents. Be particularly careful with the pronouns *this, that, which,* and *it.* Confusion often results when these pronouns have as their antecedents an entire clause. Such confusion can usually be avoided by substituting a noun for the pronoun or by following the pronoun with a clarifying noun (or nouns).

FAULTY: Bucket seats in the car were large and luxurious, with a multitude of power-operated adjustments. *They* provided comfort for occupants of all sizes and shapes.

IMPROVED: Bucket seats in the car were large and luxurious, with a multitude of power-operated adjustments. *These power adjustments* provided comfort for occupants of all sizes and shapes.

SPOT THE BLOOPER

From a local newspaper: "The driver had a narrow escape as a broken board penetrated his cabin and just missed his head. This had to be removed before he could be released."

FAULTY: We have a policy of responding to customer inquiries and orders on the day they are received. *That* keeps us busy and keeps our customers satisfied.

IMPROVED: We have a policy of responding to customer inquiries and orders on the day they are received. *That policy* keeps us busy and keeps our customers satisfied.

FAULTY: Our government contracts require work on hundreds of projects that demand constant updating and access to technical data, supplies, and references, which explains why an open office design allowing team interaction is necessary.

IMPROVED: Our government contracts require work on hundreds of projects that demand constant updating and access to technical data, supplies, and references. These needs explain why an open office design allowing team interaction is essential.

Now complete the reinforcement exercises for Level II.

LEVEL III

WRITING EMPHATIC AND COHERENT SENTENCES

In your writing you can achieve emphasis and coherence by using clause subordination, concrete words, and effective transitions.

Notice on an invoice for Cirle Alarms [Corvallis, OR]: "TERMS OF INVOICE: DO ON RECEIPT."

Emphasis Through Subordination

Subordination is a technique used by skillful writers to show the relationship between unequal ideas. Appropriate emphasis can be achieved by using subordinate conjunctions, such as *if, because, since,* and *when,* and relative pronouns, such as *who, which,* and *that,* to introduce secondary ideas or incidental information. Principal ideas should appear in independent clauses, and less important ideas in subordinate or dependent clauses.

PRINCIPAL IDEA: Micronetics recently entered the microcomputer market.
SECONDARY IDEA: Micronetics is a division of IBM.
SENTENCE: Micronetics, which is a division of IBM, recently entered the microcomputer market.

PRINCIPAL IDEA: The new Millenia performed well in government crash tests.
SECONDARY IDEA: Our bumper-basher crash test produced significant damage.
SENTENCE: Although our bumper-basher crash test produced significant damage, the new Millenia performed well in government crash tests.

SPOT THE BLOOPER

"Being moribund on arrival at the hospital, the doctor could do nothing for the patient."

PRINCIPAL IDEA: A credit card holder is not liable for more than $100 in unauthorized purchases.
SECONDARY IDEA: The credit card holder must give notice to the issuer of the card.
SENTENCE: If a credit card holder gives notice to the issuer of the card, the holder is not liable for more than $100 in unauthorized purchases.

Emphasis Through the Use of Concrete Words

As you know, concrete words (see Chapter 4) refer to specific persons, places, concepts, and actions. They bring to mind sharp images and arouse strong feelings. Abstract words, such as *honesty, freedom,* and *utilization,* because they refer to general ideas, do not call forth immediate sensory reactions or feelings. Use concrete words and constructions to make your writing emphatic, persuasive, and clear.

Use concrete words when you wish to emphasize or promote an idea. Use abstract words to soften bad news.

ABSTRACT: Repairs on your car will be completed *soon.*
CONCRETE: Repairs on your car will be completed *by May 2.*

ABSTRACT: *Utilization of improved techniques* helped reduce customer returns.
CONCRETE: *Improved product use instructions* helped reduce customer returns.

ABSTRACT: Mazda's basic warranty is *satisfactory.*
CONCRETE: Mazda's *three-year or 50,000-mile warranty includes roadside assistance.*

When an abstract word is necessary, its meaning can often be enhanced by the addition of clarifying words.

ABSTRACT: Prosecuting attorneys did not question Miss Finch's *loyalty.*
CONCRETE: Prosecuting attorneys did not question Miss Finch's *loyalty to her employer.*

Coherence Through the Use of Transitional Words or Phrases

Orderly and consistent development of ideas leads to coherency. Coherence between sentences can be attained by the use of transitional expressions such as *therefore, in this way, in addition, for example, however, moreover, for this reason,* and *on the other hand.* These words and phrases serve as flags to signal the reader that ideas are being contrasted or amplified. Notice that in the following sentences transitional words and phrases help the reader connect successive ideas.

SPOT THE BLOOPER

From the *Automotive Messenger:* "Fuel is readily available anywhere, and if you run out, you can hike to the nearest station, and carry enough back to get you going in a one gallon milk jug. Just try that with electricity!"

In 2000 B.C. ancient Babylonians created the world's first evaporative air conditioning. *Moreover,* cooling by evaporation was used extensively in ancient India.

The Gobi Desert is proving to be one of the world's richest sources of vertebrate fossils. *For example,* the first fossilized embryo of a meat-eating dinosaur was recently discovered there.

Students in Oslo, Norway, have been forbidden to use cellular phones during class. They may, *on the other hand,* use such electronic devices during breaks.

When the federal government purchases goods on a cost-plus contract, it requires detailed accounting reports. *In this way,* it can monitor operations and costs.

Now complete the reinforcement exercises for Level III.

HOT LINE QUERIES

QUESTION I just typed this sentence: *You will see in our manual where multiple bids must be obtained.* Somewhere from my distant past I seem to recall that *where* should not be used this way. Can you help me?

ANSWER You're right. *Where* should not be substituted for the relative pronoun *that.* In your sentence, use *that.* A similar faulty construction to be avoided is the use of *while* for *although* (*although* [not *while*] *I agree with his position, I disagree with his procedures*).

QUESTION When the company name *Halperin, Inc.,* appears in the middle of a sentence, is there a comma following *Inc.?*

ANSWER Current authorities recommend the following practice in punctuating *Inc.:* If the legal company name includes a comma preceding *Inc.,* then a comma should follow *Inc.* if it is used in the middle of a sentence. (*We received from Kent, Inc., its latest catalog.*)

QUESTION Where should the word *sic* be placed when it is used?

ANSWER *Sic* means "thus" or "so stated," and it is properly placed immediately following the word or phrase to which it refers. For example, *The kidnappers placed a newspaper advertisement that read "Call Monna* [*sic*] *Lisa." Sic* is used within a quotation to indicate that a quoted word or phrase, though inaccurately spelled or used, appeared thus in the original. *Sic* is italicized and placed within brackets.

QUESTION Which is correct: *I feel* (*bad* or *badly*)?

ANSWER *Bad* is an adjective meaning "not good" or "ill." *Badly* is an adverb meaning "harmfully," "wickedly," or "poorly." Your sentence appears to require *bad* (I *feel ill*), unless you mean that your sense of touch is impaired (I *feel poorly*).

QUESTION Should I capitalize *oriental* rug?

ANSWER Yes. Adjectives derived from proper nouns are capitalized (*French* dressing, *German* shepherd, *Danish* furniture). Very well-known adjectives, however, are not capitalized (*pasteurized* milk, *venetian* blinds, *french* fries, *china* plates).

QUESTION In a business report is it acceptable to write the following: *Most everyone agrees . . . ?*

ANSWER In this construction *most* is a shortened form of *almost.* Although such contractions are heard in informal speech, they should not appear in business writing. Instead, use the longer form: *Almost everyone agrees. . . .*

NAME ____________________

UNIT 6 REVIEW ■ Chapters 19–21 (Self-Check)

First, review Chapters 19–21. Then test your comprehension of those chapters by completing the exercises that follow. Compare your responses with those shown at the end of the review.

LEVEL I

Select (a) or (b) to describe the group of words that is more acceptably expressed.

1. (a) courses in Anthropology, French, and Accounting (b) courses in anthropology, French, and accounting ____

2. (a) born in Madison county (b) born in Madison County ____

3. (a) the State of Texas (b) the state of Texas ____

4. (a) during the winter break (b) during the Winter break ____

5. (a) a belgian waffle (b) a Belgian waffle ____

6. (a) the 15th of April (b) the fifteenth of April ____

7. (a) thirty dollars (b) $30 ____

8. (a) on 12th Street (b) on Twelfth Street ____

9. (a) on July 17th (b) on July 17 ____

10. (a) in view of the fact that (b) since ____

11. (a) now (b) at the present time ____

12. (a) in the amount of (b) for ____

LEVEL II

Select (a) or (b) to describe the group of words that is more acceptably expressed.

13. (a) by your Mother and Father (b) by your mother and father ____

14. (a) proceed west on Highway 5 (b) proceed West on Highway 5 ____

15. (a) our vice president, Maria Woods (b) our Vice President, Maria Woods ____

16. (a) their shipping department (b) their Shipping Department ____

17. (a) a message from Ken Kim, Marketing Manager (b) a message from Ken Kim, marketing manager ____

18. (a) a message from Marketing Manager Kim (b) a message from marketing manager Kim ____

19. (a) for the next five years (b) for the next 5 years ____

20. (a) 3 seventy-five page booklets (b) three 75-page booklets ____

21. (a) two copiers serving 11 offices (b) 2 copiers serving 11 offices ____

Each of the following sentences illustrates one of these sentence faults:

a = faulty parallel construction (such as *eating, sleeping,* and *to read*)

b = faulty phrase placement (phrase is distant from the words it modifies)

c = faulty pronoun reference (pronoun such as *this, that,* or *it* lacking clear antecedent)

Write the letter that describes the sentence fault in each of the next three sentences.

22. Inadequate ventilation, poor lighting, and hazardous working conditions were cited in the complaint. It must be improved before regulators return. _____

23. Fabric divider panels were installed in the office to provide privacy, enhance concentration, and they should effect a reduction in sound. _____

24. Robert told the doctor that he had a wart on his right hand that he wanted removed. _____

(On a separate sheet of paper, rewrite the above sentences to rectify their faults.)

LEVEL III

Select the correct group of words below and write its letter in the space provided.

25. (a) our company president, Ms. Claiborne (b) our company President, Ms. Claiborne _____

26. (a) U.S. President-Elect (b) U.S. President-elect _____

27. (a) an envelope stamped "photographs" (b) an envelope stamped "Photographs" _____

28. (a) our 40th anniversary (b) our fortieth anniversary _____

29. (a) less than 0.5 percent (b) less than .5 percent _____

30. (a) 2 quarts of motor oil (b) two quarts of motor oil _____

31. (a) an 8% return (b) an 8 percent return _____

32. (a) on her 21st birthday (b) on her twenty-first birthday _____

33. (a) under the hot sun (b) under the hot Sun _____

34. (a) arab and asian cultures (b) Arab and Asian cultures _____

35. (a) a 3/4 interest (b) a three-fourths interest _____

Hot Line Review

Write the letter of the word or phrase that correctly completes each sentence.

36. I heard that (a) most, (b) almost everyone arrived late to the party. _____

37. Analysts (a) implied, (b) inferred from the CEO's remarks that profits would fall. _____

38. Be careful not to (a) lose, (b) loose the key to the safety deposit box. _____

39. Everyone feels (a) bad, (b) badly about the proposed cutbacks. _____

40. Only the manager and (a) myself, (b) I, (c) me will be working this weekend. _____

1.b 2.b 3.b 4.a 5.b 6.a 7.b 8.a 9.b 10.b 11.a 12.b 13.b 14.a 15.a 16.a 17.b 18.a 19.a 20.b 21.a
22.c 23.a 24.b 25.a 26.b 27.b 28.b 29.a 30.a 31.b 32.b 33.a 34.b 35.b 36.b 37.b 38.a 39.a 40.b

APPENDIX Developing Spelling Skills

WHY IS ENGLISH SPELLING SO DIFFICULT?

No one would dispute the complaint that many English words are difficult to spell. Why is spelling in our language so perplexing? For one thing, our language has borrowed many of its words from other languages. English has a Germanic base on which a superstructure of words borrowed from French, Latin, Greek, and other languages of the world has been erected. For this reason, its words are not always formed by regular patterns of letter combinations. In addition, spelling is made difficult because the pronunciation of English words is constantly changing. Today's spelling was standardized nearly 300 years ago, but many words are pronounced differently today than they were then. Therefore, pronunciation often provides little help in spelling. Consider, for example, the words *sew* and *dough.*

WHAT CAN BE DONE TO IMPROVE ONE'S SPELLING?

Spelling is a skill that can be developed, just as arithmetic, typing, and other skills can be developed. Because the ability to spell is a prerequisite for success in business and in most other activities, effort expended to acquire this skill is effort well spent.

Three traditional approaches to improving spelling have met with varying degrees of success.

1. Rules or Guidelines

The spelling of English words is consistent enough to justify the formulation of a few spelling rules, perhaps more appropriately called guidelines since the generalizations in question are not invariably applicable. Such guidelines are, in other words, helpful but not infallible.

2. Mnemonics

Another approach to improving one's ability to spell involves the use of mnemonics or memory devices. For example, the word *principl<u>e</u>* might be associated with the word *rul<u>e</u>*, to form in the mind of the speller a link between the meaning and the spelling of *principle.* To spell *capitol,* one might think of the *dome* of the capitol building and focus on the *o*'s in both words. The use of mnemonics can be an effective device for the improvement of spelling only if the speller makes a real effort to develop the necessary memory hooks.

3. Rote Learning

A third approach to the improvement of spelling centers on memorization. The word is studied by the speller until it can be readily reproduced in the mind's eye.

THE 1-2-3 SPELLING PLAN

Proficiency in spelling is not attained without concentrated effort. Here's a plan to follow in mastering the 400 commonly misspelled words included in this appendix. For each word, try this 1-2-3 approach.

1. Is a spelling guideline applicable? If so, select the appropriate guideline and study the word in relation to that guideline.
2. If no guideline applies, can a memory device be created to aid in the recall of the word?
3. If neither a guideline nor a memory device will work, the word must be memorized. Look at the word carefully. Pronounce it. Write it or repeat it until you can visualize all its letters in your mind's eye.

Before you try the 1-2-3 plan, become familiar with the six spelling guidelines that follow. These spelling guidelines are not intended to represent all the possible spelling rules appearing in the various available spelling books. These six guidelines are, however, among the most effective and helpful of the recognized spelling rules.

Guideline 1: Words Containing *ie* or *ei*

Although there are exceptions to it, the following familiar rhyme can be helpful.

(a) Write *i* before *e*
(b) Except after *c*,
(c) Or when sounded like *a*
As in *neighbor* and *weigh.*

Study these words illustrating the three parts of the rhyme.

(a) *i* Before *e*		(b) Except After *c*	(c) or When Sounded Like *a*
achieve	grief	ceiling	beige
belief	ingredient	conceive	eight
believe	mischief	deceive	freight
brief	niece	perceive	heir
cashier	piece	receipt	neighbor
chief	shield	receive	reign
convenient	sufficient		their
field	view		vein
friend	yield		weight

Exceptions: These exceptional *ei* and *ie* words must be learned by rote or with the use of a mnemonic device.

caffeine	height	seize
either	leisure	sheik
financier	neither	sleight
foreigner	protein	weird

Guideline 2: Words Ending in *e*

For most words ending in an *e,* the final *e* is dropped when the word is joined to a suffix beginning with a vowel (such as *ing, able,* or *al*). The final *e* is retained when a suffix beginning with a consonant (such as *ment, less, ly,* or *ful*) is joined to such a word.

FINAL *e* DROPPED	FINAL *e* RETAINED
believe, believing	arrange, arrangement
care, caring	require, requirement
hope, hoping	hope, hopeless
receive, receiving	care, careless
desire, desirable	like, likely
cure, curable	approximate, approximately
move, movable	definite, definitely
value, valuable	sincere, sincerely
disperse, dispersal	use, useful
arrive, arrival	hope, hopeful

Exceptions: The few exceptions to this spelling guideline are among the most frequently misspelled words. As such, they deserve special attention. Notice that they all involve a dropped final *e*.

acknowledgment	ninth
argument	truly
judgment	wholly

Guideline 3: Words Ending in *ce* or *ge*

When *able* or *ous* is added to words ending in *ce* or *ge,* the final *e* is retained if the *c* or *g* is pronounced softly (as in *change* or *peace*).

advantage, advantageous	change, changeable
courage, courageous	service, serviceable
outrage, outrageous	manage, manageable

Guideline 4: Words Ending in *y*

Words ending in a *y* that is preceded by a consonant normally change the *y* to *i* before all suffixes except those beginning with an *i.*

CHANGE *y* TO *i* BECAUSE *y* IS PRECEDED BY A CONSONANT	DO NOT CHANGE *y* TO *i* BECAUSE *y* IS PRECEDED BY A VOWEL
accompany, accompaniment	employ, employer
study, studied, studious	annoy, annoying, annoyance
duty, dutiful	stay, staying, stayed
industry, industrious	attorney, attorneys
carry, carriage	valley, valleys
apply, appliance	
try, tried	**DO NOT CHANGE *y* TO *i* WHEN ADDING *ing***
empty, emptiness	
forty, fortieth	accompany, accompanying
secretary, secretaries	apply, applying
company, companies	study, studying
hurry, hurries	satisfy, satisfying
	try, trying

Exceptions: day, daily; dry, dried; mislay, mislaid; pay, paid; shy, shyly; gay, gaily.

Guideline 5: Doubling a Final Consonant

If one-syllable words or two-syllable words accented on the second syllable end in a single consonant preceded by a single vowel, the final consonant is doubled before the addition of a suffix beginning with a vowel.

Although complex, this spelling guideline is extremely useful and therefore well worth mastering. Many spelling errors can be avoided by applying this guideline.

One-Syllable Words	Two-Syllable Words
can, canned	acquit, acquitting, acquittal
drop, dropped	admit, admitted, admitting
fit, fitted	begin, beginner, beginning
get, getting	commit, committed, committing
man, manned	control, controller, controlling
plan, planned	defer, deferred (but deference*)
run, running	excel, excelled, excelling
shut, shutting	occur, occurrence, occurring
slip, slipped	prefer, preferring (but preference*)
swim, swimming	recur, recurred, recurrence
ton, tonnage	refer, referring (but reference*)

*Because the accent shifts to the first syllable, the final consonant is not doubled.

Here is a summary of conditions necessary for application of this guideline.

1. The word must end in a single consonant.
2. The final consonant must be preceded by a single vowel.
3. The word must be accented on the second syllable (if it has two syllables).

Words derived from *cancel, offer, differ, equal, suffer,* and *benefit* are not governed by this guideline because they are accented on the first syllable.

Guideline 6: Prefixes and Suffixes

For words in which the letter that ends the prefix is the same as the letter that begins the main word (such as in *dissimilar*), both letters must be included. For words in which a suffix begins with the same letter that ends the main word (such as in *coolly*), both letters must also be included.

Prefix	Main Word	Main Word	Suffix
dis	satisfied	accidental	ly
ir	responsible	incidental	ly
il	literate	clean	ness
mis	spell	cool	ly
mis	state	even	ness
un	necessary	mean	ness

On the other hand, do not supply additional letters when adding prefixes to main words.

Prefix	Main Word
dis	appoint (*not* dissappoint)
dis	appearance
mis	take

Perhaps the most important guideline one can follow in spelling correctly is to use the dictionary whenever in doubt.

400 MOST FREQUENTLY MISSPELLED WORDS*
(DIVIDED INTO 20 LISTS OF 20 WORDS EACH)

List 1	List 2	List 3
1. absence	21. afraid	41. applying
2. acceptance	22. against	42. approaches
3. accessible	23. aggressive	43. appropriate
4. accidentally	24. all right	44. approximately
5. accommodate	25. almost	45. arguing
6. accompaniment	26. alphabetical	46. argument
7. accurately	27. already	47. arrangement
8. accustom	28. although	48. article
9. achievement	29. amateur	49. athlete
10. acknowledgment	30. among	50. attack
11. acquaintance	31. amount	51. attendance, attendants
12. acquire	32. analysis	52. attitude
13. across	33. analyze	53. attorneys
14. actually	34. angel, angle	54. auxiliary
15. adequately	35. annoyance	55. basically
16. admitted	36. annual	56. beautiful
17. adolescence	37. answer	57. before
18. advantageous	38. apologized	58. beginning
19. advertising	39. apparent	59. believing
20. advice, advise	40. appliance	60. benefited

List 4	List 5	List 6
61. biggest	81. companies	101. description
62. breath, breathe	82. competition	102. desirable
63. brief	83. completely	103. destroy
64. business	84. conceive	104. development
65. calendar	85. conscience	105. difference
66. capital, capitol	86. conscientious	106. dining
67. career	87. conscious	107. disappearance
68. careless	88. considerably	108. disappoint
69. carrying	89. consistent	109. disastrous
70. cashier	90. continuous	110. discipline
71. ceiling	91. controlling	111. discussion
72. certain	92. controversial	112. disease
73. challenge	93. convenience	113. dissatisfied
74. changeable	94. council, counsel	114. distinction
75. chief	95. cylinder	115. divide
76. choose, chose	96. daily	116. doesn't
77. cloths, clothes	97. deceive	117. dominant
78. column	98. decision	118. dropped
79. coming	99. define	119. due
80. committee	100. dependent	120. during

*Compiled from lists of words most frequently misspelled by students and businesspeople.

List 7	List 8	List 9
121. efficient	141. February	161. happiness
122. eligible	142. fictitious	162. hear, here
123. embarrass	143. field	163. height
124. encourage	144. finally	164. heroes
125. enough	145. financially	165. hopeless
126. environment	146. foreigner	166. hoping
127. equipped	147. fortieth	167. huge
128. especially	148. forty, fourth	168. humorous
129. exaggerate	149. forward, foreword	169. hungry
130. excellence	150. freight	170. ignorance
131. except	151. friend	171. imaginary
132. exercise	152. fulfill	172. imagine
133. existence	153. fundamentally	173. immediately
134. experience	154. further	174. immense
135. explanation	155. generally	175. importance
136. extremely	156. government	176. incidentally
137. familiar	157. governor	177. independent
138. families	158. grammar	178. indispensable
139. fascinate	159. grateful	179. industrious
140. favorite	160. guard	180. inevitable

List 10	List 11	List 12
181. influential	201. leisurely	221. mechanics
182. ingredient	202. library	222. medicine
183. initiative	203. license	223. medieval
184. intelligence	204. likely	224. mere
185. interest	205. literature	225. miniature
186. interference	206. lives	226. minutes
187. interpretation	207. loneliness	227. mischief
188. interrupt	208. loose, lose	228. misspell
189. involve	209. losing	229. mistake
190. irrelevant	210. luxury	230. muscle
191. irresponsible	211. magazine	231. mysterious
192. island	212. magnificence	232. naturally
193. jealous	213. maintenance	233. necessary
194. judgment	214. manageable	234. neighbor
195. kindergarten	215. maneuver	235. neither
196. knowledge	216. manner	236. nervous
197. laboratory	217. manufacturer	237. nickel
198. laborer	218. marriage	238. niece
199. laid	219. mathematics	239. ninety
200. led, lead	220. meant	240. ninth

List 13	List 14	List 15
241. noticeable	261. passed, past	281. possible
242. numerous	262. pastime	282. practical
243. obstacle	263. peaceable	283. precede
244. occasionally	264. peculiar	284. preferred
245. occurrence	265. perceive	285. prejudice
246. off	266. performance	286. preparation
247. offered	267. permanent	287. prevalent
248. official	268. permitted	288. principal, principle
249. omitted	269. persistent	289. privilege
250. operate	270. personal, personnel	290. probably
251. opinion	271. persuading	291. proceed
252. opportunity	272. phase, faze	292. professor
253. opposite	273. philosophy	293. prominent
254. organization	274. physical	294. proving
255. origin	275. piece	295. psychology
256. original	276. planned	296. pursuing
257. paid	277. pleasant	297. quantity
258. pamphlet	278. poison	298. quiet, quite
259. parallel	279. political	299. really
260. particular	280. possession	300. receipt

List 16	List 17	List 18
301. receiving	321. satisfying	341. speak, speech
302. recognize	322. scenery	342. specimen
303. recommend	323. schedule	343. stationary, stationery
304. reference	324. science	344. stopped
305. referring	325. secretaries	345. stories
306. regard	326. seize	346. straight, strait
307. relative	327. sense, since	347. strenuous
308. relieving	328. sentence	348. stretch
309. religious	329. separation	349. strict
310. reminiscent	330. sergeant	350. studying
311. repetition	331. serviceable	351. substantial
312. representative	332. several	352. subtle
313. requirement	333. shining	353. succeed
314. resistance	334. shoulder	354. success
315. responsible	335. significance	355. sufficient
316. restaurant	336. similar	356. summary
317. rhythm	337. simply	357. suppose
318. ridiculous	338. sincerely	358. surprise
319. sacrifice	339. site, cite	359. suspense
320. safety	340. source	360. swimming

LIST 19	LIST 20
361. syllable	381. tremendous
362. symbol	382. tried
363. symmetrical	383. truly
364. synonymous	384. undoubtedly
365. technique	385. unnecessary
366. temperament	386. until
367. temperature	387. unusual
368. tendency	388. useful
369. than, then	389. using
370. their, there	390. vacuum
371. themselves	391. valuable
372. theories	392. varies
373. therefore	393. vegetable
374. thorough	394. view
375. though	395. weather, whether
376. through	396. weird
377. together	397. were, where
378. tomorrow	398. wholly, holy
379. tragedies	399. writing
380. transferred	400. yield

INDEX

T

U

V

W

X

Y